Jan 10, 1985

To Dr Zander

Your work in group dynamics has served as a valuable model and stimulus.

Bert Carron

MOTIVATION
Implications for Coaching & Teaching

Albert V. Carron

Canadian Cataloguing in Publications Data

Carron, A.V.
Motivation: Implications for coaching and teaching

Bibliography: p.
Includes index
ISBN 0-9691619-0-5

1. Sports - Psychological Aspects. 2. Motivation (Psychology).
3. Coaching (Athletics). I Title.
GV 706.4.C37 1984 796'.01 C84-098180-5

Layout & Typesetting by: Pear Creative Ltd.

Printed in Canada by Pear Creative Ltd., 534 Adelaide St., London, Ontario (519) 434-4744

TABLE OF CONTENTS

PREFACE

When individuals carrying out research and teaching sport psychology at the college level are approached by students, teachers, parents, coaches, and administrators of sport programs for advice or assistance, one of the most frequently requested topics is motivation. The questions may take many forms. For example, the following are typical:

- Why are so many kids quitting swimming at approximately 15-16 years of age?
- What would you recommend to prevent my athletes from going stale?
- How can I keep my team motivated?
- My son seems to have all the potential in the world but he just doesn't care. What can I do?

The list could go on and on. But, whatever specific form these questions take, their focus is essentially the same — how can motivation be developed, enhanced, and/or maintained? This, of course, is a fundamental concern. Certainly, motivation is a critical corner-stone for achievement in all challenging endeavors including sport, physical education, and physical activity. Thus, for the sport psychologist who wishes to assist the coach, teacher, or athlete, motivation is a natural place to begin.

But, this is easier said than accomplished. Motivation is a highly complex phenomenon. As Littman (1958) pointed out "*There are many different kinds of motivational phenomena.* It is simply not the case that the analysis of one kind of motivational phenomena provides us with the analysis of all, or even a substantial portion, of other motivational concepts. Motivation is not a unitary phenomenon in the sense that all motivational things have the same properties and enter into the same laws in the same way."

This complexity has presented me with a number of dilemmas in terms of my dealings with coaches, athletes, and teachers. The first dilemma relates to what can be described as a *fish in a fish market phenomen.* Because I like almost all types of seafood, I find it difficult to choose what to buy when I go shopping. In the same manner, because motivation is not a single phenomenon, it has made little sense to me in my discussions with interested persons to single out one aspect or motivational component and emphasize its preeminence to the exclusion of the others. Each of the fish in the fish market has its virtues and limitations. Which one should be singled out for the fish fry?

A second dilemma I've experienced can be described as a *bricks in the brickyard phenomenon.* The bricks in a brickyard become most useful when they are organized together into a wall, or driveway, or some overall structure. In a similar fashion, because each of us has a limited ability to process and use information, and coaches and teachers are no exception, it has also made little sense to me in my discussions to simply provide a comprehensive list of motivational techniques without some meaningful framework to tie them all together. Otherwise, the information simply represents another brick for the instructional brickyard. To be truly useful, information on motivation, should be subdivided and packaged into meaningful units or categories. Hopefully, then, the units or categories will represent small, more manageable informational packages. Also, the relationships between these units can be clarified.

The final dilemma I have been faced with can be referred to as the *ivory tower phenomenon.* When I was initially approached years ago by a coaching association to speak to their membership about motivation in sport, I was repeatedly (and politely) warned to avoid an ivory tower approach — to make sure that my material was practical, was useful, was applied. A legitimate request certainly. However, as a university professor committed philosophically to the belief that coaching and teaching in sport and physical activity will only develop fully through the establishment and implementation of a sound, research based foundation, I was certainly loathe to short circuit research and simply rely on my experiences.

In an attempt to resolve these dilemmas, I developed a lecture package, for my undergraduate class and talks with coaching groups, a package which also forms the basis for the present textbook. In that lecture package (and this text), I have attempted to accomplish three things; (1) to provide a comprehensive picture of the more important motivational factors which infuence performance in physical education, sport, and physical activity, (2) to provide a frame-of-reference within which these motivational factors can be more readily understood, and (3) to draw upon research findings as the basis for any claims or generalities advanced.

This book is intended for advanced undergraduate and graduate students pursuing a specialization in coaching theory and practice, for coaches, for teachers, and for the participants themselves. Insight into the psychology of motivation is beneficial for each of these groups.

I am indebted to my colleagues, Dr. Craig Hall and Dr. Chella Chelladurai for reading and reacting to the manuscript. It is extremely difficult to proofread something you have rewritten and reread on numerous occasions. You literally read sentences and paragraphs, not individual words. Thus, Craig's and Chella's comments were extremely helpful.

Finally, the reader will understand and appreciate that even someone writing about motivation needs help with motivation — particularly on those days when progress is slow or when the whole project seems to be a mistake. Over the past two years that this book has been in preparation, there have been a number of those days. I have been fortunate during those bleak periods to have the support of what my sociologist friends refer to as "significant others." To Dana, to Brett, to Pat, to Chris, to Wendy, and to Jeff, Thanks.

CHAPTER 1

Introduction

On a bright, sunny summer day, one person may choose to play tennis, another to play golf, while a third may sit by a pool and read. Or, during a marathon, one competitor may choose to push to the point of exhaustion and physical collapse while another, feeling discomfort, may choose to ease off on the pace and finish easily. And, finally, one basketball player may choose to hustle consistently throughout a game or practice whereas a teammate may decide to do so only sporadically.

The phenomenon used to account for these diverse individual behaviors is called motivation which is a derivative of the Latin word "movere" meaning "to move." In modern psychology, motivation is used to represent the reasons why people select different activities, persist in them, and carry them out with intensity. In the language of science, motivation is referred to as a *theoretical construct.* That is, it is not directly observable or measurable so its presence can only be inferred indirectly from behavior.

The first anecdote presented above helps to illustrate the selectivity dimension of motivation. The three individuals each had at least two alternatives or choices but they choose the one they did because that alternative satisfied some underlying motive, need or desire — in short, the three individuals were motivated to play tennis, golf, or to read.

The second anecdote provides an example in which the persistence dimension of motivation is illustrated. The two athletes differed in their ability to persist in the difficult, exhausting marathon. This persistence might have been a product of many different factors. For example, the underlying cause could have been differences in personality (e.g., one may have had an excessively high need for achievement, the other, only moderate), aspirations and goals (e.g., one may have set a goal of simply finishing the race whereas the second may have wanted to do so within a specific time limit), or incentives (e.g., one may have been striving for a financial reward while the second may only have wanted the personal satisfaction of completing the event), or some combination of these. Whatever the cause, however, the differences in the behavior of the two runners are assumed to be due to differences in motivation.

The final anecdote provides an example of the intensity dimension of motivation. Intensity, of course, can vary from sleep at one extreme to excessive excitement, arousal, activation, and energy at the other. The causes of motivational intensity are varied so it would be necessary to gather further information to determine why the two players differed. Nonetheless, the differences in behavior are considered to be the result of differences in motivation. One player is highly motivated and, therefore, hustles continually; the other is only moderately motivated and so only hustles periodically.

THE IMPORTANCE OF MOTIVATION

There are only two powers in the world, the sword and the spirit. In the long run the sword will always be conquered by the spirit.
Napoleon

Coaches, teachers, athletes, and sport psychologists view motivation as the single most important attribute for effective performance. But, as Alderman (1978) has pointed out "motivating the young athlete involves far more than just encouraging him with praise or punishing him with extra laps after practice. And with the young, amateur athlete, far more than just using *fear* as is done almost exclusively with professional athletes. It requires knowing what are the most imporant *factors* influencing the motivational levels in young people and it requires knowing *how* to put this knowledge to its best use" (p. 49).

But knowing the motivation factors and knowing how to put them to best use is easier said than done. Coaches and teachers who have actively tried to influence the motivation of performers realize that there are numerous techniques and strategies from which to choose. And, researchers consider motivation to be one of the most complex phenomena in psychology. A good illustration of this complexity is provided by the following comprehensive definition set out by Littman (1958):

"Motivation refers to processes or conditions which may be physiological or psychological, innate or acquired, internal or external to the organism which determine or describe how, or in respect of what, behavior is initiated, maintained, guided, selected, or terminated; it also refers to end states which such behavior frequently achieves or is designed to achieve whether they are conditions of the organism or environment; it also refers to the behavior engaged in, or aspects of that behavior, in respect of its organization, occurrence, continuation, reorganization, or

termination with regard to past or present or future organic or environmental conditions; further, it refers to the fact that an individual will learn or remember or forget certain material, as well as the rate or manner in which these processes occur and the ease or difficulty with which they are altered, as well as to some of the processes or conditions which are responsible for this behavior; similarly, it determines how and what perceptual and judgmental activities and outcomes will occur, as well as some of the conditions and determinants of such activities and outcomes; similarly, it also refers to the fact of and the determinants of the occurrence and fate of affective process; finally, it describes and accounts for various individual differences which appear in respect of the various behaviors, processes, conditions, and outcomes referred to above. Motivation refers to any one or more of the behaviors, conditions, processes, or outcomes in any combinations" (p. 136-137).

After looking over this definition, a typical reaction might be, "Where does motivation begin; where does it end; can I make any practical sense out of it?" It is certainly obvious that motivation is not a single, simple concept. And therefore, dealing with it, translating motivational theory and research into practical terms for application (as I have tried to do in this textbook) poses a number of difficult problems. These can be referred to as *the fish in the fish market phenomenon, the bricks in the brickyard phenomenon,* and *the ivory tower phenomenon.*

ISSUES IN TRANSLATING THEORY INTO PRACTICE

Those who are enamored of practice without science are like a pilot who goes into a ship without a rudder or compass and never has any certainty of where he is going.

Leonardo De Vinci

The first major dilemma which arises when research is translated into practical information, the *fish in the fish market phenomenon*, is tied in with the issue of where to begin, what motivational phenomena to emphasize, and what to ignore if motivational research is converted into practical terms for a coach or teacher. As Littman emphasized in his definition which was presented above, motivation is not a solitary, simple thing. There is a wide variety of motivational fish in the fish market and all have some attractive features. Consequently, it makes little sense to single out one and emphasize its use to the exclusion of all others. So, if we continue with the fish analogy, it also makes little sense to single out one motivational technique, such as token rewards, and suggest that it is *the* answer for all coaches or teachers. Awareness of the majority of motivational phenomena is necessary before informed choices can be made concerning which is better. Information on a number of motivational phenomena is provided in this text.

If it is taken as an accepted fact that a variety of different motivational techniques should be set out for the coach and teacher, the second dilemma, the *bricks in the brickyard phenomenon,* then becomes an issue. Each of us has only a limited ability to take in and use information. We can only retain a certain amount. For example, the number of digits that we are able to recall after one presentation is around seven (Miller, 1956). However, digits can be combined together into pairs. If this is the case, we again are only able to recall about seven. But, those seven pairs now represent a total of 14 digits.

If the facts about motivation are viewed as bricks in a brickyard, they are most easily recalled when they are organized into some overall, general structure. In the case of bricks, that overall, general structure might be a wall, house, or driveway. In the case of motivation for sport and physical activity, the overall general framework might involve looking at motivation as a product of personal and situational factors, some of which can be manipulated or influenced, some of which cannot. It should be obvious that there are probably a number of other ways to look at motivation — to organize the bricks in the brickyard. But, some organization is essential if we hope to retain a substantial amount of the information available. I have attempted to do this in this text. The organization used is presented in a subsequent section, "A Model for Motivation".

A final dilemma, the *ivory tower phenomenon,* is related to the question of how much we should (or need to) draw upon research to support our practices. In many instances, coaches and teachers have been uneasy with researchers and their discussions of research findings because that research has been considered to be ivory tower in nature — to be unrelated to events going on in the real world. In other instances, research results have seemed to simply confirm the obvious — to be the scientific equivalent of proving that birds can fly. Alderman (1978) talked about this second point when he stated:

> *"Good coaches know, or sense, what is important in motivating young athletes and they know what are the most important techniques for doing it. Though such knowledge comes mainly from experience, invariably, upon examination, the things they do are also theoretically sound and consistent with the results from scientific research. It is our contention, in fact, that the gap between what the scientific or theoretical literature tells us and what good coaches do in practice is virtually non-existent"* (p. 149).

So, the question is how much should we (or do we need to) use research as a basis for arriving at decisions about the role of motivation in sport and physical activity? There is no doubt that, in many instances, the gap between what science has discovered and what good coaches have learned to do through common sense is virtually non-existent. But, there is also no doubt that if coaching and teaching in sport and physical activity are to develop fully, they must do so through the development and implementation of a sound, research-based foundation. I have drawn on research for the conclusions set out in this textbook. Common sense may be essential in our day-to-day activities but it is never an adequate substitute for the scientific method.

COMMON SENSE VERSUS THE USE OF RESEARCH

To most men, experience is like the stern lights of a ship which illuminate only the track it has passed.

Samuel Taylor Coleridge

Kerlinger (1973) highlighted why experience is never an adequate substitute for research when he discussed the differences between science and common sense. His discussion is worth repeating here. One of the significant differences Kerlinger talked about is the way in which common sense and scientific theories are developed. Whereas a scientist systematically builds theoretical models, tests them for internal consistency, and then subjects them to analysis, the person in the street establishes theories concerning the way things are in a more relaxed, looser fashion. For example, some coaches hold to the theory that punishment is a highly effective motivator. In fact, it is assumed by many that punishment is the equivalent of rewards — it is only common sense. However, a significant body of research evidence now supports the viewpoint that punishment can impede learning and performance, that it is not the equal of rewards.

A second difference between science and common sense lies in the way they test their theories. Scientists systematically and repeatedly test their theories in a continuous search for alternative explanations for why things are as they are. In fact, it has been suggested that science only advances by disproof, that hypotheses are set out so that they can be disproven (Landers, 1983; Popper, 1959). The layperson, on the other hand actively seeks out verification of his/her theories. Thus, for example, people holding stereotypical "theories" about minority groups, selectively use positive examples to verify their beliefs while ignoring discrepant evidence.

A third difference lies in the concept of control. If a special condition is introduced, some reference point, comparison group or baseline measure is necessary in order to establish the impact of that condition. This is known as control. A scientist uses control; the layperson typically does not. If a coach believes a particular technique is effective, for example, he/she may introduce it to the whole team. Then, if improvement is evident at some later stage, this improvement will be attributed to the effects of the technique. A scientist, on the other hand, would be interested in determining whether some other factor or factors were equally responsible. Could the improvement be simply a natural consequence of practice? Maturation? The athletes expectations that they should get better? There is no way of answering these questions without some form of experimental control.

Another difference between science and common sense is that the former is continually involved in the search for relationships. A scientist might ask, "If I.Q. is related to school achievement, what other factors are associated with I.Q.?" "How can I.Q. be enhanced?" "What other factors predict school achievement?" And, so on. In contrast, the layperson is usually content with simple cause-effect relationships.

A final difference between science and common sense, lies in the tendency to use metaphysical explanations; explanations which cannot be tested. For example, a coach's suggestion that "It was God's will" or "It was in the cards" would be a metaphysical type of explanation. The scientist would avoid these. This is not to say that the metaphysical explanation is not correct; only that scientists only concern themselves with events and situations which are observable and measurable.

A MODEL FOR MOTIVATION

The improvement of understanding is of two ends: first, our own increase in knowledge; secondly, to enable us to deliver that knowledge to others.

Locke

What the preceeding discussion has intended to highlight is that, first, research based conclusions are essential; second, motivation is complex and, consequently, no single aspect is exclusively useful; and, therefore, third, a frame-of-reference provides obvious advantages in the communication of ideas. First, complex issues can be simplified and more readily explained and understood. Secondly, it is possible to more readily draw assumptions about how the individual components are related to each other. And, finally, it is easier to determine what is known and unknown about the topic and what possible directions subsequent research might take.

A framework that is appropriate for motivation in sport and physical activity is presented in Figure 1.1. One aspect of this model is that it incorporates the long accepted view in psychology that behavior is a result of contributing factors from within the individual as well as contributing factors from within the individual's situation (environment).

A second aspect of this model is that it acknowledges that many things which contribute to individual motivation — within the individual and within the situation — are not directly under the coach's or teacher's control. For example, two factors within the sport situation which can contribute to a participant's motivation are the presence of an audience and the type of practice set out. A coach has little or no control over whether an audience is present or how loud and supportive it is. But, the coach has very direct control over the type of practices which are held. Similarly, two personal factors (factors within the performer) which contribute to an overall level of motivation are the personality trait of need achievement and the degree of intrinsic motivation present. A individual's personality is very stable and changes minimally; therefore, the teacher or coach have little or no control over it. However, it is possible

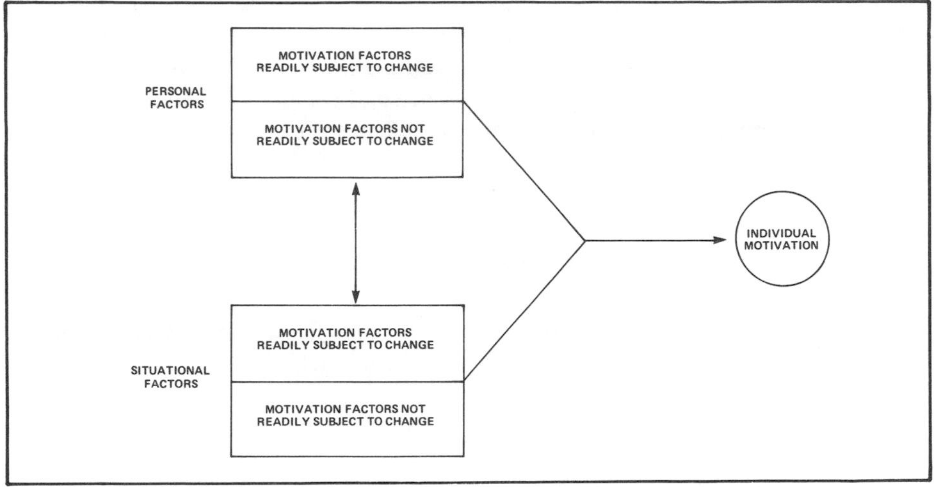

Figure 1.1
A Model for motivation in sport and physical activity.

to have a direct impact on the level of intrinsic motivation of the participant.

What this frame-of-reference serves to emphasize is that the sources of potential motivation for the participant in sport and physical activity are numerous and complex. And, the coach and teacher have an impact on selected aspects only. Thus, the task of the teachers and coaches is, first, to be aware of the potential sources of motivation, especially those over which they can have some influence. Secondly, the coach and teacher must be acknowledgeable about the relative effectiveness of each. Finally, decisions must be made regarding where and when each specific technique might be put to best use. An attempt is made to help in these decisions with the present text.

PROLOGUE

In creating, the only hard thing's to begin. A grass blade's no easier to make than an oak.

James Russell Lowell

The text is composed of six chapters. In the first (or present) chapter, the frame-of-reference which provides a foundation for the remainder of the text is introduced and explained. The subsequent four chapters then deal with the various components of the frame-of-reference set out in Figure 1.1. Thus, for example, Chapter 2 contains a discussion of those major situational factors contributing to motivation over which the teacher and coach have some control. Various factors which have the potential to contribute to the individual's overall level of motivation are introduced, the research findings pertinent to each factor are outlined, and practical implications for the coach and teacher are then set out. An identical format is adopted in Chapter 3 (situational factors over which the coach and teacher have no control), Chapter 4 (personal factors over which the coach and teacher have some control), and Chapter 5 (personal factors over which the coach and teacher have no control). The final chapter provides a summary or synopsis of motivation in sport and physical activity.

SUGGESTED READINGS

Carron, A.V. Motivating the athlete. In. W.F. Straub (Ed.), *Sport psychology: An analysis of athlete behavior.* Ithaca: Mouvement, 1978.

Gowen, G.R., Botterill, C.B., and Blimke, C.J.R. Bridging the gap between sport science and sport practice. In P. Klavora and J.V. Daniel (Eds.), *Coach, athlete, and the sport psychologist.* Champaign, Ill.: Human Kinetics, 1979.

Martens, R. From smocks to jocks: A new adventure for sport psychologists. In P. Klavora and J.V. Daniel (Eds.), *Coach, athlete, and the sport psychologist.* Champaign, Ill.: Human Kinetics, 1979.

CHAPTER 2

Situational Factors Readily Subject to Change

Coaches and teachers must be aware that the situations into which participants are placed can have a powerful influence upon their level of motivation. For example, from an athlete's perspective, all situations in sport — practices, games, the locker room, the field, arena, or auditorium — are motivating. This motivation is made up of two components (Alderman, 1978; Martens, 1975).

One of these can be referred to as the *objective* situation. As Alderman (1978) noted "purely objective stimuli in an actual situation can serve to motivate athletes. Physical stimuli such as the site or the facilities themselves act on an athlete, e.g., the shot and the circle to a shotputter or a swimming pool to a swimmer or a football stadium to a football player. Social stimuli such as the presence of spectators, other athletes, opponents, officials, etc. are objective, actual stimuli that contribute to increased arousal. Or the task itself (and all the feedback an athlete receives from his performances) has the potential to motivate an athlete simply because it is a natural requirement in the situation" (p. 138).

A second facet is the *subjective* situation — the perception the individual holds of the situation, its nature and significance. Two athletes might arrive at Yankee Stadium for a baseball game, for example. If one has played there for four previous seasons while the second is doing so for the first time, it is probable that the situation would have a different motivational impact on each of them.

It should be obvious that some aspects of the situation, both objective and subjective, cannot be influenced, while others can. In this chapter, the potentially motivating factors in the situation that can be manipulated are discussed. These include the use of token rewards, goal setting, variable practice sessions, social reinforcement, and specific coaching behaviors.

TOKEN REWARDS AS A MOTIVATOR

Teaching is the arrangement of contingencies of reinforcement under which students learn. They learn without teaching in their natural environments but teachers arrange special contingencies which expedite learning, hastening the appearance of behavior which would otherwise be acquired slowly or making sure of the appearance of behavior which would otherwise never occur.

B.F. Skinner

A fundamental assumption in education, industry, or sport is that rewards can be used to influence behavior — by withholding or providing inducements to the individual, it is possible to elicit, modify, or eliminate specific behaviors. Not surprisingly, this viewpoint is almost as old as psychology itself. For example, it formed the basis for Edward L. Thorndike's (1913a; 1913b) theory of learning (commonly referred to as connectionism). The role of rewards also forms the cornerstone of most of the major learning theories in psychology — Hull's (1943) drive theory and Skinner's (1938) behaviorism theory, for example. Today, this general topic of study is referred to by a number of names: behavior modification, operant psychology, token economies, and contingency management.

In sport and physical activity, the primary method of influencing the behavior of athletes through rewards is referred to as *contingency management* where a contingency is a relationship between a behavior and its consequences (Siedentop, 1978). As Siedentop (1978) suggested:

> *"It is the management of these relationships that is important for improving athlete productivity in practice settings. Coaches, or coaches and athletes working together, decide on what has to happen during practices. Athletics is full of potential rewards that can be used as incentives. The trade-off between practice performances and the earning of rewards is then established and a system to monitor practice performance is perfected. Those athletes that meet the contingencies earn the rewards. Those that don't perform in practice go unrewarded"* (p. 49-50).

Studies outlining those instances where contingency management programs have been successfully implemented are numerous. Those studies lead to a number of propositions which have applicability for the coach and teacher.

PROPOSITION: Undesirable behaviors can be eliminated through the use of token rewards.

In a classroom or gymnasium situation, the disruptive behaviors of a single individual or the total group can ruin the learning environment. The use of token rewards such as candy, decals, stars, trinkets, and access to special treatment in the form of free time, special events, special privileges, and so on can result in the elimination of these undesirable behaviors when other approaches have failed. For example, O'Leary, Becker, Evans, and Saudargas (1969) reported on a project in which a second grade teacher successfully used token rewards to control disruptive behavior after more conventional procedures such as ignoring the disruptive behavior, introducing behavioral rules, changing the educational situation, and using praise for appropriate behaviors were unsuccessful.

In a similar fashion, O'Leary and Becker (1967) outlined a program in which candy, comics, and pennants were used by a teacher to control the disruptive behavior (inappropriate talking, pushing, noise making, and eating in class) of a class of emotionally disturbed third grade children. Similar results for classroom situations (McLaughlin and Malaby, 1972a; Ringer, 1973) and with single individuals (McLaughlin and Malaby, 1972b) have also been reported.

Another, more sport specific example, was outlined by McKenzie and Rushall (1974). A token reward system was implemented to reduce tardiness and early departures and increase attendance and work output among swimmers. An attendance board was posted and swimmers were required to sign in and out. Also, behavioral games were introduced in practice so that squads competed for tokens. The program was extremely successful in bringing about the desired changes in the target behaviors; attendance increased, tardiness and early departures decreased, and performance times were improved.

PROPOSITION: Desirable behaviors can be enhanced through the use of token rewards.

An improvement in specific behaviors which are viewed as positive by the coach and teacher has also been successfully implemented through the use of token rewards. For example, in a study reported by Rolider (1978), the focus was on improving the atmosphere in a physical education basketball class. Using incentives to reinforce positive behaviors on the part of the students increased player-to-player encouragement by 128 percent. In a similar study with a high school basketball team (Siedentop and Dawson, 1978), positive communications among players were increased five fold when a point system was introduced and the recipients of these points received public recognition through a daily posting of the results.

In studies concerned with academic achievement in the classroom, token rewards have proven to be successful in improving study behaviors (Arwood, Williams, and Long, 1974; Broden, Hall, Dunlap, and Clark, 1970; Sloggett, 1971). These include activities such as class attendance, punctuality, bringing the necessary study materials, being in the correct place, attending to the teacher and facing the blackboard, and actually carrying out the work assigned. Not surprisingly, improvements in these behaviors were associated in most instances with improved school achievement.

PROPOSITION: Token rewards can have a spillover effect so that non-target behaviors are also positively affected.

Although a token reward is always introduced either to eliminate specific inappropriate behaviors or to increase the likelihood that specific desirable behaviors will appear, there are numerous instances reported where non-target behaviors also have been positively influenced. In short, there is a spillover effect.

A study carried out by Jones (1977) is a good example. A token reward system was set up at a summer sports camp in an attempt to improve basketball skills in teenage girls. The program was highly successful in achieving this objective. However, in addition, positive changes were noted in such non-target behaviors as increased interest, enthusiasm, and socialization.

A number of other indirect positive outcomes relating to student behavior have been observed including increased satisfaction (McLaughlin and Malaby, 1972b), improved attendance (Sloggett, 1971), improved attitudes toward school (Miller and Schneider, 1970) and increased pressures toward conforming to the rules (Sloggett, 1971).

In addition, a number of indirect positive outcomes relating to teacher behavior have been observed. These include an increase in teacher-student social interaction (Mandelker, Brigham and Bushell, 1970), and an increase in approving statements and a reduction in disproving ones (Chadwick and Day, 1971).

PROPOSITION: Individual performance can be improved through the use of token rewards.

A final important area in which token rewards can serve an important function is to improve performance. Undoubtedly, this occurs because each of the three aspects of motivation — selectivity, persistence, and intensity — are influenced by the rewards. For example, the selectivity aspect becomes involved because the use of rewards serves to direct the individual's attention and behavior to correct or important aspects of performance. The rewards also improve task persistence and provide the incentives to develop performance strategies. Finally, increased interest occurs because the performer works to obtain the reward.

In studies concerned with academic achievement, improved performance has been observed across a wide cross-section of academic areas (e.g., Chadwick and Day, 1971; Glynn, 1970; Staats, 1973). Further, these improvements have been shown to persist long after the token reward program was terminated. In a study by Dickinson (1974) the positive impact was still being felt two years after the completion of the program.

Studies in sport and physical activity have also provided evidence of the effectiveness of token rewards. For example, McKenzie and Rushall (1974) found that the introduction of behavioral games where squads within a swimming team competed for tokens led to improvements in swimming performance times. Similarly, Brock, Brock, and Willis (1972) reported that the performance of two teenage pole vaulters improved when points were awarded and practice results recorded (the points could be exchanged for milk shakes and released time from practices). And, Komacki and Barnett (1977) found that the execution of three football plays improved — from 62 to 82 percent, 54 to 82 percent, and 66 to 80 percent for the option, power sweep, and off tackle respectively — when the component parts of these plays were broken down in analysis and praise and recognition given for good execution. Finally, Jones (1977, 1978) examined the impact of colored plastic rings, which could be exchanged for a variety of rewards, upon the performance of a variety of basketball skills such as rebounding and passing. Large improvements in performance were observed.

Implications for the Coach and Teacher

From the foregoing discussion it seems obvious that behavior can be changed through the use of a token reward system. And as McKenzie (1979) pointed out "these systems have been successful in changing a wide variety of behaviors that are the concerns of physical educators, including numerous academic, social and physical skills. Token systems can be implemented with ease, and with the availability of no cost reinforcers such as free time, special privileges, and access to games, can be inexpensive to operate. Evidence also indicates that, for the most part, pupils enjoy participating in token economies. In addition, teachers, administrators and the general public have expressed satisfaction with most token applications" (p. 111-112).

Some care must be exercised, however, in setting up a token reward system. Siedentop (1978), who has been extensively involved in research on this issue has set out a series of guidelines.

Define the target in observable units. Because the token reward program is concerned with the modification of specific behaviors, a preliminary first step for the coach and teacher is to determine the specific target behaviors. While this may be difficult for things like sportsmanship, fair play, and so on, the token reward program cannot proceed until this step has been completed.

Explain the target behaviors clearly to the participants. As was the case above, the group must clearly understand what specific behaviors must be eliminated or improved. This is not to say that a coach or teacher shouldn't state that he/she is concerned about sportsmanship, for example. But, what is also necessary is a clear explanation of the specific behaviors or activities that are important. Thus, for example, a coach might say "I'm interested in improving sportsmanship so I'm going to keep track of the number of times each of you criticizes the officials."

Monitor the target behaviors consistently. Once the program has been started, it is important to maintain supervision. This can be carried out by the coach or teacher through student assistants or even by having people monitor themselves. When the supervision stops, the effectiveness of the program declines.

State the contingency clearly. The athletes must be clear about the contingency or reward system. Thus, when the target behavior is identified, the contingency is also laid out. So, for example, a coach might state "If you come to practice prior to the starting time of 4:30 p.m., you will receive one point. When you have accumulated 10 points, you can exchange these for a milkshake."

Use a simple reward system. The rewards should be tokens such as stars, points, public recognition and not major items such as T-shirts, plaques, and medals.

Think small. Because monitoring and supervision are critical to an effective program, it is advisable to begin with something small and manageable. It is then possible to add to the system.

Be consistent. Once a program has been implemented, it is important to follow through. A system is destroyed quickly through inconsistent application.

What the above guidelines tell us essentially is that it is important to identify the specific behaviors which are critical, to set up a token reward system in which an appropriate behavior leads to a specific reward, to outline this clearly to the group, and then, to consistently follow the program through to completion.

GOAL SETTING AS A MOTIVATOR

Make no little plans; they have no magic to stir man's blood. Make big plans, aim high in hope and work.

David H. Burnham

While the coach and teacher have a number of possible techniques to use in order to motivate a participant, some seem much more effective than others. Goal setting is one of these. As Locke[1], Shaw, Saari and Latham (1981) have pointed out, "the beneficial effect of goal setting on task performance is one of the most robust and replicable findings in the psychological literature. Ninety percent of the studies showed positive or partially positive effects. Furthermore, these effects are found just as reliably in field settings as in the laboratory" (p. 145). In research carried out in the business context, the improvements in performance obtained through goal setting programs have varied from 16 to 40 percent. Obviously, it isn't possible to achieve those kinds of increases with highly elite athletes because they are often operating close to their optimum. But even a one percent improvement can prove decisive in many instances and, of course, younger or less competent participants have a higher potential for improvement.

What are the main generalities which should be kept in mind about goal setting? On the basis of available research in a business and management science context (Locke et al., 1981), there appears to be a number of propositions which have application for sport.

[1]Locke et al (1981) have provided a comprehensive summary of the research carried out between 1969 and 1980 on goal setting and task performance in industrial settings. The present discussion draws heavily from their work.

PROPOSITION: Goal setting contributes to performance effectiveness.

a) **Specific, hard, challenging goals are better than specific easy goals, do-best goals, or no assigned goals.**
b) **Individuals must have sufficient ability to attain (or closely approximate) their goal.**
c) **Goals are most effective when they are stated in specific, quantitative behavioral terms rather than as vague intentions.**
d) **Intermediate goals or subgoals should be used as a link to long term or end goals.**
e) **Feedback is necessary if goals are to have maximum effectiveness in improving performance.**

In their comprehensive review of studies dealing with goal setting, Locke et al. (1981) found that in 99 out of the 110 research studies they examined, specific, hard goals produced better performance than medium, easy, do-your-best, or no goals. It should also be taken as a given fact, of course, that the individual must have the necessary ability to achieve the goal; the goal should be hard and challenging but it also must be within the person's potential for attainment.

Depending on the difficulty of the goal and how easy it will be to attain it, setting up intermediate or subgoals can be beneficial to long term goal attainment. If an athlete wants to be a tennis champion, for example, some intermediate targets must be laid out. The use of subgoals serves to provide the individual with feedback, helps to direct attention toward the important factors to practice on, and maintains interest, facilitates persistence, and affords a built-in strategy-for-action. However, on the potentially negative side, there is a possibility that the individual will treat a subgoal as the "ceiling" and be satisfied with its attainment.

Feedback (knowledge of results, KR) is also necessary with goal setting (Becker, 1978; Erez, 1977; Nemeroff and Cosentino, 1979; Strang, Lawrence, and Fowler, 1978). Locke et al. (1981) have observed that the research evidence supports

> "*one unequivocal conclusion: neither KR alone nor goals alone is sufficient to improve performance. Both are necessary. This view of goals and feedback as reciprocally dependent seems more useful and more accurate than Locke's (1968) earlier position, which viewed goals as mediating the effects of feedback on performance. Together, goals and feedback appear sufficient to improve task performance (given the obvious contextual variables such as adequate ability and lack of external blocks to performance). The studies demonstrate that action is regulated by both cognition (knowledge) and motivation*" (p. 135).

A study which illustrates the importance of feedback in conjunction with goal setting as well as the usefulness of setting up intermediate goals was the Bandura and Simon (1977) work with individuals striving to lose weight. They found that dieters who kept daily records of their food consumption and then set goals based on that information (i.e., feedback plus goal setting), decreased their food consumption significantly in comparison to a group who simply kept daily records (i.e., feedback only) and a control group that did not maintain records or set any goals. Moreover, weekly goals were only effective when daily goals were also established.

PROPOSITON: Token rewards are effective for increasing commitment in performance toward a specific goal.

In the previous section, it was pointed out that token rewards can be used effectively as a motivator to eliminate undesirable behaviors, improve desirable behaviors, and improve performance. Further, since the target, whether it is behavior or performance, must be stated in observable, measurable units, it represents a clearly defined goal. Thus, the effectiveness of goal setting can be improved through the use of token rewards.

The two conditions — goal setting and token rewards — are both effective on their own. Token rewards can influence performance without a goal setting program, and vice versa (Locke, Feren, McCaleb, Shaw, and Denny, 1980; Terborg, 1976; Terborg and Miller, 1978). It seems likely that the token rewards provide an additional incentive which, in turn, leads to an increased commitment to the task (Locke et al., 1981).

PROPOSITON: Supportiveness from the coach and teacher and goal acceptance by the participant are important positive factors in goal setting.

Three issues which are of interest to coaches and teachers involved in goal setting are: a) the relationship of the participant's participation in goal setting to the program's subsequent effectiveness, b) the relationship of the participant's acceptance of and commitment to the goal and the program's subsequent effectiveness, and c) the relationship of the coach's or teacher's supportiveness to participant effectiveness. Intuitively, it would seem that all three — participation, supportiveness, and acceptance — are directly associated with the effectiveness of any goal setting program. This is not necessarily the case; at least, it's not necessarily the case in research carried out in laboratory and business settings.

Goals arrived at in an autocratic fashion by the leader have not proven to be any less effective than goals arrived at in a consultative fashion by leaders and their followers (Locke and Schweiger, 1979). It may be that subordinates do not have an overall perspective of the task or they are unable to objectively assess their own skill level and potential. McClements and Botterill (1979) supported this viewpoint for an athletic situation when they observed that insofar as performance outcomes are concerned "coaches should not assume that athletes are capable of evaluating success on their own, because athletes often have inadequate reference-points and cannot be objective about themselves" (p. 201-202).

Goal acceptance or commitment is related to both a person's expectations for success and the incentive attached to that success (Locke et al., 1981). Thus, easy goals have little incentive value and, therefore, if they are accepted, are pursued with minimal commitment. Similarly, if the assigned goal is too difficult, the expectations for success are reduced, the possibility of a failure is increased, and, consequently, there is very little chance that the individual will accept it (Forward and Zander), 1971; Lopes, 1976; Zander, Forward and Albert, 1969). Thus, while the coach may set a goal for the athlete in an autocratic fashion, that goal should be attainable or the athlete will reject it.

Supportiveness on the part of the teacher or coach is important in order for a participant to reach his/her goal (Locke et al., 1981). This supportiveness can be shown through encouragement, friendliness, and by asking for advice from the performer (Latham and Saari, 1979). In this way, the coach or teacher serves as a facilitator in the goal setting process (Weinberg, 1982).

PROPOSITION: The positive effects of goal setting are produced independent of individual differences in age, sex, education, and personality.

A number of studies have examined the impact of several individual difference measures on the effectiveness of goal setting and the only consistent conclusion to emerge according to Locke et al., (1981) is that there is an inconsistency in the pattern of findings. In short, goal setting is effective in producing improved performance across all age levels (Ivancevich and McMahon, 1977), in both sexes (Ivancevich and McMahon, 1977; Steers, 1975), and with individuals who have broad ranges of education (Steers, 1975).

Insofar as personality is concerned, a number of different personality traits have been analyzed to determine if they influence the degree to which goal setting is an effective motivator. The traits studied include need for achievement (Sales, 1970), need for independence (Latham and Yukl, 1976), self esteem (Latham and Yukl, 1976), and perception of personal control (Latham and Yukl, 1976). No systematic differences were observed so, again, goal setting seems to be equally effective for individuals with a wide cross section of personality dispositions.

PROPOSITION: Competition among individuals for goal achievement produces greater commitment and better performance.

Sport and physical activity are competitive; not only does competition exist between groups but it is usually present in varying degrees within a group. Deutsch (1968) highlighted this point when he noted that "the members of a basketball team may be cooperatively interrelated with respect to winning the game but competitive with respect to being the 'star' of the team". Coaches and physical education teachers could profit from the competition which exists in sport and physical activity if they combined goal setting and competition. In a study by Latham and Baldes (1975) in which goal setting and feedback were used, competition occurred spontaneously among the participants. Also, White, Mitchell and Bell (1977) found that the direct introduction of competition resulted in an improvement in performance beyond that resulting from goal setting alone.

Implications for the Coach and Teacher

Reasons for Goal Setting. There are a number of reasons why a program of goal setting should be introduced (Coaching Association of Canada, 1979). These are illustrated in Figure 2.1

A number of these payoffs relate directly to coaching and teaching because they produce improvements in the group's *climate* or *general atmosphere.* For example, problem behaviors such as tardiness, laziness, lack of discipline, and unsportsmanlike conduct are prevented because the participants unite in pursuit of their personal and/or group goals. Communication is improved and empathy for the rights of others develops as information is shared about successes, setbacks, and possible strategies to use. Confidence and morale are enhanced and individual satisfaction is increased when the individual achieves particular standards, subgoals, or goals.

Other payoffs relate more to the *personal growth* which the participant experiences. For example, a person involved in a goal setting program develops increasing maturity in the form of self-discipline, self-control, and self-management. In turn, the person's coping capabilities — ability to adapt to difficult situations — are aided through the experiences gained. Moreover, the potential for using goal setting or long range planning procedures can spill over into other aspects of the person's life. Another payoff benefits the coach or teacher. *Leadership* becomes more enjoyable and the leader's effectiveness is improved as a direct result of the factors listed above. Quite simply, it's easier to work with participants who know what they are doing, are motivated to do it, and who experience success in the process.

Also, a number of payoffs revolve around the *group's goals and objectives.* For example, through goal setting, specific goals and priorities are clarified for all group members. The relative importance which a coach or leader attaches to individual outcomes, group outcomes, social experiences, and performance outcomes are clearly laid out through a goal setting program. Because goals are expressed in specific terms, measurable success is assured. And, clear, acceptable goals also lead to increased commitment and motivation on the part of the participant.

Although the impact of goal setting is extremely important from a performance/production perspective, there also may be compelling, humanistic reasons for coaches

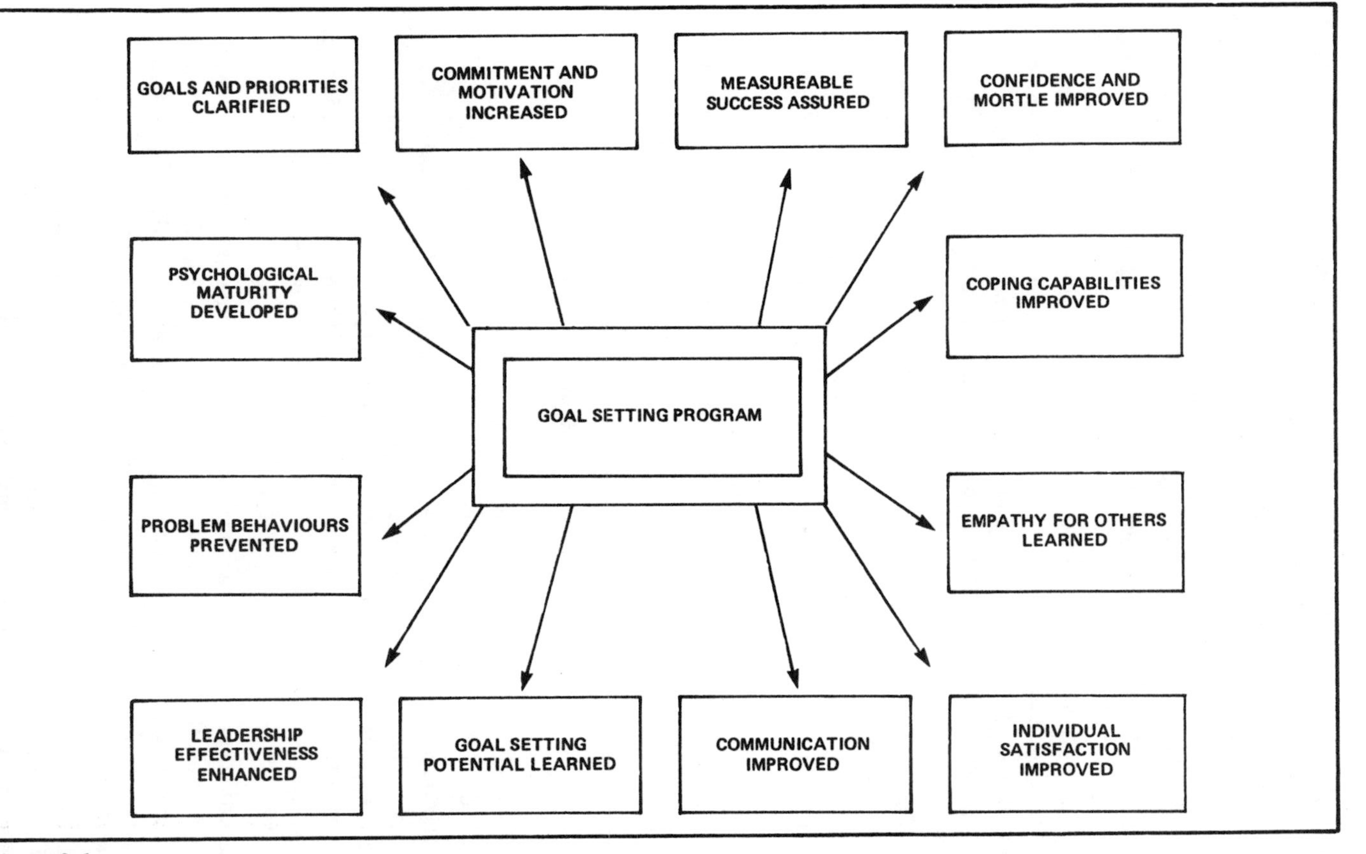

Figure 2.1
Benefits of goal setting programs (Adapted from Coaching Association of Canada, 1979).

and teachers to become sensitive to the need to establish individual goals for the participants. McClements and Botterill (1979) have argued that "if sport and competition have social values, then *each individual has the right to be successful.* Proper setting of goals and evaluation of this attainment can facilitate this right. Each person involved with sport has the responsibility to promote the right to be successful. In order to ensure the opportunity for success, the planning process should include the goal setting and evaluation as equal partners with skill learning, physical training and teamwork" (p. 199). Rather than use an absolute standard for performance (such as winning) which permits only an elite minority to experience success, the coach and teacher should establish individual standards which are relative to each participant's age, experience, ability, and aptitude. Through effective goal setting, all participants can then experience the satisfaction which is derived from successful achievement of an objective.

Mechanisms Associated with Goal Setting. There are four reasons why goal setting works (Locke et al., 1981). These are shown in Figure 2.2. As this diagram illustrates, one aspect of goal setting is that it serves to *direct attention and action.* It is one thing to tell an athlete to come back to training camp in "good physical shape" but this is not as effective as setting out specific goals. These specific goals might include time or improvement expected for speed events such as the 40 yard sprint, time expected for endurance events like a two mile run, and, specific kilogram improvement expected for strength events like the bench press. Through goal setting, the athlete's attention and actions are directed toward those individual components of getting in shape that the coach has set the highest premium on.

This was illustrated in a study on drivers reported by Locke and Bryan (1969). Feedback was provided for five different aspects of driving performance but goals were established for only one of these. Improvement in that one aspect was found to be significantly greater than for the other four.

The second mechanism associated with goal setting is a *mobilizing of energy.* Not only is the individual's attention and action directed toward the goal but the necessary effort is also expended to achieve that outcome. More difficult goals produce better performance in terms of speed, work in a given period of time, and perceived effort than do easy goals or no goals because the individual simply works harder for the difficult goals (Locke et al., 1981).

Goal setting also influences *persistence* which is a combination of the previous two — the direction of effort expended by the individual over an extended period of time. Participants who have specific, challenging but attainable goals will persist for longer periods of time than participants who are not given goals or who are simply told to "do your best."

The final way in which goal setting influences task performance is by *motivating the individual to develop performance strategies or plans-for-action.* A swimmer who is given a goal which requires five one-hour weight training sessions per week must

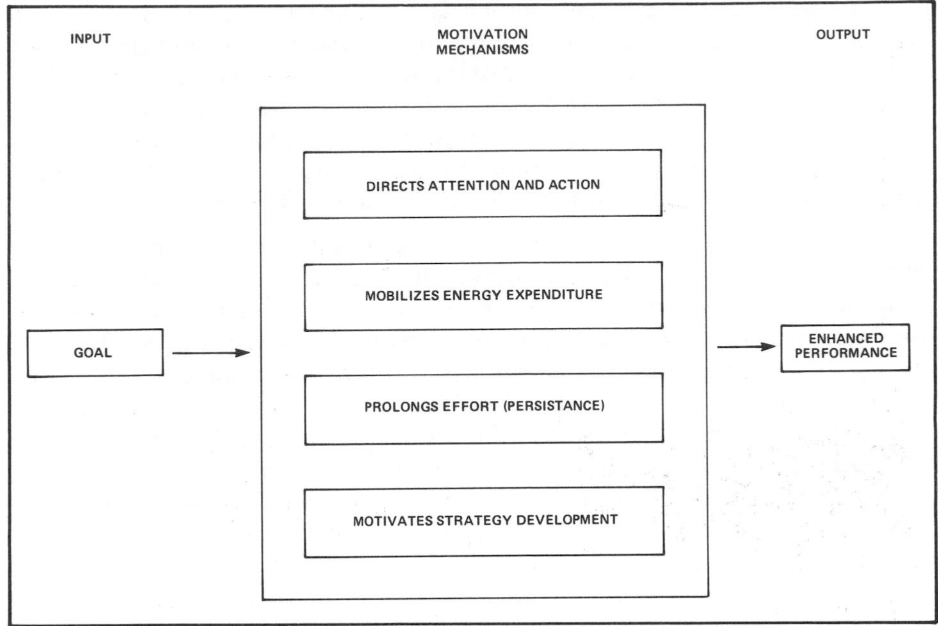

Figure 2.2
The motivational mechanisms associated with a goal setting program (Adapted from Locke, Shaw, Saari, and Latham, 1981).

develop an overall weekly timetable in order to accommodate this goal within a schedule that might also include swim practices, school, a social life, and homework.

This was illustrated in the study by Bandura and Simon (1977) of individuals on a diet. When the subjects were given set quotas for number of mouthfuls of high-calorie foods, they changed their eating patterns both in terms of types of food eaten and the amount eaten at specific times. This was done through the development of an overall plan for action.

The Dynamic Nature of Goal Setting. A goal setting program must be dynamic, not static in nature. That is, periodic evaluations should be undertaken at various stages in order to assess the relative effectiveness of the program. Adjustments can then be made to the situation if they are required. Thus, for example, a basketball player's defensive goal may be to limit an opponent to 15 points. If the opponent has scored 13 points by the end of the first half, reevaluation and adjustments to the goal must be made both in terms of the program (i.e., the way in which the player is carrying out the assignment) and the goal for the second half of the game. Similarly, a long term goal such as improving the team's free throw percentage to 75 percent might have to be adjusted upward if that standard is achieved readily.

The dynamic nature of goal setting is illustrated in Figure 2.3. A goal is determined for a class or game (short term goal) or season (long term goal) and an appropriate program or strategy is planned in order to help with goal attainment. This program is then evaluated against the goal. Is the goal possible given the individual's skills? Is the program appropriate? If the answer to these and other related questions is "no", it is necessary to start over. Either the goal or the program must be modified. If the answer to these questions is "yes", the program can then be initiated.

The participant would then carry out the program by training, competing or performing. If this is not being done, the coach or teacher must again reevaluate the goal or the program. However, if the program is being carried out, the coach or teacher can then evaluate the participant's progress. This evaluation is carried out from two major perspectives: *effort* and *performance.* Effort is the more important of the two —if the performer makes the effort, success has been achieved. According to McClements and Botterill (1979) "the evaluation of performance is only meaningful if the [person] has made the effort to complete the program. *It is crucial to evaluate effort before evaluating performance...* [When performance is considered] it is very important ...to avoid the *either-or* thinking that leads to labeling success or failure. It is more important to determine the degree of success and to identify the cause, that is, the program, commitment, opportunity, long term goal, or individual potential" (p. 202).

Prediction of Performance. One of the most difficult aspects involved in setting difficult but attainable goals is in estimating where the person should be at some future point in time. Goal setting involves prediction — the prediction of future performance (McClements and Laverty, 1979; McClements and Botterill, 1979). Prediction might be easy if skill acquisition occurred in a regular fashion. For example, a regular improvement would be present if a high jumper showed a 4 cm. increase in jumping ability from 10 to 11 years; another 4 cm. increase from 11 to 12 years; another 4 cm. from 12 to 13 years; and, so on. With each unit of time (years in this example), the improvement is constant.

However, almost without exception, when a skill is learned, improvement is not regular. There is a rapid initial improvement, then a tapering off (see Figure 2.4). In short, learning follows the *law of diminishing returns* (McClements and Laverty, 1979). As the absolute performance limits are approached by a learner — and these limits are fixed by the learner's body structure, physiological potential, and genetic make-up — it becomes more difficult to show performance improvements. Therefore, goal setting must take this into account.

McClements and Laverty (1979) provided a mathematical example of how this might be done using the hypothetical case of a speedskating athlete who, in 1976, has a longterm goal of competing internationally by 1984. As Figure 2.4 illustrates, the index of improvement which is associated with this long term goal (which is marked by a Y on the horizontal axis) is 28 when the current level of performance, the starting point, (which is marked by an X on the horizontal axis) is 0.

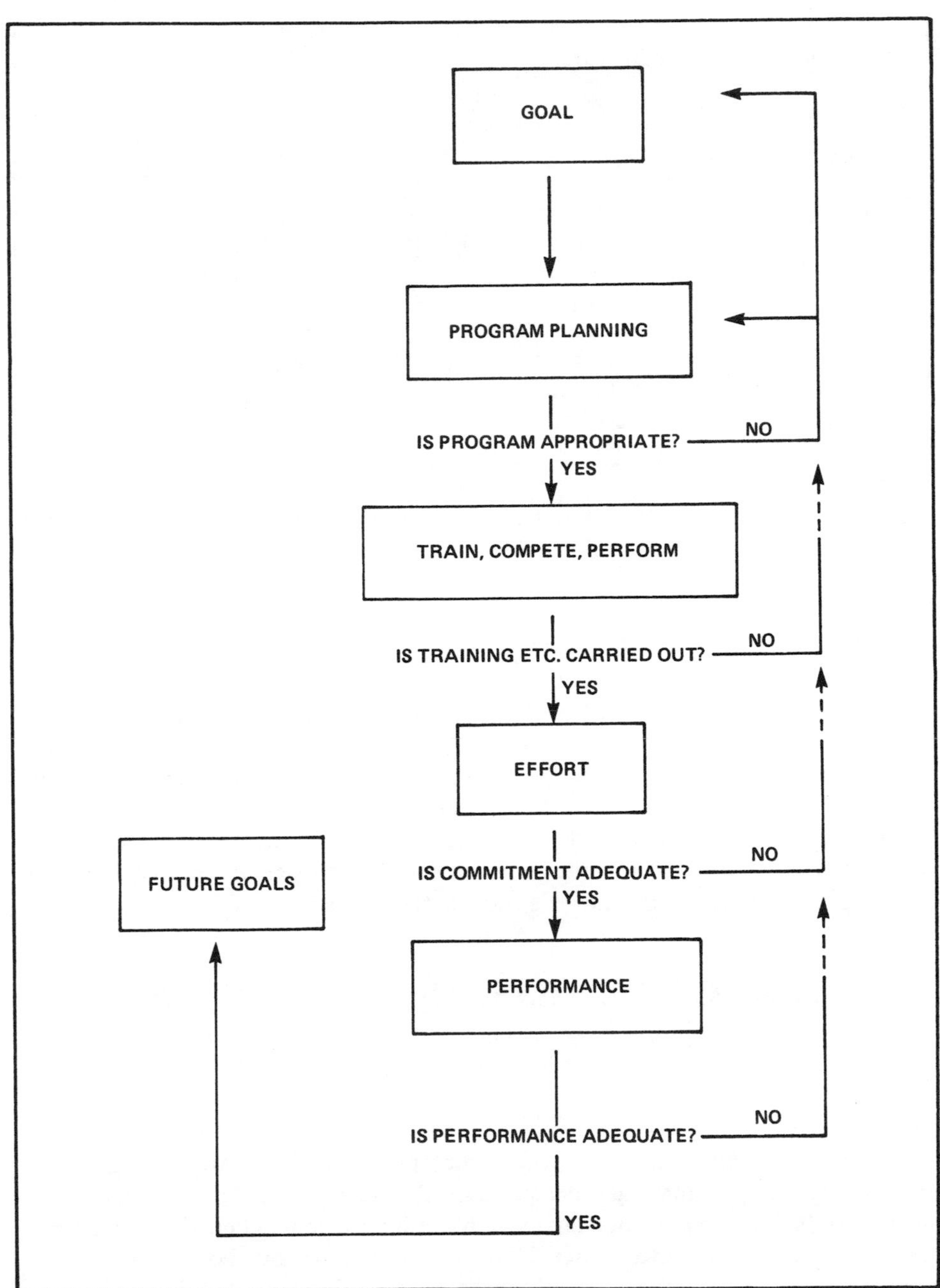

Figure 2.3
The goal setting process (Adapted from McClements and Botterill, 1979).

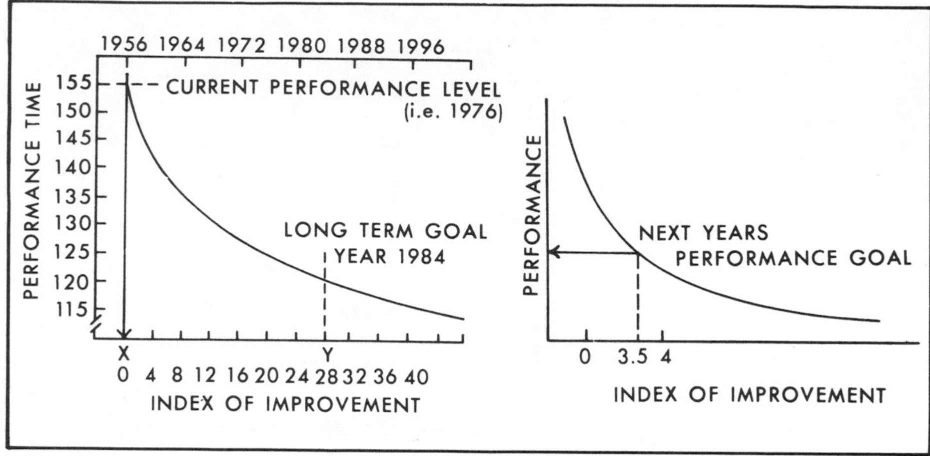

Figure 2.4

Goal setting for athletes: (a) An individual goal setting curve; (b) The performance goal for the coming season (From McClements and Laverty, 1979; Used with permission).

Since the athlete is 28 index units from the goal and there is 8 years available to achieve the goal, 3.5 units (28 divided by 8) represents the first year goal. In order to determine how the 3.5 units are translated into actual performance expectations, a line is drawn upward from the horizontal axis to the performance curve and then taken across to the vertical axis (see Figure 2.4). In each subsequent year, a similar process would then be undertaken. McClements and Laverty have correctly pointed out that in this way, short term performance goals could be used to evaluate both performance and training programs at the end of a short term period.

THE PRACTICE SESSION AS A MOTIVATOR

In the NHL there is so much repetition. You can almost predict what the practices will be before you go. They go over and over the same thing.

Fred Arthur

With older, more experienced (or elite) performers who are undergoing an intense regimen of training and competition, the challenge of the coach is often to insure that boredom and mental fatigue don't build to a point where they can detract from effective performance. Tom Watt (1979), a university hockey coach and, subsequently a coach in the National Hockey League, highlighted this problem in a discussion of the critical issues facing coaches, issues which he would like to see addressed by sport psychologists:

"As a hockey coach faced with a long schedule, I need to know more about motivational theory. How can you maintain the players' motivation over a long period of time? It is a problem for us at the university level with a season of 35 to 40 games but it must be a greater problem in professional sport with 80 or 100 games played in a season" (p. 11).

Roger Neilson, coach of Vancouver Canucks of the National Hockey League also addressed this same issue and provided what he considered to be a possible solution to the problem:

"In hockey you're practising every day, so variety is a key. Some parts have to be fun drills and new ideas. There's a drill practice that has to be hard working, a short 45-minute deal. If the players really are working hard all the time that's about all they can take. You have the teaching type practice, where in part, you'll work on something like powerplay or penalty killing, shot blocking, checking, passing or whatever. They take a lot longer, maybe two hours. Or you can have a conditioning practice where you do maybe 30 minutes work on aerobics" (Newman, 1982, p. 11).

Neilson's suggestion about the need for variety is sound. There is research evidence to back it up, and, thus, it represents a general proposition for consideration.

PROPOSITION: Motivation can be increased through the introduction of novelty, a change in routine and/or, by providing special attention to the participant.

Historically, in industrial psychology, the main support for this proposition has come from research carried out from 1924 to 1932 at the Western Electric Company's Hawthorne Plant in Chicago (Roethlisberger and Dickson, 1939). The general purpose of that research program was to examine the influence of different components or aspects of the work environment upon employee morale and, ultimately, upon their work output and productivity. The important conclusion drawn from that research program, however, was that the specific aspects of the work environment were not as critical as insuring that change was introduced periodically — the special attention paid to employees served as a motivating device.

This phenomenon of increased motivation resulting from changes in the environment has come to be called the *Hawthorne effect.* And, as Rice (1982) noted, it has "helped to launch a whole new approach to human relations in industry, an approach that underlies current attempts by American industry to motivate workers and increase productivity by redesigning job conditions" (p. 70).

Rice also pointed out, however, that the Hawthorne effect was never actually scientifically demonstrated in the original study. There were serious gaps and flaws in the published reports and, more importantly perhaps, any improvements in performance could be attributed to the presence of other factors. For example, slower workers in the original sample were replaced, no attempt was ever made to separate improvements due to learning (simply getting better at the task) from improvements due to motivation, and the selective introduction into the experimental situation of rewards and incentives and the use of performance feedback and goal setting might have accounted for any motivation and performance results. Therefore, it does not seem reasonable to draw on the Hawthorne effect alone as the only source of support for the above proposition. Two other avenues of research also provide considerable support for the proposition.

Stimulus seeking behavior, which includes the need for *activity, curiosity, exploration, manipulation,* and *contact,* is a basic requirement of all species. Unlike physiological motives such as *hunger, thirst, pain avoidance, sleep,* and *sex* which are also basic, the stimulus motives are more independent on conditions from outside the organism rather than from within. Consequently, they serve a function beyond simple survival of the organism or species. They provide us with the necessary push to investigate and manipulate our environment (Morris, 1976).

Because the need for stimulation and change in the environment are basic, the curiosity and exploration motives propel all organisms to seek out or choose unfamiliar situations (and stimuli) over more familiar ones. For example, research has shown that if a rat is placed in a black maze and allowed to become familiar with it, on a subsequent trial when it is given a choice between a black and a white maze, it will choose the white one (Dember, 1965). Similarly, give a choice between more complex versus more simple situations, animals also show a greater preference for complexity (Dember, Earl and Paradise, 1957). That complexity provides greater opportunity to satisfy the curiosity motive.

This basic need for change is also apparently associated with the way in which humans focus their attention and take in information from their surroundings. For example, attention will be directed toward those stimuli or events in the environment which are unusual or have unusual characteristics — probably because they provide the greatest stimulation to the sense organs (Kahneman, 1973). Situations or conditions which are highly familiar or commonplace do not attract attention until they move or change in some way.

The second avenue of research which provides support for the proposition that novelty and change should be introduced into a practice session has been reported under the heading *optimal level theory* (Berlyne, 1960; Duffy, 1962; Hebb, 1949; Leuba, 1955; Malmo, 1959; and, Walker, 1964). While it is often assumed that there is one optimal level theory which deals with the amount of arousal associated with the most effective performance, there are actually a number of different ones (Carron, 1980). Each of these deals with the state of the individual — the amount of muscle tension, the degree of physiological arousal, the level of sensory stimulation or complexity — preferred by the individual.

Two principles have been developed from research on the optimal level theories. Both of these provide support for the suggestion that periodic changes should be introduced into the participant's situation.

In the *simplification principle,* it is stated that as a result of repeated exposures, stimuli or situations become less complex, less stimulating, or less arousing. In short, the person adapts. Thus, for example, professional basketball players soon find that the regular season contests are not highly motivating. They find it harder and harder to retain their motivation unless their opponent represents a special challenge.

The generalization in the *habituation principle* is that those individuals who are more experienced with a stimulus or situation show greater preference for change and an increase in complexity. Thus, for example, professional athletes with the greatest experience show the greatest preference for the beginning of the playoffs.

Studies in which subjects have been placed in situations with severely reduced enviornmental stimulation (referred to as sensory deprivation) clearly illustrate some aspects of these principles (e.g., Bexton, Heron, and Scott, 1954; Heron, 1961; Lilly, 1956). For example, Bexton, Heron, and Scott (1954) paid volunteers to lay on a bed for 24 hours a day in a quiet cubicle, wearing translucent goggles over their eyes, gloves on their hands, and cuffs over their forearms to reduce stimulation. For most subjects, the situation become intolerable within two or three days and the experiment had to be terminated. The disorientation experienced as a result of the sensory deprivation also persisted for some time after the subjects were removed from the environment.

Similarly, Berlyne (1951, 1958, 1960, 1969) has carried out a series of experiments on selective attention which also illustrates these principles. For example, in the initial phase of a three-phase experiment, subjects responded to lights in four windows by pressing a lever as quickly as possible. During each of the final two phases, one of the lights was replaced by a novel stimulus light which differed in either shape or color from both its predecessor and its cohorts. The results showed that a response was much more likely to occur to a novel than to a familiar stimulus.

Berlyne (1960, 1969) has also reported that novelty and variety have an impact on the speed of learning. Stimuli of greater intensity or novelty were found to serve as more effective rewards for learning than familiar stimuli. And, in another experiment, when three-to-nine-month old children were presented with oblongs which differed in geometric design and complexity, the most complex one was always examined first (Berlyne, 1958).

Implications for the Coach and Teacher

It is possible that the repetitive presentation of drills over the course of a teaching year or coaching season might not detract from the participant's performance because other motivational factors are undoubtedly in operation. For instance, those individuals with exceptional intrinsic motivation or a high need for achievement or those individuals on a good goal setting program or receiving token rewards might maintain sufficient motivation for effective performance. But, there is no doubt that, in the general case, monotony of routine and a repetition in approach will detract from motivation. Certainly, there seems to be no doubt that constant repetition will do little or nothing to enhance motivation.

Many coaches and teachers are sensitive to the need for an occasional change particularly when individual or group motivation might be low. For example, football coaches switch their linemen to the backfield (and vice versa) or have their team play soccer rather than football during an occasional practice. Although the athlete's task has been changed and, therefore, the payoff in football skill acquisition is negligible, the increased motivational benefits far outweigh the negative aspects.

Roger Neilson, in the quote leading off this section, talked about using variety in a practice session — variety from the point of view of type (or purpose of the practice), duration of time spent, and intensity. The range of practices he suggested encompassed fun drills, intense conditioning sessions, practices devoted to highly specific aspects of the game (e.g., the power play, penalty killing), and sessions devoted to standard hockey drills. Each of these had a different fundamental purpose and, more importantly, provided for novelty, variety, and change.

Having another person teach your class or coach your team occasionally is also a good idea. Commenting on the idea that coaches might consider taking time away from their teams during the course of the season, Neilson stated that "it's probably not a bad idea when you think that there are so many games in baseball or hockey. A week break would be good for everybody, if you could have someone else step in and do the job while you were gone" (Newman, 1982, p. 10). This represents a radical departure from tradition. Also, the coach would have to be mature (and secure) enough to recognize that any motivational benefits resulting from the temporary departure would be an inevitable by-product of the novelty and change; not an indication of improved coaching by the replacement!

While the above examples represent dramatic illustrations of a coach utlizing novelty and change to enhance motivation, other more subtle examples are available. For instance, most teachers or coaches who have taught a skill for an extended period of time are rather restricted in the number and variety of drills they use. The process is gradual. Through experience in teaching and coaching, efficient, effective drills may be added and modified and less useful drills eliminated. The result is that many experienced teachers and coaches may have a fixed, minimal repertoire of drills which are used repetitively. On occasion, the teacher and coach should consider a trade-off. That is, a less effective drill (in terms of teaching potential) might be better in some instances because it is a change and, therefore, is potentially more motivating.

SOCIAL REINFORCEMENT AS A MOTIVATOR

I don't praise other teams. I'm considered somewhat of an authority. If I build up another team, they're liable to believe me.
Woody Hayes

Reinforcement is considered to be "a neutral term referring to one of the operations that will increase the strength of a response. A *positive reinforcer* is any stimulus which, when it follows a response, will increase the strength or maintain the occurrence of that response. A *negative reinforcer* is a stimulus, the removal of which increases the strength of a response" (Martens, 1975, p. 52). From this perspective, *social reinforcement* in a sport and physical activity can be viewed as all the positive and negative comments or reactions made by coaches, teachers, parents, and fellow players which serve to convey information of an evaluative nature to the participant. Consequently, they serve as motivators. This information can be transmitted both verbally and by facial expressions — through praise, encouragement, favorable gestures, smiles, frowns, reproof, criticism, or disinterest.

Martens (1975) has pointed out that the terminology and language used in discussing reinforcement has not been consistent and this has led to some confusion in the past. For example, not only can reinforcement be positive or negative but each of these types of reinforcement can be presented or withdrawn. This results in four outcomes; two classes of rewards and two classes of punishment (see Table 2.1).

Positive reinforcement — the quadrant in Table 2.1 which results from the presentation of reinforcement of a positive nature to the person — can be viewed as a reward. This occurs when a teacher or coach smiles, congratulates and/or pats the participant on the back after a good performance.

Negative reinforcement also can be viewed as a reward, a reward which occurs when the negative reinforcement is terminated or withdrawn. Thus, a coach may be continuously critical of an archer's inaccurate attempts. Then, when a perfect shot is made by the archer, the coach might say and do nothing. Removing the negative reinforcement would represent a negative reward.

Punishment may occur in two ways (Table 2.1). In one, negative reinforcement is presented to the participant. A teacher who criticizes a student for a poor performance

Table 2.1 The terminology of social reinforcement (Adapted from Martens, 1975).

TYPE OF REINFORCEMENT	MANIPULATION	CONSEQUENCES
POSITIVE	Presented	Reward
	Withdrawn	Punishment
NEGATIVE	Presented	Punishment
	Withdrawn	Reward

is one example of this type of reinforcement. In the second instance, punishment is present because positive reinforcement normally given is withdrawn. For example, a baseball coach may be in the habit of saying something positive to every child after they have taken their turn at bat. If the coach suddenly doesn't do this for the child —the child may simply be ignored — the result would be a form of "punishment."

There is little doubt that the impact of social reinforcement upon behavior and performance has been an issue which has intrigued researchers for some time. As Kennedy and Willicutt (1964) observed "experimental studies using various incentives for motivating discrimination, learning, and performance in human and animal subjects compose the greater part of the literature of psychology. The history of child psychology is spanned by studies seeking to evaluate the effectiveness of praise and blame as incentives for school children" (p. 323). What this research has shown us is that social reinforcement does not consistently result in a modification or improvement in motor skill performance. There are a number of factors which influence the degree to which social reinforcers have an impact on the learning and performance of physical skills.

PROPOSITION: Social reinforcement is an effective motivator for behavior and performance under selected circumstances.

a) **Younger children profit more than older ones from social reinforcement.**
b) **Social reinforcement has a greater impact when it is administered by an individual who is less well known to the recipient.**
c) **Social reinforcement has a greater impact when it is administered by significant people of the opposite sex.**
d) **Social reinforcement is more effective in tasks that are very simple, well learned, boring, or where feedback is not otherwise readily available.**
e) **Children who are the recipients of positive social reinforcement gain better self esteem and more positive perceptions of their coach.**

There are a number of research studies in which social reinforcements had no effect on adult subjects. For example, Roberts and Martens (1970) had university students practice on a motor task. Four experimental groups were formed: positive social reinforcement, negative social reinforcement, no social reinforcement (knowledge of results was given but no evaluative comments were made by the experimenter or four confederates), and control (only the experimenter was present during testing and knowledge of results was given but no evaluative comments were made). There were no differences among the four groups.

Younger children do appear to be more sensitive to the use of social reinforcement than older children or adults (Kennedy and Willicutt, 1964; Martens,

1975). This may be because social reinforcers used frequently (and possibly, indiscriminantly) lose their informational and/or motivational impact. The teacher who says "very good" after every performance by every student may create a positive, humanistic environment. However, ultimately that encouragement will hold little incentive value and convey no information about performance effectiveness to the student.

In a comment related to this point Panda (1971) noted that "if in the past the child has learned that social comments have little informational value because of their indiscriminate use and unreliable occurrence he will ignore them and turn to more reliable cues ... [The effectiveness of reinforcers depends on] how reliable they are used to discriminate the forthcoming positive events and extent to which they are contingent on the child's response" (p. 60). This may also account for the fact that social reinforcement received from individuals who are unfamiliar to or even disliked by the recipient possess greater motivational impact (Stevenson, 1965).

The type of task being carried out and the sex of the person providing the reinforcement are also factors to consider. Stevenson (1961) and Stevenson and Allen (1964) found that childrens' performances on speed of movement tasks were superior when social reinforcement was introduced. This general result has been replicated with sufficient frequency that Stevenson (1965), in a review of the literature, concluded that social reinforcement improves performance in simple or quantitative tasks (i.e., tasks involving easily measured outcomes such as strength and speed).

The critical factor may not be whether the task is simple or complex, qualitative or quantitative but whether it is *intrinsically interesting.* Stevenson (1965) suggested that "if interesting tasks are used it is likely that ... supportive comments will initially have only minimal effect and will gain in effectiveness only after the child has played with the materials long enough to become satiated" (pp. 98-99). In other words, when interest starts to decrease or the dramatic improvements associated with initial learning begin to diminish, social reinforcement will be more effective.

Wankel's (1975) results from a study with grade seven and eight boys using a balance task called the stabilometer are consistent with this suggestion by Stevenson. Three groups were tested under positive, negative, or no social reinforcement conditions. Five blocks of five trials represented the test period. No differences were present among the groups during the first three blocks — the period when the most dramatic improvements in performance were occurring. In the final two blocks, however, the positive reinforcement group was superior to the negative reinforcement group and the control group.

Gerwitz and Baer (1958), Stevenson (1961), and Stevenson and Allen (1964) have all found that elementary school children show greater improvements in performance when social reinforcement is administered by people of the opposite sex. It may be that there is either greater incentive in obtaining reinforcement from someone of the opposite sex or that a person of the same sex leads to increases in performance anxiety which, in turn, detracts from performance (Hill and Stevenson, 1965).

Because the effects of social reinforcement are so elusive — present under some conditions for some subjects in some studies, absent in others — some social scientists have even questioned their usefulness as a general motivational phenomena. Martens (1975), addressing this issue, provided one sound reason why the use of positive reinforcers should be encouraged for coaches and teachers:

> *"Perhaps you may now conclude that social reinforcements should be eliminated when teaching motor skills, but no such interpretation is intended. Social reinforcements may play a very important indirect role in the learning of motor skills. The judicious use of positive social reinforcement is probably very important in the development and maintenance of positive interpersonal relations between the learner and teacher. Although we often overlook this point, in many voluntary learning experiences the development of negative or even neutral interpersonal relations will result in the learner discontinuing his efforts. Possibly good interpersonal relations may indirectly facilitate learning by maintaining a relationship between the teacher and learner in which the learner will heed the information provided him by the teacher"* (p. 65).

The importance of creating a positive environment in sport and physical activity was vividly illustrated by Smith, Smoll and their colleagues (e.g., Curtis, Smith, and Smoll, 1979; Smith, Smoll, and Curtis, 1978; Smith, Smoll, and Hunt, 1977). After initially developing an inventory which could be used to code and classify coaching behaviors in practices and games — called the *Coaching Behavior Assessment System* (see Table 2.2) — subsequent studies were carried out to assess the relative frequency with which these behaviors occurred with coaches and the impact of these behaviors upon athletes. Finally, a training program was initiated with a group of Little League coaches to sensitize them to the impact that their behaviors could have on athletes and then to counsel them in the use of positive behaviors. In this last aspect, another group was used that did not go through the training program and it served as a control.

A number of important results came out of the project but for purposes of the present discussion, the following are most pertinent:

- The coaches who were trained to emphasize more positive coaching behaviors were perceived by their athletes as providing more reinforcement, more encouragement, and more instruction. Also, they were perceived as more knowledgeable and as better teachers of baseball skills.
- The coaches who were not trained were perceived as using more punishment and as more frequently ignoring a good performance.
- The athletes playing for the coaches who were trained expressed greater satisfaction with the coach and a stronger desire to play for that coach again.
- A difference in the perception of the general team environment was also present; athletes who played for the trained coaches rated their teams as higher in the degree

Table 2.2 The Smith, Smoll, Curtis, and Hunt COACHING BEHAVIOR ASSESSMENT SYSTEM

Origin of the behavior	Specific Stimulus Event	Type of Coaching Response	Description
Reactive Behaviors (Response by coach to an Athlete Behavior)	Desirable performance	1. Positive Reinforcement	Verbal or non-verbal Positive Reaction
		2. Nonreinforcement	Failure to Reinforce Positive Behavior
	Mistakes/Errors	3. Mistake Contingent Encouragement	Encouragement Following a Player's Mistake
		4. Mistake Contingent Technical Instruction	Providing Instruction to a Player After a Mistake
		5. Punishment	Verbal or Nonverbal Negative Reaction
		6. Punitive Mistake Contingent Technical Instruction	Combination of Negative Reaction and Instruction
		7. Ignoring Mistakes	Failure to Respond in any Way to a Mistake
	Misbehaviors	8. Keeping Control	Responses Designed to Maintain Order
Spontaneous Behaviors (Behavior Spontaneously Initiated by The Coach)	Game Related	9. General Technical Instruction	Communication on Techniques or Strategy
		10. General Encouragement	Spontaneous Encouragement
		11. Organization	Communications of an Administrative Nature
	Game Irrelevant	12. General Communication	Interactions Unrelated to the Sport or Game

of interpersonal attraction present among teammates.
- Athletes playing for coaches who were trained showed an increase in self esteem over the course of the season.

Smoll and Smith (1979) have pointed out "like other kinds of human interaction, coaching involves trying to influence others in desired ways ... the *positive approach* is designed to strengthen desirable behaviors by motivating people to perform them ... the *negative approach* involves attempts to eliminate negative behaviors through the use of punishment and criticism. The motivating factor in the second approach is fear. Both of these approaches are used by coaches, but there are a number of reasons why the positive approach is preferred. First, it works much better! Second, it creates an enjoyable climate" (p. 5).

It is obvious that the training program with the Little League coaches was highly successful in producing a positive climate. The athletes saw themselves, their teammates, their coaches, and the sport in a more positive light. And, of course, in most sport programs involving young children these are the fundamental objectives emphasized by the general organization, and most coaches and parents.

Implications for the Coach and Teacher

It seems clear that social reinforcement, particularly positive, social reinforcement, is not as powerful a motivator of performance as some other factors discussed in this book. It also seems clear that a major reason for this is that it is often used frequently and sometimes indiscriminantly and unreliably by coaches, teachers, and parents. Most coaches and teachers strive to develop a supportive climate which emphasizes praise, encouragement, and a great deal of instruction. Consequently, social reinforcers may lose their motivational and informational impact.

Vince Lombardi used praise sparingly and, as a result, when it was given, it was prized by the athletes. This is vividly illustrated in an entry in a diary kept by Jerry Kramer during the 1967 NFL season (Schaap, 1968):

> *"More than anything else, I suppose, Lombardi is a psychologist. Maybe a child psychologist. Today he kept telling Bob Hyland, the big rookie, how great he is. 'Fantastic, Hyland, fantastic,' he kept saying.*
>
> *Hyland has come in for a lot of praise from the old man - and only from the old man. Actually, he's made a couple of blocks that were sort of medium, semi-good, and Coach has told him that they were great. Lombardi has a habit of praising the young people when they do anything at all. He was that way with Gillingham last season - everything Gilly did was fantastic - but now he's riding Gilly every day, chewing him, chewing him, chewing him. The courtship is over, the romance is gone, and Gilly's got to work his ass to the ground. The strange thing, and maybe it isn't*

strange at all, is that Gilly is twice the ballplayer this year that he was last year. He's taken Fuzzy's job away for good.

Vince has always chewed Fuzzy and me pretty hard, and once we stopped and figured out why. First, Vince was an offensive coach before he was a head coach, so he's tougher on the offense. Second, he played the line himself, so he's tougher on linemen. Third, he was a guard, so he's tougher on guards. And fourth, from my own point of view, he was a right guard, so he's tougher on me than anybody.

In 1959, his first year, he drove me unmercifully during the two-a-days. He called me an old cow one afternoon and said that I was the worst guard he'd ever seen. I'd been working hard, killing myself, and he took all the air out of me. I'd lost seven or eight pounds that day, and when I got into the locker room, I was too drained to take my pads off. I just sat in front of my locker, my helmet off, my head down, wondering what I was doing playing football, being as bad as I was, getting cussed like I was. Vince came in and walked over to me, put his hand on the back of my head, mussed my hair and said, 'Son, one of these days you're going to be the greatest guard in the league.' He is a beautiful psychologist. I was ready to go back out to practice for another four hours." (pp. 78-79).

Coaches and teachers must initially decide the extent to which they want to use their social reinforcers as a motivator. If the answer is "a great deal", then the approach used should be consistent with sound reinforcement principles. That is, it should be *meaningful* to the participant (it cannot be indiscriminately given), *contingent* (based on performance), and *immediate* (given after only a minimal delay). Used in this way, social reinforcement has the greatest potential to positively enhance performance.

With young participants, performance effectiveness is not always the most important objective. The research project directed by Smith and Smoll clearly showed that positive social reinforcers frequently administered helped to produce a better team climate and increased self esteem in the athlete. Ultimately, these may be the most important criteria of sport success with young athletes. It is certainly a basic objective in teaching physical education. Smith and Smoll (1979) have urged coaches

"Be liberal with reward. Look for positive things, reward them, and you'll see them increase. Praise the little things that others might not notice. Reward that is sincerely given does not spoil people; rather, it gives them something to strive for. Have realistic expectations and consistently reward players when they succeed in meeting them. Reward positive things as soon as they occur, since immediate reward is more potent. But even delayed reward is better than none at all. Remember, whether children show it or not, the psychological rewards you give them help to reinforce the good feelings they have about themselves" (pp. 6-7).

Thus, all coaches and teachers have to assess the extent to which they want to use social reinforcement for *performance* purposes and for *social psychological* purposes. The solution does not have to be an either/or one, of course. But at one end of the continuum — positive social reinforcement provided sparingly — the performance benefits are maximum while at the other end — positive social reinforcement provided liberally — the social psychological benefits are maximum.

LEADERSHIP BEHAVIOR AS A MOTIVATOR

We will either find a way or make one.
Hannibal

The traditional view of leaders has been that they serve as the sensitive balance point between two units or forces. One of the forces is the general organization itself. A primary responsibility of any leader is to ensure that the organization's requirements — productivity, performance, work output — are met. Therefore, one measure of leader effectiveness is the degree to which this has been successfully carried out. And, of course, leaders who consistently fail to meet the organization's requirements are soon replaced.

A second force is the group or team the leader must influence. The primary responsibility of the leader in this respect is to insure that the needs and aspirations of those individuals are achieved and they are satisfied with their involvement in the organization. And, again, a second measure of leader effectiveness is the degree to which this aspect has been successfully carried out. Thus, every leader must be sensitive to both the task demands and the people involved.

Not surprisingly, modern approaches to the study of leadership in industrial situations have paid special attention to the leader's task-oriented and person-oriented behavior. For example, a paper and pencil questionnaire was developed in the Ohio State study of leadership which was called the *Leader Behavior Description Questionnaire,* or *LBDQ* (Hemphill and Coons, 1957). It assesses the relative degree to which a leader engages in *initiating structure* behavior which is task related behavior and *consideration* behavior which is person related behavior. Similarly, a basic assumption in Fielder's (1967) Contingency Theory of Leadership is that all leaders have a unique, preferred way of interacting with their subordinates. The *Least Preferred Coworker Scale (LPC),* which was developed by Fiedler to assess interaction style, discriminates between those leaders who have a style of interacting which involves placing maximum emphasis on task performance as opposed to those leaders who have a style of interacting which involves a maximum emphasis on interpersonal relations.

Researchers attempting to assess the behaviors most characteristic of leaders in sport and physical activity have also identified task-and-person-orientations. However, because of the unique nature of sport and physical activity and its specific leadership demands, a greater number and type of coaching behaviors have been identified. For example, in both the *Coaching Behavior Assessment System* (which is presented in Table 2.2) developed by Smith, Smoll, and Hunt (1977) and the *Coach*

Observation Schedule (COS) developed by Rushall (1977), 12 types of behaviors were set out as characteristic of coaches. In the *Leadership Scale for Sports (LSS)* presented by Chelladurai and his colleagues (Chelladurai and Saleh, 1980; Chelladurai and Carron, 1981), five kinds of coaching behaviors preferred by athletes were identified: training, social support, rewarding, democratic, and autocratic behavior (see Table 2.3). Training behavior represents the task-oriented responses of coaches, social

Table 2.3 The Chelladurai LEADERSHIP SCALE FOR SPORT

Dimension	Description
Training and Instruction Behavior	Behavior of the coach aimed at improving the performance of the athletes by emphasizing and facilitating hard and strenuous training; by instructing them in the skills, by clarifying the relationship among the members; and by structuring and coordinating the activities of the members.
Democratic Behavior	Behavior of the coach which allows greater participation by the athletes in decisions pertaining to group goals, practice methods, and game tactics and strategies.
Autocratic Behavior	Behavior of the coach which involves independence in decision making and which stresses personal authority.
Social Support Behavior	Behavior of the coach characterized by a concern for individual athletes, for their welfare, for positive group atmosphere, and for warm interpersonal relations with members.
Rewarding (Positive Feedback) Behavior	Behavior of the coach which includes providing reinforcements for an athlete by recognizing and rewarding good performance.

support and rewarding behavior, the person-oriented ones, and democratic and autocratic behavior reflect decision styles.

According to Chelladurai (1981) all coaches engage in these behaviors while carrying out their leadership function. Each behavior has a different impact upon motivation, performance, and satisfaction. Chelladurai suggested that in order to understand what a coach can do to influence athletes toward better performance and greater satisfaction, it is helpful to analyze the athlete's motivation pattern. An illustration of this is presented in Figure 2.5.

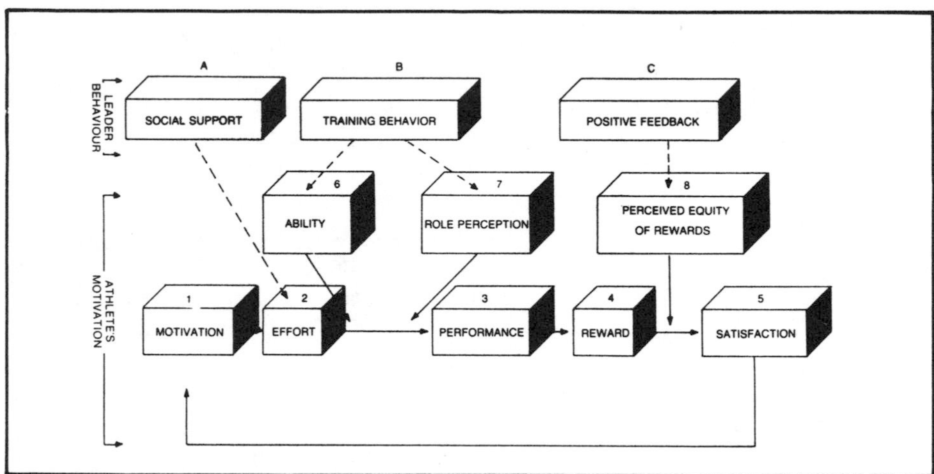

Figure 2.5
Leader behavior and motivation in athletics (From Chelladurai, 1981. Used with permission, Coaching Association of Canada).

It is assumed that athletes are essentially task motivated (Box 1, Figure 2.5). Their motivation leads to effort (Box 2, Figure 2.5) which, in turn, leads to performance (Box 3, Figure 2.5). Effective performance is then followed by rewards (Box 4, Figure 2.5) which result in satisfaction (Box 5, Figure 2.5). Chelladurai (1981) pointed out that:

> *"Of the many rewards of sport participation, excellence (doing something very well) and status (prestige and acclaim) are the rewards that are most consistent with the purpose of competitive athletics — the pursuit of excellence in sport and physical activity. An individual may be able to seek other rewards in other settings, but excellence in physical activity and the associated status and prestige are available only in competitive athletics"* (p. 1).

Although the path from motivation to performance, rewards, and satisfaction is sequential, there are also some influencing conditions. For example, common sense tells us that the amount of effort expended is not necessarily reflected in the performance of the participant. Often some of the hardest working athletes have little success in the way of relative or absolute performance improvements to show for their efforts. In short, the athlete's physical traits (height, weight, speed, strength), personality, and ability (Box 6, Figure 2.5) serve to influence the effort-performance relationship.

Another influencing factor is role perception. The athletes must have a clear understanding of their responsibilities on the team — setters versus spikers in volleyball; checkers versus goal scorers in hockey; the pace setter in distance events; the sixth man on a basketball team. They must also have the necessary ability to carry out these roles (Box 7, Figure 2.5).

The final influencing factor is called perceived equity of rewards (Box 8, Figure 2.5). While rewards should lead to satisfaction, that satisfaction "is either enhanced or diminished depending on whether the athlete perceives these rewards to be equitable ... In other words, an athlete compares the rewards received with some standard and decides whether the rewards are equitable or not. It can be expected that the athlete will compare the total cost (time and energy) with benefits derived. This benefit may be based on a personal cost-benefit balance and within the frame of reference of the cost-benefit balance of other teammates. If the rewards match the standard internalized by the athlete, they are perceived to be equitable and satisfaction is enhanced. With enhanced satisfaction, the athlete is motivated to put forth more effort; with lowered satisfaction, motivation and effort is reduced" (Chelladurai, 1981, p. 2).

The model presented in Figure 2.5 and research on leadership in sport teams does provide the basis for a number of generalizations.

PROPOSITION: Social support behavior on the part of the leader is related to motivation.

a) **The most experienced athletes show the greatest preference for social support behavior from their coaches.**
b) **Male athletes show a greater preference for social support behavior than female athletes.**

Social support is behavior by the coach which is characterized by a concern for individual athletes, for their welfare, for the development of a positive group atmosphere, and for the development of warm interpersonal relationships. The longer athletes have been in the athletic setting and the more experienced they are, the greater is their preference for social support behavior on the part of the coach.

Chelladurai and Carron (1983) found this was the case in a study of male basketball players who were competing at either a high school midget level (approximately 14 years of age), a high school junior level (approximately 15 years of age), a high school senior level (approximately 17 years of age), or at university (approximately 20 years of age). A similar result was reported by Chelladurai and Carron (1982) for university basketball players, wrestlers, and track and field athletes with varying amounts of athletic experience.

In their work with the *Coaching Behavior Assessment System* (Table 2.2), Curtis, Smith, and Smoll (1979) found that younger players were more sensitive to incidences of negative behavior from their coaches; older players, more sensitive to encouragement. The coaches rated as most popular by their players were those who provided a great deal of encouragement and technical instruction; the least popular were those who frequently used punitive behaviors.

Chelladurai's (1981) explanation for this is that as athletes become more involved in their sport, their sources of satisfaction for their social needs become more and more restricted to the team; affiliation with other groups is reduced. Consequently, social interactions with the team become increasingly important. And, since coaches are the most dominant, most significant members of the team, athletes show increasing preference for social support as their level of experience increases. The implications for elite athletes who are on demanding, time consuming training schedules are obvious. Social support behavior (Box A, Figure 2.5) from the coach becomes increasingly tied in with motivation and effort.

Chelladurai and Saleh (1978), in a study with university college students found that females preferred a coach who did not provide a great deal of social support behavior. It is not clear whether these findings are true reflections of sex differences or the fact that female athletes in many instances are coached by males.

PROPOSITION: Coaching behavior that emphasizes training and skill instruction is related to athlete motivation.

Training and instruction is behavior by the coach which is aimed at improving athlete performance by emphasizing hard and strenuous training, by providing skill instruction, by clarifying group roles, and by structuring and coordinating the activities of the group. Athletes want to learn, to improve their ability. An analysis of thousands of children from the ages of 11 to 18 years revealed that regardless of age, sex, type of sport, and culture, the pursuit of excellence was rated as one of the two strongest and most consistent incentives motivating athletes (Alderman, 1978; Alderman and Wood, 1976). Thus, it is probably no surprise that Curtis, Smith, and Smoll (1979) found that the most popular coaches were those who provided encouragement mixed with useful technical instruction.

In the effort and performance relationship then, training behavior from the coach (Box B, Figure 2.5) is necessary to insure skill acquisition and to clarify group roles and responsibilities. As Chelladurai (1981) pointed out "the coach may organize all the relevant bits of abilities and talents into a comprehensive whole and plan a set of strategies for the team. But the implementation of these plans can be successful only if the athletes have a clear grasp of their individual roles and how they fit into the total picture" (p. 3).

PROPOSITION: Positive feedback (rewarding) behavior from the coach is related to athlete motivation.

Positive feedback was dealt with in some depth in the previous section ("Social Reinforcement as a Motivator"). There is no purpose in repeating that discussion here. Insofar as its relationship to the motivation-performance relationship (see Box C, Figure 2.5), Chelladurai suggested that positive rewards from the coach are critical because fans and the media "are not always equitable in bestowing their rewards on athletes. Individual stars are singled out and showered with acclaim and support sometimes without reference to the contributions made by other members of the team ... Coaches must be cognizant of this inequity and realize that their Positive Feedback Behavior is the most potent of all rewards" (p. 3).

PROPOSITION: The coach's decision style influences level of motivation.

a) **Male athletes show a greater preference for an autocratic decision style on the part of coaches than female athletes.**
b) **Older, more experienced athletes show a greater preference for an autocratic decision style on the part of coaches than younger, less experienced athletes.**
c) **In periods of stress, an autocratic decision style is preferred.**

When Chelladurai and Saleh (1978) had university students indicate their level of preference for various leadership behaviors, they found that females expressed a preference for a leader who permitted greater participation in the decision-making process. Similar findings were reported by Arnott (1982) in a study with male and female intercollegiate basketball players and Erle (1982) in a study with male and female ice hockey players.

There is also strong evidence that with increasing experience, athletes show increasing preferences for a more autocratic approach from their coaches. This has been reported in studies by Chelladurai and Carron (1983) with high school midget, junior, and senior and intercollegiate basketball players, Chelladurai and Carron (1982) with intercollegiate basketball players, wrestlers, and track and field athletes, and Erle (1982) with intercollegiate ice hockey players.

There are a number of possible explanations for this general finding. One is that since coaching is essentially an autocratic enterprise, athletes who are in opposition to this approach gradually weed themselves out. What is left are individuals who prefer an autocratic approach. Another possibility is that athletes learn through experience that an autocratic approach in sport and physical activity is the norm. Thus, when they express a preference, they are simply indicating something with which they are most familiar and most comfortable. A final possibility is that athletes may simply develop a preference for an autocratic approach due to its speed and efficiency. The group can quickly focus its attention and energies on the task at hand and the more experienced performers prefer this.

This latter explanation may also help to account for the fact that under conditions of stress, a group seeks out or is more receptive to more authoritarian styles of leadership. When the stress diminishes, preference for a more participative decision style increases (Foder, 1976; Korten, 1962; Lowin and Craig, 1968; Rosenbaum and Rosenbaum, 1971). The stress could be a result of some external threat or pressure on the group. For example, Rosenbaum and Rosenbaum (1971) found that when the competitive nature of the group task was emphasized, group performance was improved substantially under an authoritarian decision style.

Extending the above principle to sport, the greatest amount of stress is present during games and competition. Consequently, the greatest preference (and best performance) of the athletes would be associated with a more authoritarian approach. In practice situations, the stress is reduced somewhat and, therefore, more input — a more participative approach — is preferred by the athletes. (This latter point is discussed in greater depth in Chapter 4 in the section entitled "Intrinsic Interest as a Motivator".)

Implications for the Coach and Teacher

There is little doubt that participants are most satisfied, most motivated and most productive in an environment which is characterized by warmth, positivism, respect, and support from their coach or teacher and in which the opportunity for personal growth and skill learning is maximized. Thus, practice and teaching sessions should be marked by leadership activity which emphasizes instruction giving, error correction, encouragement, positive feedback, and support. If coaches and teachers simply started and ended a practice session or class and said or did little in between, the result would be rapidly diminished interest and motivation on the part of performers. An active, involved coach and teacher serves as a strong motivator for the group.

While there is some evidence that athletes show a preference for a more autocratic approach, this is by no means an either/or situation. Decision style should vary with the situation because there are advantages and disadvantages to any style adopted.

For example, four advantages are present if a participative style of decision making is utilized (Chelladurai, 1981). First, a decision arrived at by the group generally has greater *group acceptance* and, therefore, is implemented with less resistance. Second, participation in decision making contributes to *feelings of responsibility and self determination* which form the basis for intrinsic motivation. Third, the *information base* is broader which means that more solutions can be generated and each of these can be subjected to broader scrutiny. Finally, the *quality of decision* is also improved because the divergent orientations of group members contributes to the increased likelihood that original and creative solutions will be generated.

In turn, there are also disadvantages to group participation in decision making. One obvious one is that *time* is required and, often, time is not available in sport situations. If a decision must be arrived at quickly, the discussions (and possible arguments) associated with a participative decision style would rule against its use.

A second disadvantage arises if the problem is *complex* and a series of interrelated decisions are required. This would be the case when a swimming coach with a large team is permitted to enter each athlete in only a limited number of events. Setting out the best team would require a number of sequential decisions. (For example, because John Smith is in three events, he cannot be entered in the relay). There is strong evidence supporting the contention that in this type of situation the coach acting alone would arrive at a better decision than the group as a total unit.

A third problem is that groups often arrive at a *compromise solution.* The consensus decision may be best for group cohesion but be far from optimal for group productivity and performance.

Finally, and somewhat related to the above point, self interest on the part of group members could contribute to *intragroup conflict.* In turn, group productivity and performance would be negatively effected.

SUMMARY

The situations into which participants are placed can have a strong impact upon their motivation level. In the present chapter those factors in a participant's situation which the coach or teacher has the potential to manipulate were discussed. These included token rewards, goal setting, the practice session, social reinforcement, and coaching behavior. On the basis of available research, a number of general propositions have been supported:

1. Undesirable behaviors can be eliminated through the use of token rewards.
2. Desirable behaviors can be enhanced through the use of token rewards.
3. Token rewards can have a spillover effect so that non-target behaviors are also positively affected.
4. Individual performance can be improved through the use of token rewards.
5. Goal setting contributes to performance effectiveness.
   a) Specific, hard, challenging goals are better than specific, easy goals, do-best goals, or no assigned goals.
   b) Individuals must have sufficient ability to attain (or closely approximate) their goal.

   c) Goals are most effective when they are stated in specific, quantitative (behavioral) terms rather than as vague intentions.
   d) Intermediate goals (or subgoals) should be used as a link to long term or end goals.
   e) Feedback is necessary if goals are to have maximum effectiveness in improving performance.
6. Token rewards are effective for increasing commitment in performance toward a specific goal.
7. Supportiveness from the coach or teacher and goal acceptance by the participant are important positive factors in goal setting.
8. The positive effects of goal setting are produced independent of individual differences in age, sex, education, and personality.
9. Competition among individuals for goal achievement produces greater commitment and better performance.
10. Motivation can be increased through the introduction of novelty, a change in routine and/or by providing special attention to the participant.
11. Social reinforcement is an effective motivator for behavior and performance under selected circumstances.
    a) Younger children profit more than older ones from social reinforcement.
    b) Social reinforcement has a greater impact when it is administered by an individual who is less well known to the recipient.
    c) Social reinforcement has greater impact when it is administered by significant people of the opposite sex.
    d) Social reinforcement is more effective in tasks that are very simple, well learned, boring, or where feedback is not othewise readily available.
    e) Children who are the recipients of positive social reinforcement gain better self esteem and more positive perceptions of their coach.
12. Social support behavior on the part of the leader is related to motivation.
    a) The most experienced athletes show the greatest preference for social support behavior from their coaches.
    b) Male athletes show a greater preference for social support behavior than female athletes.
13. Coaching behavior that emphasizes training and skill instruction is related to athlete motivation.
14. Positive feedback (rewarding) behavior from the coach is related to athlete motivation.
15. The coach's decision style influences level of motivation.
    a) Male athletes show a greater preference for an autocratic decision style on the part of coaches than female athletes.
    b) Older, more experienced athletes show a greater preference for an autocratic decision style on the part of coaches than younger, less experienced athletes.
    c) In periods of stress, an autocratic decision style is preferred.

While this list of propositions is extensive, it is still possible to utilize all of the techniques discussed. Emphasizing social reinforcement and having sensitivity to the effectiveness of specific leadership behaviors are two ongoing concerns for every coach and teacher. They are a consideration at every practice, class, and competition or game. Thus, coaches and teachers only have to become familiar with the specific conditions under which they are maximally effective and then, make a point of using them.

Insofar as the three remaining factors are concerned — introducing change, implementing a token reward system, and setting out a realistic goal setting program — some planning (either prior to the season or prior to a class or practice session) is necessary. Also, following through to completion requires additional effort. But the benefits in terms of improved athlete motivation should be worth the effort.

SUGGESTED READINGS

Carron, A.V. Motivating the athlete. *Motor Skills: Theory into Practice,* 1977, *1,* 23-24.

Chelladurai, P. The coach as a motivator and chameleon of leadership styles. *Sports Science Periodical on Research and Technology in Sport (Social Psychology Bu-2).* Ottawa: Coaching Association of Canada, 1981.

Locke, E.A., Shaw, K.N., Saari, L.M., and Latham, G.P. Goal setting and task performance: 1969-1980. *Psychological Bulletin,* 1981, *90,* 125-152.

Martens, R. *Social psychology and physical activity.* New York: Harper and Row, 1975, Ch. 4.

Siedentop, D. The management of practice behavior. In W.F. Straub (Ed.), *Sport psychology: An analysis of athlete behavior.* Ithaca: Mouvement Publications, 1978.

CHAPTER 3

Situational Factors Not Readily Subject to Change

Situations differ markedly in the degree to which they are objectively and subjectively exciting, interesting, challenging, or stress provoking. For example, a physical education student who comes into an empty gymnasium to shoot baskets is faced with a different environment than the basketball player who comes with a friend, or the one who is practicing with teammates under the critical supervision of a coach, or the one who is competing in a game in front of a packed auditorium. This total spectrum of situations would be characterized by increasing differences in motivation and arousal on the part of the participant.

In the previous chapter, it was pointed out that in many instances the coach and teacher can intervene directly and manipulate the situation or selected aspects within the situation in order to improve or maintain the participant's motivation. But, there are also instances where the environment is highly motivating or even stressful and yet the coach or teacher has no direct control over it. The best that can be hoped for is that awareness and sensitivity on their part can contribute to the participant's ability to cope with the situation. Three factors in the participant's environment which can serve as a source of motivation but which the coach and teacher have little or no control over are the presence of spectators, the participant's competitor, and the general group environment.

THE PRESENCE OF OTHERS AS A MOTIVATOR

When the fans tell me I'm no longer filling the bill, I'll quit.
Miller Huggins

Social psychologists have been interested in the impact of what is referred to as *social presence* upon performance since the beginning of the twentieth century. In fact, it was one of the earliest experimental issues pursued in social psychology. Triplett (1897), a fan of cycling was intrigued by what he felt was a discrepancy in performance times for individuals cycling alone in comparison with when they cycled in the presence of others. In order to test his suspicions, he used official data from the Racing Board of the League of American Wheelman and compared unpaced performances with paced and paced-competition performances. In the unpaced situation, a cyclist raced alone against time. The cyclist also raced against time in the paced situation but a tandem bicycle containing 3 or 4 teammates was permitted. In the paced-competition situation, the cyclists also raced against each other but, again, pacers were used.

Triplett found that the two paced conditions were 35 to 40 seconds per mile faster than the solitary, unpaced condition. After considering a number of physical, physiological, and psychological possibilities, Triplett settled on an explanation he called *dynamogenesis* — a proposal that the bodily presence of another cyclist not only serves to arouse a competitive instinct but also helps to release suppressed nervous energy.

Subsequently, another significant contribution — at least from the point of view of the terminology used — was made by Allport (1924). In the early and mid 1920s, Allport carried out a series of experiments (primarily with verbal and mental tasks). He reported that the presence of another individual carrying out the same task (a situation referred to as coaction) produces *social facilitation* and *rivalry.* Allport defined social facilitation as a faster, more intense response which is triggered by the sights and sounds of others doing the same task. Rivalry referred to a competitive drive which Allport felt is an inevitable byproduct of all coactivity.

Over the first six decades of this century, the research focus on social presence was expanded and the impact of both coactivity and spectators upon performance was examined. Researchers during this period concluded that no clear pattern of findings was present; the results seemed to be generally confusing with some authors reporting improved performance from social presence, others, just the opposite effect.

In 1965, Robert Zajonc (1965) examined the research findings and then proposed that the results from previous studies were not confusing; that a common pattern was actually present. Essentially, Zajonc suggested that the mere presence of others serves to increase arousal level. Under this increased arousal, dominant, well-learned responses would be improved, but poorly learned, more tentative responses would be disrupted. The underlying logic here is that a person might know how to do something well but because of lowered motivation, performance level is down. When people begin watching, motivation is increased and performance improves. If, on the other hand, a person has not learned a task very well, the presence of others will be distracting, stressful, or anxiety producing. So, depending upon the level of proficiency or the stage of learning of the performer, the presence of others could be harmful or beneficial (see Figure 3.1).

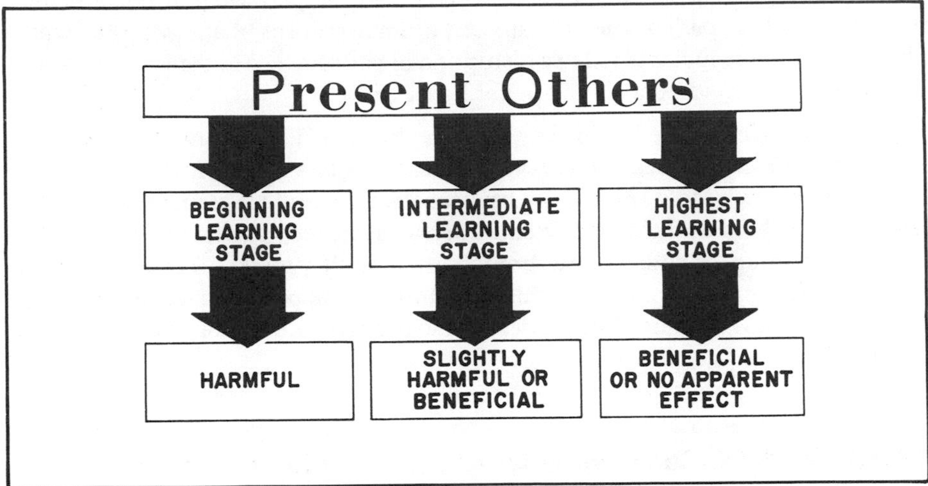

Figure 3.1
Influence of others present on performance and learning of motor skills (Adapted from Singer, 1975).

Research in laboratory and nonlaboratory experiments has tended to support this proposal. However, an important refinement has been advanced by Cottrell (1972). Although Zajonc felt that the mere presence of other people produces increased arousal, Cottrell has argued that it is *evaluation apprehension* — the expectation that the people who are present will form judgments about the quality of the performance — that leads to the arousal increase. The association between the presence of others and apprehension that we are being evaluated is considered to be learned. From birth, the presence of others comes to be associated with praise, blame, rewards and punishment. Therefore, when a task must be carried out in the presence of others, anxiety about evaluation contributes to an increase in arousal level which, in turn, influences the effectiveness of performance on that task.

PROPOSITION: The presence of others influences motivation and performance effectiveness.

a) **The presence of others improves performance in tasks in which the required responses are simple or well learned.**
b) **The presence of others causes a disruption in performance in tasks in which the required responses are complex or not well learned.**

A number of studies have provided support for the above propositions (e.g., Haas and Roberts, 1972; Martens, 1969). For example, Martens (1969) used a timing task where subjects had to respond when two targets were in line. An audience of 10 passive spectators was present during the learning phase (the initial period when rapid improvements were occurring with each trial) and the performance phase of the experiment (a later period when the amount of improvement, if any, was minimal). The presence of an audience led to a disruption in performance in the learning phase but produced improvements in the performance phase.

Similar findings were obtained by Haas and Roberts (1972) in another laboratory experiment. Female college students were tested on a task which involved tracing a six-sided star which could only be seen by means of a mirror. One group practiced this task until they became highly proficient. Then an audience was brought in to watch. For another group, an audience was brought in when they were still unfamiliar with the task. The introduction of the audience improved the performance of the group that had previous learning but hindered the performance of the group with no previous learning.

PROPOSITION: Characteristics of the individuals present influences the participant's motivation.

a) **The size of the group watching has an influence on the motivation of the performer.**
b) **The expertise of the people present has an influence on the motivation of the performer.**
c) **The supportiveness of the people present has an influence on the motivation of the performer.**

The introduction of an audience during performance is assumed to produce an increase in arousal. However, characteristics of that audience influence the extent of its impact. Previous research in this regard (mostly carried out in tightly controlled laboratory settings) has revealed that the size of an audience, its expertise, and supportiveness are important considerations; the sex of the audience is not.

For example, McCullagh and Landers (1976) observed that as audience size increased, the nervousness and arousal of the performers also increased. That is, as the size of the audience was systematically increased from one to six, the level of nervousness and arousal of the performer progressively increased. Similar findings were reported by Brenner (1974). Arousal, as reflected by voice patterns in public speaking situations, increased steadily for audiences of 0, 2, 8 and 22 spectators.

Also, when others who are present (whether in the form of an audience or as coactors) are thought to possess competence or to have a greater potential to evaluate, the level of arousal in the performer is increased. For example, in the study by Haas and Roberts (1972) which was discussed earlier, the mere presence of an audience (a group of four blindfolded students) had substantially less impact than an evaluative audience (a group of four students described as physical education majors brought in to evaluate the person's performance for a class project). This difference between what are commonly referred to as "mere presence" and "evaluative potential" audiences has been observed in numerous other studies (e.g., Cottrell, Wack, Sekerak, and Rittle, 1968; Henchy and Glass, 1968; Klinger, 1969; Martens and Landers, 1972).

It is often assumed that when the others present are of the opposite sex they represent a different psychological and motivational situation for the performer than do members of the same sex. In laboratory studies this has not been the case. Bird (1975), using manual dexterity and hand steadiness tasks, Cox (1966), using a marble dropping task, Harney and Parker (1972), using a ball roll-up task, and Rikli (1974), using hand steadiness and grip strength tasks, found that the sex of the audience had no special impact upon the performer.

However, the extent to which an audience is thought to be supportive is important.[1] For example, as early as 1923, it was observed that a razzing audience produced decrements in coordinated movements (Land, 1923). More recently, it has been found that professional baseball, football, hockey, and basketball teams, and college football and basketball teams win substantially more games playing in their home arena or on their home field than they do away (Koppet, 1972; Lefebrve and Passer, 1974; Schwartz and Barsky, 1977; Varca, 1980).

Varca (1980) has suggested that the difference between home and away performance lies in the level and type of aggressive play exhibited by the two teams. His study of men's basketball teams in the United States Southeastern Conference during the 1977-78 season provided evidence in support of this viewpoint. Only home and away games against the same conference opponent were examined. Although the home teams won 70% of the games, this superiority was not due to field goal percentages, free throw percentages, and turnovers — there were no differences between the teams in these measures. However, the home team outperformed their opponents in what Varca referred to as *functional aggression* measures — rebounds, blocked shots, and steals. On the other hand, Varca found that visiting teams committed more fouls — a *dysfunctional type of aggression.*

If the home crowd is negative or abusive toward its own team, negative results follow — essentially, the home crowd advantage disappears. Thirer and Rampey (1979) observed that the home team committed an increasing number of fouls and

[1]The terminology used in any scientific area is important because it helps to insure that researches are examining and reporting on the same phenomena. So, in analyzing the impact of others present, a clear distinction is usually made between situations in which an audience is simply present but does not interact in any way with the performer and those in which the audience cheers, razzs, supports, criticizes, and so on. The former represents a social facilitation situation; the latter, the spectator situations most typical of sport. The propositions and discussion in this general section deal with results from both areas of research.

performance deteriorated when it was subjected to abusive spectator behavior.

PROPOSITION: The presence of others is relaxing in highly stressful situations.

While the presence of others does result in an increased arousal level, there are also situations in which the reverse can occur. For example, Schachter (1959), in his research on the conditions influencing affiliation behavior, has observed that individuals in highly stressful situations will seek out the company of others. In turn, the presence of these other individuals has a reassuring effect and the end result is a lowered level of arousal.

One explanation which seems to account for this is that individuals are most comfortable with arousal levels in an intermediate range (Cottrell, 1968). Thus, when the initial level of arousal of the individual is normal (and, therefore, relatively low), the introduction of others into the situation leads to an increase. However, when the initial level of arousal of the individual is excessively high, the introduction of others serves to produce a reduction. If the others present are also anticipating the same anxiety-producing situation and they are relaxed and calm, the reduction in arousal level is even more pronounced.

Implications for the Coach and Teacher

Competition contains a large number of elements which cause anxiety in the performer. These generally fall into the five categories contained in Table 3.1 (Kroll, 1979). It should be apparent from an examination of Table 3.1 that the items in the bodily complaints category are related solely to discomfort arising from an awareness by the performer of personal bodily reactions. Therefore, bodily complaints are not necessarily directly associated with the presence of others. On the other hand, when others are present, either as performers or spectators, the fear of failure, feelings of inadequacy, loss of control, and a tendency to feel guilt are all more likely to be experienced. Competing in front of others is a stress producing event.

Because spectators and other performers are inevitable in many sport and physical activity situations, there is little a coach or teacher can do to eliminate this source of stress. But, acclimatization to having others present can occur. And, coaches and teachers have as much responsibility to help the performer prepare in this area as they do in their preparation of the physical and skill areas. Specific teaching techniques for this preparation have been outlined by Cratty (1983). These can be categorized under the two old adages *knowledge is power* and *practice makes perfect*. In short, the performer can be taught and can practice mentally and physically to handle the stresses of an audience.

If knowledge and understanding are power, then the coach and teacher should:

Table 3.1 Factors in the competitive situation which cause anxiety and stress in the performer (Adapted from Kroll, 1979).

CATEGORY	REPRESENTATIVE FACTORS	
Bodily complaints	tightness in neck nervousness urge to urinate	throwing up sore muscles training
Fear of failure	losing performing to ability making a mistake	living up to expectations presence of friends/relatives criticism by coach
Feelings of inadequacy	remembering instructions being afraid getting tired	physical appearance poor fit of equipment coach ignoring me
Loss of control	being outcoached conduct of opponents behavior or spectators	poor spectator turnout noisy locker room people asking questions
Guilt items	sportsmanship losing my temper not being mean enough	hurting an opponent spectators booing making opponent look foolish

- Inform participants about the physiological reactions they will experience when they are performing in front of a group of people. An awareness that anxiety, stress, and discomfort are normal and generally experienced by everyone and that they will gradually become more comfortable with it can be reassuring. Also teaching relaxation techniques and attention control strategies is also beneficial in this regard (e.g., Nideffer, and Sharpe, 1978).
- Inform performers how an audience usually leads to a faster response thereby producing errors in simpler movements and timing tasks. For example, an individual driving the family car in front of friends for the first time may press the gas pedal or brake pedal too vigorously because he/she is anxious to "perform" well.
- Inform participants that a hostile audience can produce increased feelings of anxiety and stress. With advance knowledge, there is a reduced likelihood that the participant will respond with anxiety or hostility to a nonsupportive audience.

While knowledge helps, practice does make perfect. Thus, the more experience a performer has in front of spectators, the quicker acclimatization can occur. With this in mind, the coach or teacher should:

- Teach new skills until they are overlearned before having the participant attempt them in front of an audience.
- If skills are repetitive, simple, or well learned, introduce a group of spectators during practice. This will serve to increase motivation.
- Arrange for *audience training* by gradually introducing audiences of increasing size during the initial weeks and months of practice.
- Precondition athletes (if it is possible) to abusive crowds by introducing a hostile crowed or by playing tape recordings from a hostile crowd during practice.
- Arrange for a low anxious, calm person to associate with any performer who seems excessively stressed prior to competition; the presence of that person will have a relaxing effect.

An overriding consideration for all of the above guidelines is the *principle of specificity* which states that the more similar a practice drill or situation is to the real event, the greater will be the benefit. Conversely, the greater the difference between the real event and the practice situation, the less the person will be able to transfer the skills learned. This truism holds for both the learning of actual skills and learning to handle the stresses and pressures of performance. A coach or teacher should try to model the competitive situation as closely as possible in practice to achieve the best possible transfer.

THE COMPETITION AS A MOTIVATOR

> *A good opponent [is] a rare and treasured thing for any team or player. For a good opponent defines a player or team. By forcing you to be as good as you can be, such an opponent stretches the boundaries of your emotional and playing experiene, giving you your highest highs and lowest lows; your best and worst and hardest moments.*
>
> Ken Dryden

When the motives and drives that account for human behavior are discussed, a distinction is generally made between *primary drives* and *secondary drives.* The primary drives are unlearned; they emerge naturally in the organism. Examples of these include any of the physiological drives such as hunger, thirst, and sleep. On the other hand, secondary drives are those that are acquired through learning — through the positive and negative experiences and reinforcements received during the process of growth and development. Some examples of secondary drives are the affiliation drive, the need for achievement, the need for social approval, and the competitive drive.

Competition is a predominant feature of our modern industrial society. In fact, it is so predominant, so ingrained in us that it is often assumed to be a primary drive which has a biological basis. That is not the case, however. The degree to which a competitor and/or the competition itself serves to increase a participant's motivation is learned.

The term competition has come to be viewed as a synonym for sport. As Cratty (1981) pointed out "the term *competition* is used in sport by coaches, fans, and athletes alike. The word competitor is often substituted for the term *athlete* when speaking of members of sports teams. Within the vernacular there is general agreement on the meaning of competition: it denotes the process of trying hard to win, to get something someone else wants" (p. 62). This is unfortunate because it is inaccurate. Competition is not synonomous with sport and/or physical activity. What is meant by the term "competition" then?

A number of authors have attempted to clarify this term. For example, in discussing what constitutes a competitive situation, Deutsch (1949a, 1949b) used a cooperative situation for contrast. He stated that in cooperative social situations, the skills and subsequent successes of one individual serve to bring rewards to the total group and those rewards are then distributed evenly among all group members. On the other hand, in a competitive social situation, if the skills and successes of one individual or group lead to rewards, these are enjoyed singly and there is a reduction in the rewards obtained by others.

There are gradations or combinations of these two processes, of course. Luschen (1970), in discussing competition, referred to *zero sum situations* and *non-zero sum situations.* In zero sum situations, a win or reward obtained by one individual or group is balanced against a loss or negative outcome for another individual or group. In *non-zero sum situations* a number of individuals share in the reward outcome to varying degrees.

Another view of competition was proposed by Ross and Van den Haag (1966). They differentiated between *indirect competition* where an individual strives against a personal standard (such as a previous best in golf) or some norm (such as the par on the golf course) and *direct competition* where the individual is pitted directly against an opponent.

Whether an individual competes directly against one or more other individuals, against self-imposed standards, or against fixed norms is relatively unimportant. These targets, goals, or standards represent a strong source of motivation — a source which is referred to in the subsequent discussion as the participant's *competitor* or *competition.* In most instances, the teacher and coach have very little direct control over the choice of a competitor or competition. A number of factors influence the degree to which a competitor contributes to intensity, selectivity, and persistance of a participant's behavior. These are outlined in the propositions which follow.

PROPOSITION: Competitiveness is a learned behavior.

a) **The competitive drive varies in intensity in individuals from different cultures.**
b) **The competitive drive increases in intensity in children as they get older.**

c) **The competitive drive varies in intensity according to the personality of the participant.**

Evidence that competitiveness is learned comes from studies comparing individuals of different ages, from different cultures, and/or with different personality types. Competitiveness initially appears at approximately 4 to 6 years of age and the number of children who exhibit competitiveness then increases progressively from that point until early adolescence. By mid-adolescence, a strong motivation to compete is present in almost all children (Greenberg, 1932; Piaget, 1932; White, 1960).

In an early study carried out by Greenberg (1932), a block stacking task was used with young children and competitive behavior was largely absent in all children at ages 2 to 4 years. But, by 5 years, it was present in 69% of the cases. By 7 years, 87% of the children displayed competitive behavior.

Other evidence that competitiveness is learned comes from a comparison of individuals from different cultures. This was the approach taken by Madsen and Shapira. They found that American children had a much greater tendency to be competitive than Mexican or Israeli children (Madsen and Shapira, 1970; Shapira and Madsen, 1969). In fact, American children even competed when it was not to their advantage to do so. As a further example, McNally and Orlick (1975) found that when competitive games were modified to emphasize cooperation and then introduced to children from Central Canada and Northern Indian children living within 100 miles of the Arctice Circle, the latter group reacted more positively and expressed considerably more satisfaction with the experience.

And, finally, because personality is partly acquired through the social experiences an individual has, differences in personality also contribute to the suggestion that the competitive drive is socially learned. In this regard, the personality traits of *need to achieve* and *need to avoid failure* are particularly important because they are associated with the orientations people have toward achievement situations (Atkinson, 1964; McClelland, 1961). A person with a high need for achievement actively seeks out challenging, competitive situations where there is uncertainty about success and failure. On the other hand, a person with a high fear of failure tries to avoid these types of situations.

Development of the need for achievement has been associated with child-rearing practices (McClelland, 1955; Rosen and D'Andrade, 1959; Winterbottom, 1953). For example, Winterbottom (1953) found that when mothers expected their children to be self-reliant and independent from an early age — to make their own friends, to find their own way around the city — the children developed a high need for achievement. The need for achievement as a motivator is discussed in greater detail in Chapter 5.

PROPOSITION: The performer's ability in relationship to the challenges in the task has an influence on the competitive drive.

a) **The competitive drive is most strongly aroused when both participants feel that they are relatively equal in ability.**
b) **The performance of individuals with high ability at a task improves when competition is introduced; those with low ability gets worse.**

In general, the competitive drive is most strongly aroused when the two participants both hold the perception that they have a chance for success.[2] If one person does not see any possibility for success, there is very little likelihood of competition occurring (Cratty, 1967). In this type of situation, the competition will usually revert to an attempt to improve the weaker person's skill through some form of cooperative performance. For example, if two tennis players or golfers have great differences in ability, the "game" often reverts to the better player helping the other with tips and coaching instructions which are designed to improve the weaker player's game.

Using results from an experiment involving a cooperative weight lifting task, Kohler (1927) suggested that the perception of similarity, expressed as a ratio, must be in a range from 65:100 to 75:100 in order for competition to occur. When the differences are greater than this, competition decreases and cooperation increases.

Individuals who do not have sufficient ability for the task at hand show a deterioration in performance when competition is introduced while those with high ability profit. The competition probably serves as motivation for the high ability person but is simply one additional stressor to be dealt with by the low ability person. This result was demonstrated in a laboratory study carried out by Wankel (1972). The results are presented in Figure 3.2. In comparison to a low ability group that did not

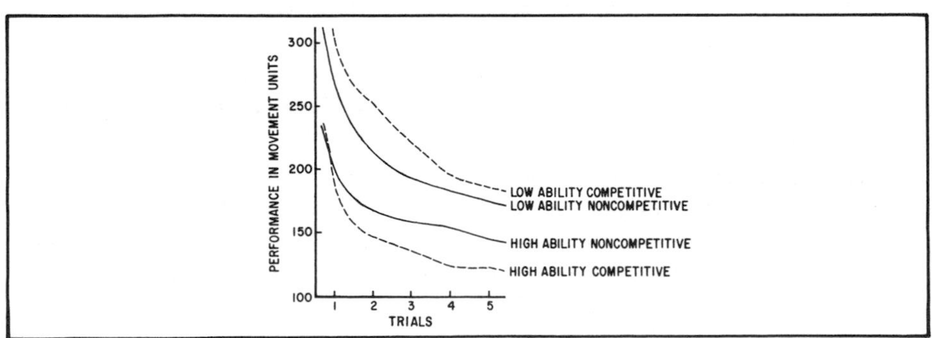

Figure 3.2
The interaction between ability of the performer and competition (Adapted from Wankel, 1972).

[2]An exception to this general condition is discussed in Chapter 5 in the section entitled "The Need to Achieve as a Motivator." Essentially, this exception is associated with fundamental personality differences between competitors — differences in the degree to which individuals possess a fear of failure and a need for achievement.

compete, the performance of a low ability competitive group got worse. However, in comparison to a high ability group that did not compete, the performance of a high ability competitive group improved.

PROPOSITION: Early success contributes to the development of the competitive drive; early failure contributes to a decrease.

Human behavior is shaped by outcomes. Thus, behaviors or responses which are successful and, consequently, are rewarded become progressively stronger. On the other hand, unsuccessful behaviors or responses are discarded. In sport and physical activity, one of the most powerful consequences or rewards for competitiveness is success.

Managers of young boxers — successful amateurs who have turned professional, for example — are fully aware of this fact. The young boxer is initially matched against opponents who are virtual pushovers. Thus, a program of development is chartered which follows a progression from fights against "never was" or "never will be" opponents to "has been" and then to other "young prospects". With continued successes, the young boxer is then matched against highly ranked contenders.

Research evidence from studies carried out with young animals provides strong support for this approach. Young, noncombative animals have been trained to become more and more vicious through successful experiences gained in a series of bouts with progressively more experienced opponents. Typically, in the initial stages, the noncombative animals were matched against weakened or physically restrained opponents. But, as their fighting skills improved and greater success was experienced, continuously, more difficult opponents were introduced — opponents who were also vicious and persistent. The final product was a vicious, highly aggressive, highly persistant fighter — a dramatic change from the original, passive and noncombative animal (Ginsburg and Allee, 1942; Kahn, 1951; Scott and Marston, 1953).

Research evidence from these same studies has also shown that defeat at an early age acts as a strong inhibitor for subsequent aggressiveness. And, the earlier, the more frequent and/or the more painful the initial defeat, the more passive the animal becomes. In short, early experience can have a powerful and permanent impact (Kahn, 1951; Scott and Marston, 1953).

Similar results have been found with young nursery school children although the experimental approach obviously was not the same. Patterson, Littman and Bricker (1967) found that initially passive children who retaliated against their aggressors and were successful, became more aggressive. On the other hand, passive children who either were not the object of aggressive behavior or were unsuccessful in their counterattacks remained passive.

Implications for the Coach and Teacher

One dominant feature of competition is that it is motivating. Participants are challenged by their competitors and the competitive situation. They strive to beat a standard — either a personal one or one fixed by the task — or an opponent. A second dominant feature is that the competitive drive, competitiveness, is learned and improved through positive experiences. These two elements have some important implications for coaching and teaching young participants.

One implication is related to the emphasis placed on competition for young children. Many authors feel that it is too great. Orlick (1978), for example, has pointed out:

> *"As the factory has come to be a model for the organization of so much of Western life, so too have children's games been industrialized. The emphasis on production, machine orientation, and overspecialization has become as widespread in games as in industry. Games themselves have become rigid, judgmental, highly organized, and excessively goal-oriented. There is no freedom from the pressure of evaluation and the psychological distress of disapproval. In the end, the focus on squeezing the most out of every individual leaves no room for plain old fun. Pitting children against one another in games where they frantically compete for what only a few can have guarantees failure and rejection for the many. Many children's games and programs are in fact designed for elimination. Many ensure that one wins and everyone else loses, leaving sport 'rejects' and 'dropouts' to form the vast majority of our North American population. To make things worse, the games are now beginning to destroy even the winners. Children are encouraged to delight in others' failures. They hope for it, they help it happen, because it enhances their own changes of victory. Exposing young children to irrational competition does not teach them how to compete in a healthy manner, it merely pressures them into competition. As they grow older, they have been so conditioned to the importance of winning that they can no longer play for fun, for enjoyment. They don't know how to help one another, to be sensitive to another's feelings, or to compete in a friendly, fun-filled way, even when they want to. If failure ensues, and it often does, many children learn to avoid competition, to withdraw. Failure at games may also 'teach' children totally unjustified 'bad things' about themselves."* (p. 5)

If the Orlick perspective is endorsed, then teachers and coaches should try to promote more cooperation in young children's games for at least four reasons. First, sport inevitably leads to failure experiences for a number of participants and, in turn, those failures lead to a reduction in competitiveness (Kahn, 1951; Patterson, Littman and Bricker, 1967; Scott and Marston, 1953).

Second, competition is associated with the development of many negative behaviors, while cooperation is associated with the development of numerous positive ones. For example, it has been observed in a number of studies (Deutsch, 1949a, 1949b; Julian, Bishop and Fiedler, 1966; Meyers, 1962; Sherif, Harvey, White, Hood and Sherif, 1961) that competition is associated with an increase in hostility, stereotyping, and conflict and a decrease in friendliness, communication, and general goodwill among participants. Cooperation produces results which are opposite in nature — cohesiveness is enhanced, positive social interaction skills developed, interpersonal relationships are improved.

Third, cooperation is superior to competition and individualism[3] (a situation in which an individual is rewarded on the basis of personal merit, independent of the rewards received by other individuals who also profit according to their merit) in promoting productivity and achievement. Traditionally, it has been assumed that cooperation is more effective insofar as social factors are concerned but that competition leads to more effective performance. This is not the case.

Johnson, Maruyama, Johnson, Nelson and Skon (1981) carried out a total analysis of the results from 122 studies on competition, cooperation, and individualism. The latter two were not found to differ from each other in terms of effectiveness and both were superior to competition.

Johnson and his colleagues identified some additional variables which further contributed to the superiority of cooperation over competition for performance and achievement. For example, cooperation was most superior to competition when the task demands required cooperation on the part of the group. (A sport like basketball "requires" cooperation; one like bowling does not because no ball or puck needs to be exchanged among teammates.) Also, with small groups, the superiority of cooperation was even greater. Finally, the younger the person, the greater the superiority of cooperation over competition.

Fourth, competition can be highly stressful for young participants. As Passer (1981) pointed out:

> "*Although many players are very confident of success, others are uncertain about performance outcomes (Scanlan and Passer, 1979a, 1981). Further, the structure of most athletic contests is such that certain achievement demands (e.g., winning) cannot be satisfied by all children at all times. If threat represents the perception that important values and goals are endangered, it is clear that the youth sport setting will, at times, be perceived by some children as threatening*" (p. 234).

In his summary of the research on competitive stress in young children, Passer (1981) set out six conclusions:

- Stress prior to competition is greater for participants in individual sports than for those in team sports.
- The importance of the situation is directly related to the development of feelings of stress. Prior to important competitions and at critical points in competition, stress increases.

[3]An example of individualism is what occurs in the typical classroom situation. All students are graded according to their own ability and contributions. Thus, a teacher might give all students an "A" grade if their work met a certain standard. Or, all students might receive an "F" if their work was not adequate.

- The outcome of the competition has an impact on stress. Winning leads to a decrease; losing and tieing lead to an increase. A loss in a close game is the most stressful situation.
- Precompetition stress is greatest for young participants with higher competitive trait anxiety, lower self-esteem, and lower expectancies for success.
- For a minority of young participants, the stress of an impending competition leads to a disruption in sleeping and eating patterns and subsequent impairment in performance.
- The stress associated with youth sport is similar to that experienced in other achievement situations. (As evidence for this claim, Simon and Martens (1979) had 9 to 14-year old boys complete a self report anxiety inventory prior to seven nonschool organized sport activities and four school activities. It was found that 82% of the subjects had scores below the midpoint of the test scale; see Table 3.2.)

Table 3.2 State anxiety associated with various sport and nonsport activities (Adapted from Simon and Martens, 1979).

ACTIVITY	AVERAGE STATE ANXIETY SCORE*
Wrestling	19.5
Basketball	18.5
Baseball	16.2
Hockey	16.0
Gymnastics	18.5
Football	15.8
Swimming	17.0
Band Solos	21.5
Band Groups	18.0
School Test	16.4
Physical Education Softball	14.5
NORMATIVE MEDIAN**	18.8

*Scores can vary from 10 to 30 with higher scores reflecting greater state anxiety.
**This is the 50 percentile for this age group.

All of the above may appear to be an argument in favor of eliminating youth sports for children. This is certainly not the intent. If a distinction is made between *physical activity* and *sport,* then more physical activities should be promoted for young children which emphasize cooperation. There are too many positive outcomes associated with cooperative activities to leave them to chance.

Sport is, by nature, competitive. But, the degree of competitiveness should be reduced for young participants. For example, in a soccer program in our community which involved 6- and 7-year old boys and girls, the children on one team practiced on the same field at the same time as another team. To increase communication and friendliness, the children were combined into one group on many occasions for instructions and drills, players were exchanged for the practice games, and the coaches were liberal in their praise of all children on both teams. During the regular season, no formal records were maintained for winning, losing, or goal scoring. Rotations were made freely among all the positions and all children were substituted equally. So, while competitions was present, active attempts were made to deemphasize it.

In the introduction to this section, it was pointed out that competition is motivating and that competitiveness can be acquired through positive learning experiences. These factors also have important implications for coaching older athletes. For example, the approach taken with the young boxer can be generalized to other sport situations. Young athletes advancing to a higher level in sport (e.g., from one age level grouping to another, from high school to college) should be brought along slowly, if possible, to insure that some initial success does occur. Professional players acquired through a trade are often introduced into the team's roster for away games to eliminate the pressure of playing in front of the home crowd. Many coaches give young players their first game experience when the outcome is not in doubt —their team is winning or losing by a substantial margin. The result is that less pressure is placed on the competitor.

From a team perspective, the coach should also try to schedule relatively easier opponents in preseason exhibitions if it is possible. Not only is competitiveness influenced but success has a strong influence on the development of cohesiveness (Carron and Ball, 1977).

THE TEAM AS A MOTIVATOR

Many coaches have a motto that the test of their team — and their coaching — is whether the last substitute has good morale. If he has, it means everybody has.

Tutko and Brun

A fundamental message in this textbook is that athlete motivation is a complex phenomenon. The participant's level of motivation is influenced through a number of sources — personal considerations, the teacher, the crowd, the coach, teammates, classmates. The sources have been categorized and subdivided into a number of different sections — environmental factors, personal factors, factors readily subject to change, and factors not readily subject to change. As pointed out previously, this general organization helps to facilitate the discussion, provides a framework for better understanding, and simplifies the exceedingly complex phenomenon of motivation.

It is important to also keep in mind, however, that real situations are not easily categorized. Motivation factors that are apparently not readily subject to change could be manipulated by a particularly creative teacher or coach; conversely, factors that the teacher or coach should be able to influence may prove to be out of their direct sphere of control if the participant is uncooperative or resistant to suggestions. In short, there are no absolutes about motivation.

This dictum certainly applies to the present section in which the team environment as a motivator is discussed. Any successful coach not only motivates athletes as individuals but also the team as a collective unit. *And, it is important to bear in mind that these are two separate concerns.* Alvin Zander (1971), a psychologist who has carried out one of the most comprehensive testing programs on groups, provided an interesting comment on this point:

> *"Members' motives to achieve success ... are not merely dispositions to obtain personal gains; they are also indicators to help the group attain satisfactory outcomes ... most relevant research has been based on the assumption that a member thinks only about his own interests while participating in a group; he competes, bargains, negotiates, or cooperates with colleagues in order to achieve personal ends. Group objectives in this view, are only an indirect product of the agreements among self-centered individuals. And, when the members of goal-setting bodies indulge in self-seeking, group objectives do become a compromise among preferences based on personal motives. When one observes group decision making, however, one notes that members often suppress any inclination to put their own needs first, pay little attention to each other's personal desires, and believe it to be an ethical matter to behave in this way. They concentrate instead upon what the total group should do. Choices are made on the basis of what is "good for the group", a matter which can itself generate disharmony and differences. It is understandable then that members' motives to achieve success may not only be dispositions to obtain personal rewards, but may also be inclinations to attain satisfactory outcomes for the group."* (p. 2)

Thus, the successful coach strives to motivate the athlete as an individual as well as to motivate the group as a whole. Independent of what the coach says or does, however, the group's motivation also has an impact on the athlete's level of motivation (see Figure 3.3). For example, Zander found that if the group as a total unit sets

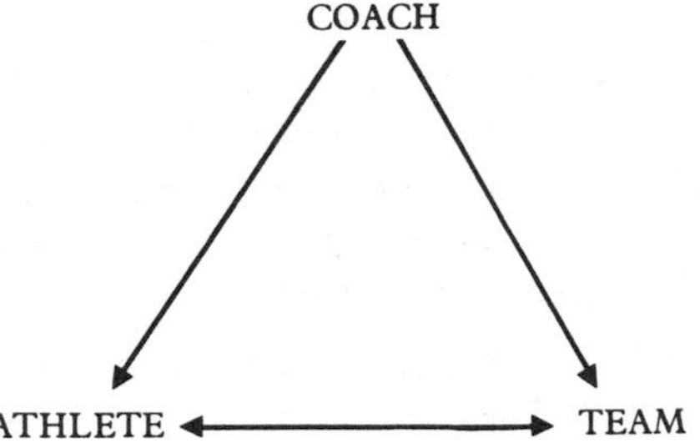

Figure 3.3
Motivational impact of the coach and the team on the athlete.

extremely easy goals, has a low level of aspiration, and/or has experienced repeated failures, the motivation of individual group members is negatively affected. Under these conditions, the level of aspiration that individual group members personally hold for themselves decreases, confidence in the group and interest in the group's activities declines, and active participation in the group is slowly reduced. The coach-as-a-leader could try to stop or reverse this process but the influence of the group is extremely powerful. And, thus, the team environment, as a motivator, does represent a factor not readily subject to change.

PROPOSITION: Similarity among members of a group can have both a positive and a negative effect upon the group's atmosphere and the group's productivity.

Because this proposition says that both homogeneous and heterogeneous groups can be effective, it is essentially of little value to the coach or teacher. This is unfortunate, but it is the only conclusion that can be drawn from available research.

For example, Eitzen (1973) found that high school basketball teams with athletes who were similar in terms of such socio-economic and personal factors as father's occupation, family prestige in the community, religion, and place of residence, had fewer cliques and were more successful. Conversely, however, Fiedler (1967) reported that high school basketball teams in which members were close personal friends were not as effective — team members tended to pass to each other on the basis of friendship. Fiedler suggested that "the team with overly close interpersonal ties among teammates tends to set up shots for team members on the basis of friendship rather than ability or advantage to the team, i.e., the particular boys who are 'set up' might not be the best players on the team — in close games this will, of course, be decisive" (p. 68).

Klein and Christiansen (1969), Zander (1971), and Martens (1970) also have examined the degree to which the general orientation or motivation held by group members is associated with the group's effectiveness. Klein and Christiansen, for example, found that basketball teams in which the members possessed similar levels of aspiration were not as successful as teams in which the members were mixed in their aspirations. It was proposed that in those teams where all members universally held a similar aspiration level or need for achievement, intragroup conflicts could arise. That is, it wouldn't be possible for every team member to be satisfied simultaneously. On the other hand, in mixed groups, it would be possible for members with low needs to defer to those members with higher needs or aspirations.

Zander's work with problem solving groups has led him to a conclusion which is almost completely opposite from Klein and Christiansen. Zander assessed not only individual motives (the need to achieve and the need to avoid failure) but group motives as well (the desire for group success and the desire to avoid group failure). The desire for group success is the tendency on the part of a group member to feel pride and satisfaction if the group is successful in accomplishing a challenging task. The desire to avoid group failure is the tendency on the part of a group member to feel embarrassment or dissatisfaction if the group is unsuccessful. Zander found that after a series of trials or performances by the group, those members with individual motives not in harmony with the group became tense. In sport, if an athlete has an overwhelming desire to be successful but this is not shared by his/her teammates, a feeling of frustration, anger, and stress will result. Thus, there is certainly a strong suggestion that similarity between a member and the group in terms of needs and aspirations contributes to a positive group atmosphere.

The focus in Martens' research was somewhat different from the above. He examined the relationship of individual task motivation and individual affiliation motivation to group success and satisfaction. In one aspect of the study, 144 intramural basketball teams were classified as high, moderate, and low on task motivation on the basis of the average response of individual team members. It was observed that in contrast to teams categorized as low or moderate, the high task motivated teams were more successful and more satisfied. Also, when a similar analysis was undertaken with the 144 teams categorized on the basis of affiliation motivation, Martens found that teams classified as high on affiliation motivation were more satisfied but less successful than the teams classified as low or moderate.

Carron (1981) has suggested that "the critical factor may not be homogeneity or heterogeneity per se, but whether the team fractionates into cliques or produces social isolates" (p. 249). Certainly from a skill perspective, having athletes who can carry out a wide variety of roles is essential. No hockey team can be successful without both checkers and goal scorers, no volleyball team can function without both setters and spikers, no basketball team can be effective without shooters, rebounders, and playmakers. And in most instances, the same athlete cannot carry out these different roles. Thus, the division of responsibility present on sport teams requires a wide cross-section of skills. So, heterogeneity seems preferable except in these instances where that heterogeneity has the potential to produce cliques.

PROPOSITION: The group's goals and successes and failures influence the individual member's level of motivation.

Groups, like individuals, set goals for themselves. Thus, a hockey team might have a long term goal such as a reduction in its goals-against average, a decrease in penalty minutes per game, or an improvement in the ratio of shots taken to shots on goal. Or their goal might be short term such as increasing the number of body checks in an upcoming period. Each of these goals is set out for the total team and not for any specific individual. But, the goals set by the team and the successes or failures experienced also influence the individual members' motivation.

In his research on this issue, Zander (1971) used laboratory tasks as well as the results from real organizations like the United Fund. His laboratory research used a ball rolling task which required three to six individuals to collectively push a ball up a ramp using an aluminum pole. The object was to get the ball to stop in a hole lying in the upper section of the ramp. Nine numbered holes were set above this target hole and nine numbered holes were set below. Thus a group score could be obtained and a group aspiration established. Also, in some experiments a series of wires and dials were attached to the pole (supposedly to assess individual competence and effort). Fictitious feedback was then transmitted to the individual group members concerning their personal contributions to the group's performance.

Zander's results from the laboratory groups and real life organizations revealed that the group's level of aspiration changed with success and failure. In fact, it generally conformed to the rule: "succeed, raise; fail, lower". But, there was a greater tendency to raise aspirations after a success than to lower them after a failure. The group outcome also has a large impact on member motivation. For example, when a group or organization consistently fails more than it succeeds, the following outcomes are observed:

- When a new level of aspiration is established for the group, members express reduced confidence in the group's ability to achieve it.
- Members express a desire to leave the situation and avoid the responsibility for the group's performances.
- Minimal pride is expressed in the group.
- Members express an unwillingness to continue setting goals for the group.
- Less importance is attached to the attainment of the group's goals or the group's success.
- Less attention is paid to the chances for the group's success when a group goal is selected.

Zander (1971) summarized his results by stating:

> *"After repeated failure, members are less inclined to be concerned about the probabilities of future failure, or success; instead, they seek means that will help them avoid the unfavorable consequences of failure. They tend to: lower their group's goals or stick with the one they have failed to reach, giving an unapproving evaluation to their group's performance, see the activity as less important, believe that success on the task is less desirable, are less attracted to their own group, and would like to judge the group in relation to its past performance rather than its goal attainment - they would gladly abandon altogether the practice of setting aspiration levels. Members in such a group have a distinct preference for unreasonably difficult tasks in the light of their past performance, making them highly vulnerable to subsequent failures"* (p. 200-201).

From a psychological point of view, the individual in a failing group retreats from that group and its work. An attempt is made to either ignore the failure experience, reduce the importance attached to achieving success, or decrease the degree of involvement, association, and personal contributions to the group. Success, of course, leads to reactions which are opposite in nature.

Implications for the Coach and Teacher

It is of little benefit to suggest that a sport group or physical education class should be as similar or dissimilar as possible. An essential factor in teaching and coaching is working with what is available. Occasionally, minor changes can be made by a coach to a team roster through trades, retirements, or cuts, but usually coaches have very little flexibility. (Ironically, it's probably coaches who are the most disposable parts of a team. Annually, the sport pages of newspapers contain a reference to this fact when owners of losing teams are quoted: "We felt a change was necessary and we can't fire the whole team, so we let Coach go".)

What the coach or teacher must do is insure that similarity or dissimilarity among group membership does not detract from the group concept. A number of points are relevant in this regard. First, individual members of sport teams should clearly understand their role in the group. The third line in hockey may be a checking line, the sixth man in basketball may be a defensive specialist, and the bullpen pitcher may be used for short relief only. Each group has a number of assignments or responsibilities which must be fulfilled if the group is to be successful. Not all of these may be equally attractive to the individual. But, athletes must be informed of their respective roles and their overall importance to team success.

Second, when it is possible, individuals should be selected for their ability to fulfill specific roles. Managers of Olympic hockey or basketball teams, and World Cup soccer teams keep this in mind when they establish their rosters. They are not foolish enough to select only the top scorers for their teams. The complement of individuals they select have the potential to fill all the various roles.

Third, care must be taken if dissimilarity (heterogeneity) is present on socio-economic and personal factors among team members — religion, race. Cliques, social isolation, and disharmony can wreck the solidarity of the group. Techniques which have been used to reduce this likelihood in professional and amateur teams generally involve mandatory interaction. Thus, roommates are rotated, locker room assignments are designed to maximize communication, and attempts are made to have the group socialize as a unit.

This latter point was clearly illustrated in an anecdote told by football player Ahmad Rashad of the Minnesota Vikings (Rashad and Deford, 1982):

"I started the day by skipping the team breakfast so I could order grits back in my room. Then in the afternoon, I went to our team pregame meal. I seldom eat much there. I want to be lean and hungry when I'm playing. Today I didn't eat a thing; but

later I ordered Southern fried chicken from room service. I must have eaten a whole chicken. I raised hell at the team meal because when I came in I looked around and almost every table was all-white or all-black. 'What is this?' I hollered. 'I thought Jim Crow was dead!' And then I designated certain table integrators. But don't get the wrong impression ... This sort of thing is much more a case of social choice than of any real racism ... The trouble is, if this gets to be a habit the people end up eating together every meal and in the long run that's not good for the team" (p. 89-90).

Consistently winning or losing can have a signficant impact on the motivation athletes hold personally and for the team as a unit. Thus, it is extremely important for the coach and team to set realistic goals and objectives. An important point in this regard is that success and failure are not absolutes — they are highly related to the expectations the individual holds (Carron and Chelladurai, 1982). Thus, the process outlined in Figure 2.4 is equally applicable for teams. Is the goal realistic? Is the program appropriate? Are the training program and preparation adequate? Is the team committed? Is team effort sufficient? Is team performance adequate?

If the season has been particularly unsuccessful, or a loss is especially unsettling, the coach may have to pay special attention to the emotional needs of the athletes. This is often difficult. The reactions of a coach on a losing team are no different than those of the athletes. Association with the team is viewed as unattractive, confidence in the ability of the team to achieve any new aspirations is minimal, and there is an increased desire to withdraw from the situation and avoid the consequences of more failures. Dealing with this type of failure situation may be a coach's most challenging task.

Dickie (1982), in an article concerned with losing and its consequences, has pointed out that "whether a coach works with a novice or an international caliber athlete, one of his primary responsibilities is to cure the emotional side effects of losing in sport" (p. 19). She also provided a number of insightful quotes from coaches to illustrate this point. One was from Jack Donohue, the Canadian Olympic men's basketball coach. Donohue recalled his team's loss to Cuba in the 1975 Pan-American Games when a silver medal was at stake:

"Losing is part of the sport. We played badly and that really hurt. Although it was a traumatic day, it was not as though the sun would not come up again. We had a job to do the next day ... If anyone reacted violently, I would spend personal time with him. It is important to define winning and losing for your players. You must reinforce the fact that mistakes are part of development and the learning experience. Defeat is more of a learning situation than a setback" (Dickie, 1982, p. 19).

Another quote was from John Stockdale, coach of the senior men's water polo team from British Columbia. Stockdale's team was favored to win the championship from eight-time winner Hamilton, but they lost 5-4 in overtime in the semi-finals. Stockdale recalled that the loss was a big surprise and an even bigger letdown:

"Our pride was on the line. We were the favorites because we had a lot of national team talent. Players made some key mistakes that cost us the game. They were very

hurt and some were on the verge of tears ... Some had to be talked to and others needed physical contact — a hug or a pat on the back. Anger was expressed towards the referee through a barrage of yelling. Others were not in control, but that passed in minutes. Blame was directed at themselves and at me. Everyone was hurting, so we needed an emotional talk ... I didn't want them to pretend that it didn't hurt. Forget the stiff upper lip type of thing. I could have told them to go home and forget it, but it was too important. We failed and that was okay. It was time to get off our cloud and get back into the game. At the end of our talk, the players who were seemingly distant, uncaring and unresponsive, had regained their pride" (Dickie, 1982, p. 18).

The final quote was from Jack Walters, Canadian national speedskating coach. Walters discussed events following the 500-metre final at the world championships. His athlete, Gaetan Boucher, who had previously set a world record over the same distance, fell after leaning too far on a turn:

"*The first thing I did after Gaetan's fall was check for injuries and then I tried the best I could to tell him that the competition was not that important. We had to realistically look at the next season. Since he is always in the top three in the world, his performance goals are easy to set. We had to analyze the past season — why he fell and discuss the important components of training, especially those which worked for him*" (Dickie, 1982, p. 19).

What these three quotes clearly show is that the coach must be a stabilizing influence when the athlete or team is under stress from events such as losing.

SUMMARY

The situations into which participants are placed can have a strong impact upon their motivation level. In this chapter those factors in the situation that the coach or teacher has reduced or no opportunity to manipulate were discussed. These included the presence of others, the competition, and the team environment. On the basis of the available research, a number of general propositions were outlined:

1. The presence of others influence motivation and performance effectiveness.
   a) The presence of others improves performance in tasks in which the required responses are simple or well learned.
   b) The presence of others causes a disruption in performance in tasks in which the required responses are complex or not well learned.
2. Characteristics of the individuals present influence the participant's motivation.
   a) The size of the group watching has an influence on the motivation of the performer.

   b) The expertise of the people present has an influence on the motivation of the performer.
   c) The supportiveness of the people present has an influence on the motivation of the performer.
3. The presence of others is relaxing in highly stressful situations.
4. Competitiveness is a learned behavior.
   a) The competitive drive varies in intensity in individuals from different cultures.
   b) The competitive drive increases in intensity in children as they get older.
   c) The competitive drive varies in intensity according to the personality of the participant.
5. The performer's ability in relationship to the challenges in the task has an influence on the competitive drive.
   a) The competitive drive is most strongly aroused when both participants feel that they are relatively equal in ability.
   b) The performance of individuals with high ability at a task improves when competition is introduced; those with low ability deteriorates.
6. Early success contributes to the development of the competitive drive; early failure contributes to a decrease.
7. Similarity among members of a group can have both a positive and a negative effect upon the group's atmosphere and the group's productivity.
8. The group's goals and successes and failures influence an individual member's level of motivation.

Although the factors referred to here as *present others,* the *competitor,* and the *team* are not directly subject to modification and manipulation, it is possible for the coach and teacher to have some influence over them over an extended period of time. The negative impact of an audience can be reduced through a program of acclimatization. Also, if young participants are brought along slowly, the competitive drive can be nurtured. And, finally, any positive programs the coach develops to motivate the team should also serve to motivate individual athletes. But, patience is a requirement. Not only will it be difficult to definitely determine whether these programs have had an impact, any impact will be slow in developing.

SUGGESTED READINGS

Carron, A.V. Motivating the athlete. *Motor Skills: Theory Into Practice,* 1977, *1,* 23-34.

Carron, A.V. Processes of group interaction in sport teams. *Quest,* 1981, *33,* 245-270.

Cratty, B.J. *Social psychology in athletes.* Englewood Cliffs: Prentice-Hall, 1981.

Cratty, B.J. *Psychology in contemporary sport: Guidelines for coaches and athletes* (2nd ed.). Englewood Cliffs: Prentice-Hall, 1983.

Zander, A. *Motives and goals in groups.* New York: Academic Press, 1971.

CHAPTER 4

Personal Factors Readily Subject to Change

The professions of coaching and teaching are exceedingly complex. All coaches and teachers, no matter at what level they are working, must assume a variety of different roles beyond those of skills instructor (Singer, 1972; Tutko and Ogilvie, 1967). These roles can include being a 1) *public relations person* in terms of interactions with such diverse groups as parents, athletes on other teams, other coaches and teachers, and possibly the media; 2) *counsellor* in terms of being sensitive to the participant-as-a-person and assisting that participant with non-activity problems, concerns, or aspirations; 3) *organizer* in terms of annual and daily practice sessions and classes, travel arrangements, and game or competition scheduling; 4) *budget manager* in terms of the financial arrangements necessary for facilities, equipment, and travel arrangements; and, 5) *motivator,* to insure that each student or athlete approaches or achieves his/her potential.

This last role, being a motivator, is generally assumed to be the most important, particularly for coaches. Tutko and Richards (1971) emphasized this point when they stated that "possibly the most important role played by the coach is that of motivator" (p. 115). In addition, in a later commentary on the athlete's internal motivation, Tutko and Richards also aptly observed that "the degree of internal motivation varies greatly among athletes. The reason for participation and the extent to which they are prepared to work to achieve success are factors with which the coach has very little to do — *at least at first* [emphasis added]. Some athletes are highly motivated internally. They will spend an enormous amount of time working to perfect their skills without ever being prodded or cajoled by the coach. Others spend very little time, and the coach must work to provide the motivation necessary to help them reach their potential" (p. 129).

The suggestion that initially a coach has little to do with athlete motivation is correct. This would also hold true for the student-teacher interaction. For example, different sports and activities have different incentive values for a participant. Thus, it is not uncommon for very young children to participate in one sport one summer and an entirely different sport in the next. This decision is usually made because the child perceives that the types of experiences he or she desires are more available in one situation than the other. Thus, a young athlete may choose to play baseball rather than swim because her friends have also made this transfer. The coach would have had nothing to do with that incentive motivation originally (but she could capitalize on it to keep the young athlete interested and involved in baseball). What is necessary then is an understanding of the internal (personal) factors which serve to motivate participants. In the present chapter, the motivational factors that can be manipulated to some extent by the coach or teacher are discussed. These include incentive motivation, the analysis of of the outcome, intrinsic interest, the expectations of others, and self confidence.

INCENTIVE MOTIVATION AS A MOTIVATOR

Running for money doesn't make you run fast. It makes you run first.

Ben Jipcho

When individuals engage in activities which have some final goal as their objective such as playing a sport, taking a university course, or carrying out a job, they consciously or subconsciously assess the incentive value attached to that activity. For example, how much satisfaction can be expected from simply engaging in the activity? To what extent will success be associated with a feeling of pride? The greater the extent to which positive outcomes are possible, the greater will be the incentive value in that activity. Thus, incentive motivation represents a powerful source of motivation for young participants in sport and physical activity. Alderman (1978) pointed out the rationale for this when he stated:

> "*Incentive motivation simply refers to the incentive value a young athlete attaches to the possible outcomes or experiences he perceives as being available to him in a particular sport. If a boy or girl perceives that particular kinds of experiences are available to them in a sport, and they feel these will be pleasant, enjoyable or satisfying to them, then they will elect to participate in that sport rather than another. If, in addition, their expectancies are confirmed from actual experiences, then they will persist in that sport and their level of motivation will remain high. If, on the other hand, their expectancies are not confirmed, or the experiences are negative, they will quit or choose another sport. It is a simple stance: namely, if young athletes get what they are seeking in a sport, then they'll be motivated to continue in that sport*" (p. 139).

A number of researchers have pursued the question of what incentives are perceived by children to be available in sport (and, more importantly perhaps, what incentives form the strongest basis for sport involvement). These include Alderman and his students (Alderman, 1976; 1978; Alderman and Wood, 1976; Garvie, 1979; Wood, 1980, 1981), Passer (1981, 1982) and Gould and his colleagues (Feltz, Gould, Horn & Weiss, 1982; Gould, 1982a, 1982b; Gould, Feltz, Weiss & Petlichkoff, 1981; Gould & Horn, 1983). Alderman's work evolved from a strong theoretical basis and involved great numbers of participants from different ages, sex, sports, and cultures. It might be useful to elaborate on it in more detail.

Initially, Alderman and Wood capitalized on an assumption proposed by Birch and Veroff (1966) that seven major incentives are the reason for persistent kinds of goal-directed behavior in humans. These incentive systems were called *sensory, curiosity, achievement, aggression, affiliation, power,* and *independence* behaviors. When Birch and Veroff's work was adapted for sport situations by Alderman and Wood, again seven kinds of experiences (or motive incentive systems as they were also called) were identified as being available and important to young participants (see Figure 4.1.) These include *independence* (doing things without the help of others),

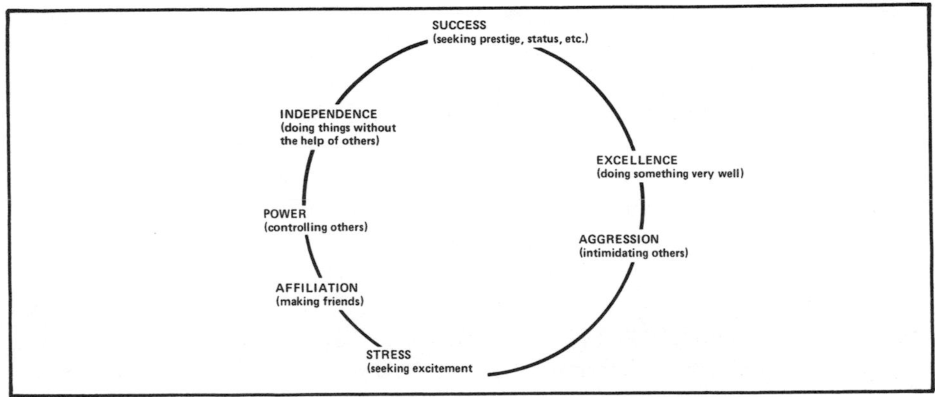

Figure 4.1
The major incentive systems in sport (Adapted from Alderman and Wood, 1976).

power (controlling others), *affiliation* (making friends), *stress* (seeking excitement), *excellence* (doing something very well), *aggression* (intimidating others), and *success* (seeking status, prestige, recognition). Thus, for example, one major attractive aspect of sport and physical activity is that it satisfies a need for independence; it contains opportunities to do things alone without the help of others. A questionnaire was also developed by Alderman and Wood to assess the extent to which each of these experiences are perceived to be important by participants of different ages and competitive experience. The results from these investigations as well as from other researchers interested in youth sports form the basis for the propositions which follow.

PROPOSITION: The majority of young participants have multiple motives for their involvement in sport and physical activity.

a) **The most dominant, consistently endorsed reasons for participation are affiliation, skill development, excitement, success and status, fitness, and energy release.**
b) **A need for independence, power, aggression, and the influence of others (such as parents) are relatively minor factors for participation.**
c) **There are no sex differences in the motives for involvement in sport and physical activity.**
d) **There are no age differences in the motives for involvement in sport and physical activity.**
e) **There are no major differences across different cultures in the motives for involvement in sport and physical activity.**

One of the most dominant conclusions which evolves from any examination of the research on children's motives for participation is that there is no one single reason. This was emphasized by Gould (1982b) in his overview of the work in this area when he stated that "children have a number of varied motives for sports participation ... [and] most young athletes have multiple motives for participation, as opposed to one single motive" (p. 2-3). Similarly, Passer (1981), in his review, identified six major categories of participation motives — affiliation, skill development, excitement, success and status, fitness, and energy release — but then pointed out that "the most general conclusion is that with the exception of energy release all of these motives are viewed by most children as important determinants of their sport involvement" (p. 232).

As indicated previously, Alderman and Wood (Alderman, 1976, 1978; Alderman and Wood, 1976; Wood, 1980, 1981) tested thousands of participants of different ages, sex, sports, and cultures to determine which of the seven incentives were perceived to be of primary importance. Their dominant findings were that, first, affiliation and skill development (excellence) were consistently the two strongest motives. Second, excitement (the motive they called stress) and success (winning, achieving recognition) were rated next. Third, aggression, independence, and power failed to achieve any degree of consistent support. And, fourth, these three findings were generally consistent across age, sex, sport, and culture.

Subsequent investigations have supported these general conclusions (see Table 4.1) although in a number of reports *to have fun* has been heavily endorsed by participants. Whether knowing that "to have fun" provides any additional insight into why children participate is questionable. What is fun? What are the elements of fun? Gould (1982b) and Passer (1981) have both addressed this issue and their opinion is that children probably experience "fun" in participating when their other primary motives are satisfied. Passer, for example, stated

"It seems likely that satisfying affiliation, skill development, success and status, and excitement needs will all contribute to players having fun" (p. 233).

In a similar vein, Gould suggested that

"Elements of the fun construct may be specific to the individual or be dependent on his or her other motives for participation. That is, a young athlete who is primarily motivated by affiliation will experience 'fun' when this need is fulfilled, while another young athlete who is success-oriented, will not experience fun until he or she attains success" (p. 5).

If fun is associated directly with the satisfactory attainment of primary incentives — affiliation, excellence, and fitness — it becomes essential for the coach and teacher to recognize the degree to which these incentives are important to their participants. However, research by Larose and Carron (1982) has shown that while high school coaches are aware of the motives of sport participants in a *global sense* (they are aware that athletes-in-general want to satisfy affiliation needs, achieve success, and so on), they have virtually no idea about the primary motives of *specific athletes.*

PROPOSITION: The reasons for discontinuing involvement in sport and physical activity are diverse and complex.

a) **The most dominant, consistently stated reason for discontinuing involvement in sport or physical activity is the development of an interest in other activities.**
b) **Among the negative reasons listed for discontinuing involvement in sport and physical activity are lack of playing time, lack of success, lack of skill improvement, lack of fun, boredom, injury, and lack of encouragement from significant others.**
c) **The negative reasons for discontinuing involvement play a more important role with younger participants.**

An alternate approach to the study of what motivates children to participate in sport and physical activity is an assessment of why they discontinue their involvement. A summary of a number of studies which have pursued this question is contained in Table 4.2

The earliest research in this area was conducted by Orlick (Orlick, 1973, 1974; Orlick and Botterill, 1975) with children who either had never participated or were what was referred to as a *sport dropout.* The children who had never participated mentioned a fear of failing and a perception that they did not have sufficient ability to get involved. The children who had participated but then elected to discontinue mentioned problems with the program (e.g., it was too serious, not enough fun,), or the coach (e.g., coach was too critical, didn't play everybody), or the development of other interests. An examination of Table 4.2 shows that in the majority of studies carried out after Orlick's original work, a *conflict of interests* was consistently mentioned as a primary reason for discontinuing sport involvement. Presumably the incentives, rewards, values associated with participation in other activities begins to outweigh the incentives, rewards, and values associated with the sport experience. This is not to say that negative reasons do not play a part — particularly with the youngest participants. In fact, as Gould (1982b) stated "some evidence reveals that these more negative motives [lack of playing time, over emphasis on competition, boredom, lack of fun, and dislike of the coach] play an especially important role in the discontinuation of younger as compared to older athletes" (p. 3).

Table 4.1 Participation motive studies of youth sports participation (Adapted from Gould, 1982b).

Author(s)	Sample Size and Characteristics	Major Findings (Motives)
1. Alderman & Wood (1976)	425 Canadian ice hockey participants (ages 11-14)	1. affiliation 2. excellence 3. arousal-stress 4. esteem
2. Alderman (1978)	2000 Canadian athletes (ages 11-18)	1. affiliation 2. excellence 3. arousal-stress-success 4. no age, sex, sport, or culture differences
3. Griffin (1978)	531 U.S. football players (ages 9-15)	1. fun 2. get in shape 3. meet new friends 4. parental pressure
4. Sapp & Haubenstricker	579 U.S. male and 479 female athletes (ages 11-18)	1. fun 2. improve skills 3. fitness benefits 4. females more friendship oriented 5. few sport differences
5. Fry, McClements & Sefton (1981)*	112 Canadian ice hockey participants (ages 8-16)	1. fun 2. scoring goals, skating, puck handling 3. winning or competition 4. meeting new people — being with friends

6. Gill, Gross, & Huddleston (1981)	720 U.S. male and 418 female athletes (ages 8-18)	1. improve skills 2. learn new skills 3. challenge 4. fitness
7. Gould, Feltz, Weiss & Petlichkoff (1981)*	365 U.S. swimmers (ages 8-19)	1. fun 2. fitness 3. skill improvement 4. team atmosphere 5. challenge 6. females more emphasis on fun and friendship
8. Robertson (1981)*	663 Australian male and 625 female Grade 7 athletes (age 12)	1. intrinsic rewards (e.g., fun, feel good fitness) 2. achievement-mastery (e.g., winning, success, playing well) 3. extrinsic rewards (e.g., praise, trophies) 4. social reciprocity (e.g., friendship)
9. Sands (1981)	96 Australian male and female track and field participants (ages 8-12)	1. being with friends — making friends 2. fun
10. Wankel & Pabich (1981)	132 Canadian baseball, soccer and ice hockey participants (ages 8-12)	1. improve skills — sense of accomplishment 2. doing the skills of the game 3. excitement 4. compare skills against others
11. Passer (1982)	316 U.S. male soccer participants (ages 10-15)	1. fun 2. do something good at 3. like to compete 4. learn new skills
12. Petlichkoff & Gould	270 U.S. male and female high school athletes (ages 12-18)	1. excellence 2. affiliation 3. arousal 4. success

*Simultaneously studied both participants and former participants.

Table 4.2 Studies assessing motives for discontinuing youth sports participation
(Adapted from Gould, 1982b).

Author(s)	Sample Size and Characteristics	Major Findings (Motives)
1. Orlick (1973)	32 Canadian non-participants in organized sport (ages 8-10)	1. fear of failure 2. never played 3. not good enough
2. Orlick (1974)/Orlick & Botterill (1975)	60 Canadian former sport participants (ages 7-19)	1. emphasis of program (e.g., too serious, lack of enjoyment) 2. coach (e.g., left people out, criticized too much) 3. conflict of interest 4. interest in other sports 5. competitive emphasis of program
3. Sapp & Haubenstricker (1978)	1183 U.S. male and female athletes (ages 11-18)	1. involvement in other activities 2. working 3. not interested 4. did not play enough
4. Ewing (1981)	254 U.S. male and 198 female high school students (ages 14-15)	1. multiple achievement orientations 2. social approval oriented children persist longer in athletics 3. ability oriented players drop out at a higher rate
5. Fry, McClements & Sefton (1981)	97 former Canadian ice hockey participants comprising a cross sectional sample (ages 8-16) and 112 former Canadian ice hockey participants comprising a longitudinal sample	1. conflicts of interest lack of skill 3. dislike of coach 3. rough play 4. organizational problems

6. Petlichkoff (1981)	32 former high school athletes (ages 12-18)	1. conflicts of interests 2. injury 3. lack of skill improvement 4. not as good as wanted to be
7. Pooley (1981)	50 former Canadian soccer participants (ages 10-15)	1. conflicts of interests 2. overemphasis on competition 3. poor communication 4. motives differ by age
8. Roberts, Kleiber & Duda (1981)	143 male and female elementary school children (ages 9-11)	1. sport participants higher in perceived competence 2. no significant relationship between perceived competence and athletic experience
9. Robertson (1981)	405 male and 353 female Australian former athletes (ages 12)	1. program emphasis (e.g., no fun, boring, never played) 2. conflicts of interest
10. a) Gould, Feltz & Horn (1982) b) Feltz, Gould, Horn & Weiss (1982)	50 U.S. former swimmers and 357 swimmers (ages 10-18)	1. other things to do 2. not good enough 3. not enough fun 4. wanted to play another sport 5. relationships between experience and competence 6. male dropouts higher competence than female dropouts
11. Robinson & Carron (1982)	98 male high school football players	1. lack of enjoyment and sense of belonging to a group perceived to be very close knit 2. lack of encouragement from significant others (fathers and teachers) 3. perception of coach as autocratic 4. low perception of ability

Implications for the Coach and Teacher

It must be kept in mind that motivation is simply a concept (or construct to use the more scientific terminology) which is used to explain why a behavior occurs. The question "Why is Dana playing baseball?" might receive the answer. "Because she enjoys it." While the term motivation is never mentioned in this sequence, it is implicit in the answer. A further question of "Why? What does she find enjoyable about baseball?" could receive a host of answers such as "Her friends are playing", "She's learning a lot", or "It's good exercise." Again, motivation is never mentioned in any of these answers but the reasons can be thought of as the basis for the behavior. In short, they are rewards, valued outcomes, incentives. And, if a coach or teacher is concerned that participants stay involved in sport and physical activity and that they get the most out of their involvement, knowledge of incentive motivation is critical. The sequence if reasonably simple. As Wood (1981) stated:

> "*An understanding by coaches as to why individuals are participating in competitive sport and a willingness to structure the competitive sport environment to provide the participants with the experiences they are seeking may contribute to significantly improving the motivation of these athletes. Thus coaches who satisfy their athletes' reasons for participation will very likely at the same time enhance the motivation of their athletes. Enhanced motivation may contribute to improved personal satisfaction from participating and improved levels of performance. As well, increased motivation may also contribute to obtaining more consistent and optimal effort from these participants*" (p. 7).

The evidence from research on participation motivation contributes to a suggestion that most individuals have a variety of motives for being involved in sport. But, certainly, in almost all cases, affiliation, skill development, excitement, success and status, fitness, and energy release are at the forefront. Further, power, independence, aggression, and pleasing other people who are influential are relatively inconsequential. To a large extent, outcomes such as affiliation, skill development, excitement, success and status, fitness, and energy release are natural byproducts of sport and physical activity. It is also possible, however, for the coach and teacher to set up situations which increase the opportunities for these outcomes to occur (Wood, 1981).

For example, a coach can contribute to the satisfaction of affiliation needs by continually emphasizing the value and importance to the total team effort of all roles — the starters and nonstarters, setters and spikers, defensive and offensive specialists, managers and participants. This contributes to a sense of unity and the development of a team identity. Although it is more difficult in a youth sport situation, nonsport social get-togethers are also effective for promoting a sense of team closeness and unity.

Skill development (or excellence as Alderman and Wood referred to it) is a particularly strong incentive. Participants can encounter difficulty in the satisfactory attainment of this incentive if their standards are inappropriate. For example, a participant may use an older brother or an outstanding classmate as a reference and become discouraged because with every improvement, he or she is still in the same place relative to that reference. If the teacher outlines realistic goals based on individual performance standards, this problem can be reduced, and the participant can be provided with objective evidence that he or she is improving. Since skill improvement is often slow and subtle, it is advantageous to advocate self-recording progress charts (Wood, 1981). A critical point in goal setting is that a *relative* rather than an *absolute* standard of performance must be emhasized.

The two physical incentives, energy release and fitness, are, of course, present in most sport and physical activity situations. But, all too often the practice session or physical education class can become passive if some care isn't taken. For example, there is often a tendency on the part of highly experienced teachers and coaches to overteach — the participants spend a large part of the session listening while the coach or teacher goes into excessive detail about techniques and strategies. Or a less experienced coach or teacher might not take maximum advantage of the equipment and facilities. Thus, the participants spend a great deal of their practice session standing in line waiting for their turn to bat, shoot or skate. The coach and teacher can maximize satisfaction by maximizing movement, participation, and involvement during a class, practice or game.

The incentive of excitement can be achieved by "setting up interesting challenges, using novelty and fun events to combat boredom, and providing a practice atmosphere that has stimulating sensations — sights, sounds, physical surroundings. Providing different ways to practice various skills, changing the order of events in practices, and periodically providing unexpected events in practices all contribute to providing sensation for the participants. The ways to make practices a source of excitement for the competitors is limited only by the creativeness of the coach and athletes" (Wood, 1981, p. 9).

The final group of incentives endorsed by participants, success and status, also warrants some comment. The question of whether winning should be treated as an important outcome in youth sports has been an issue of some concern. Educators, parents, and coaches have had mixed reactions to this issue. But, children have not.

For example, in their interviews of youth sport participants, Scanlan and Passer (1980a, 1980b) noted that 94% of the females and 91% of the males felt winning was either very important or important. Similarly, Alderman (1978), in his analysis of 2000 athletes found that success was consistently rated among the top four motives. Thus, while winning should not be overemphasized in competition, it cannot be ignored. Children want to compete, to test themselves against each other and this incentive must be accommodated. As Passer (1982a) cautioned, however, "it must be remembered...that children become and stay involved in organized sports for multiple reasons, and for many players, other objectives are as or even more important than success and status" (p. 233). The challenge for the educator is to strike a balance between winning and the other incentives.

ANALYSIS OF THE OUTCOME AS A MOTIVATOR

During spring training, you watch who you follow in batting practice, how many minutes you pitched, whether the morning workout is more important than the afternoon. The Yankees would divide the squad into morning and afternoon groups and they'd always say it didn't mean a thing ... I never saw a guy hit or pitch himself off the afternoon list.

Jim Bouton

A significant change in the study of motivation since the 1960's has been an increased interest in understanding cognitions — what the individual thinks and/or what the individual knows. It has been assumed, quite rightly, that what we think, the way that we perceive things, and the information that we come to accept as "fact", can have a direct influence on our motivation and behavior. For example, a domineering, overbearing parent may continually criticize his son's clothes selection, his grooming, his posture, and so on. The son may then eventually come to believe that he is not a very attractive or competent person and act accordingly. As a second example, a young girl may come to believe that she is a good athlete because of some early successful experiences in sport. Subsequently, when she is learning a new skill and early difficulties are encountered, she may show dogged persistance because of her expectation that success will eventually occur. And, as a final example, people become convinced that they can't quit smoking, lose weight, learn a second language, or make friends readily. That certainty, of course, contributes to a half-hearted effort when any new project is initiated. And, the result is then usually another failure and further confirmation of the belief.

Figure 4.2 contains a schematic representation of how cognitions can come to

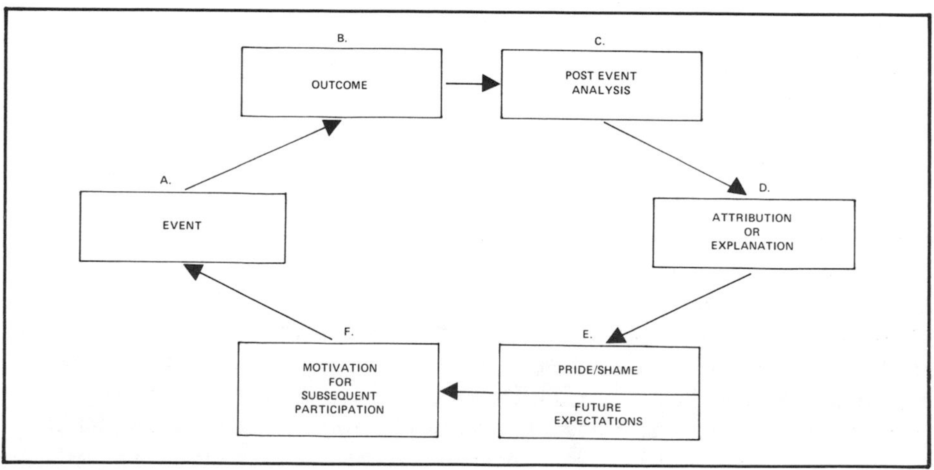

Figure 4.2
The attribution process (Adapted from Carron, 1981).

influence expectations and behavior. An event (Box A) takes place. This may be the son coming to breakfast after selecting his own clothes, or the young athlete starting a new task, or the adult joining a smoking cessation program. An outcome to that event (Box B) then occurs which is interpreted as a success or failure. It is important to bear in mind that success and failure are never absolute events; they are psychological states which are intimately related to the individual's expectations and perceptions (Maehr and Nicholls, 1980; Ross, 1981). For example, the young girl learning the new sport may be quite inept but still be very satisfied with her progress.

After the event occurs, the individual analyzes it (Box C, Figure 4.2) in light of the information available — previous experiences, any expectations which were held prior to the event, the impact of external factors. The outcome is then attributed to some cause (Box D). So, for example, if the parent criticizes the child's clothes selection, that child might attribute the criticism to the fact that the parent is in a bad mood or is impossible to please or to a lack of his own ability to select proper clothes.

This process of analysis and explanation (making attributions) occurs all the time in all sports situations. For example, consider the following set of quotations which appeared in the same edition of the Toronto Globe and Mail:

> "*He had a little bad luck. Maybe he wouldn't have won anyway but he might have been closer.*" [Trainer Gord Huntley discussing the third place finish of his race horse Native Fisher.]
>
> "*I got a lot of help from the outfielders today. We've got great outfielders and they ran them down and made some super catches.*" [Pitcher Bill Gullickson of the Montreal Expos baseball team discussing a victory over the Pittsburgh Pirates.]
>
> "*I was shocked. The Red Wings are trying to cut their costs and I guess they thought I couldn't make the team.*" [Hockey player Dave MacQueen after being released by the Detroit Red Wings hockey team.]
>
> "*None of these guys went through what I went through to get here. I'm not going to say that they had it handed to them but...*" [Rookie Steven Ratzer of the Montreal Expos.]
>
> "*My car was going well so I took the lead early on and was able to control the opposition.*" [Driver Nelson Piquet after winning the Italian Grand Prix.]

In each of these quotations, the speaker is outlining his perception of the factors associated with a previous event. This is referred to as the *attribution process.*

The attribution process occurs quite naturally. Also, it is an universal phenomenon — every individual engages in it. And, the perceptions of causes and the attributions made are not necessarily objectively accurate. For example, Roberts (1975) and Iso-Ahola (1977a) questioned Little League baseball players following winning and losing games. They found that after either a win or a loss the players rated their own efforts high. But, their perception of the effort expended by the total team dropped dramatically if the team had lost. Since any team is a composite of its individual members, it obviously isn't possible for all team members to be correct in their viewpoint that "I was trying to the same extent that I always do but my teammates were not."

Researchers interested in the question of why people perceive events the way they do have advanced four explanations. These are referred to as the *need to sustain self-esteem,* the *desire for social approval,* the *need to retain effective control over one's personal destiny,* and the *need to maintain a belief that we reside in a just world* (Rejeski and Brawley, 1983; Tetlock and Levi, 1982).

The first explanation is very straightforward. All individuals have a desire to enhance, protect and maintain their self-esteem. Thus, it is assumed that the frequently observed self-serving bias in analysis (in which personal credit is accepted for success but responsibility for failure is denied) is simply a reflection of this tendency to be self-protective.

It is also assumed that a desire for social approval can underlie the explanations people give — particularly those made publicly. For example, it would be an unusual athlete who, while being interviewed on T.V., admitted that he or she was almost totally responsible for a successful outcome. An athlete might secretively believe this, teammates and coaches might publicly proclaim it, and the T.V. interviewer might press this position, but the athlete would probably praise the overall team contributions. In short, athletes often endorse a viewpoint which, while possibly inaccurate, assures public approval and avoids public embarrassment.

A need to maintain effective control also helps to explain the use of attributions. A natural consequence of human activity is the desire on the part of all individuals to understand/explain past events. In turn, understanding contributes to the feeling that events which are occurring can be predicted and controlled in the future. Thus, a teacher who has had a verbal disagreement with a student mentally goes over the event in an attempt to understand why. When an explanation (attribution) is arrived at — it may be considered to be the student's personality, the teacher's approach, the timing, or some combination of these — it serves as frame-of-reference for future teacher-student interactions.

Finally, it is also assumed that the need to believe in a just world also accounts for the use of attributions. For example, through learning, people come to believe that violence and aggression are socially unacceptable. But hockey, basketball, and football fans will readily condone aggression by their favoured team if the opposition is believed to be unnecessarily aggressive and therefore, "to have it coming to them." In short, attributions can also serve the function of making unacceptable behaviors more acceptable (Rejeski and Brawley, 1983).

Although individuals typically use a wide variety of explanations (see Box D, Figure 4.2 again), most researchers have categorized these into broad dimensions and then attempted to determine whether there is a systematic pattern in the way the different dimensions are utilized after successful versus unsuccessful outcomes. For example, three dimensions have been adopted by Weiner (1979) in his research. He referred to these as *stability, locus of causality,* and *controllability.* The stability dimension takes into account the fact that a success or failure might be perceived to be caused by factors that don't change very much over time such as the difficulty of the task (a stable factor). Or, the individual may feel that the outcome was the result of a highly unstable, changing factor such as the mood he/she was in. The locus of causality dimension is an acknowledgement that outcomes can be perceived to be the result of internal factors, factors within the person such as the amount of effort expended or external factors, factors in the situation such as the home court advantage. Finally, the controllability dimension serves to recognize that people perceive that outcomes can result from factors over which they either have some control such as the level of their training or over which they have no control such as luck.

When an attribution has been made, the individual experiences pride or shame and satisfaction or dissatisfaction. At the same time an expectation develops about the potential for a successful performance at some later date (Box E, Figure 4.2). Finally, the general attribution process and the beliefs which develop as a result, influence subsequent motivation (Box F, Figure 4.2). The specific way in which this occurs is contained in the discussion of the propositions which follow.

PROPOSITION: A participant's perception of the causes for an outcome influences subsequent motivation.

a) **Positive outcomes which are perceived to be the result of internal, personal factors (e.g. ability, effort, training) rather than external environmental factors (e.g., good luck, ease of the task, officiating decisions) are associated with the greatest amount of pride and satisfaction.**

b) **Negative outcomes which are perceived to be the result of internal, personal factors (e.g., poor ability, low effort, inadequate training) rather than external environmental factors (e.g., bad luck, difficulty of the task, officiating bias) are associated with the greatest amount of shame and dissatisfaction.**

c) **Positive outcomes which are perceived to be the result of stable factors (e.g., high ability, ease of the task) rather than unstable factors (e.g., exceptional effort, good luck) are associated with the greatest expectancy for subsequent success.**

d) **Negative outcomes which are perceived to be the result of stable factors (e.g., poor ability, difficulty of the task) rather than unstable factors (e.g., poor effort, bad luck) are associated with the lowest expectancy for subsequent success.**

It has been repeatedly observed that people are very self-centered in their perceptions of the causes of outcomes (e.g., Carron and Spink, 1980; Forsythe and

Schlenker, 1977; Frieze and Weiner, 1971). That is, success is generally attributed to internal, personal characteristics such as personal ability, mood, and effort. On the other hand, failure is generally attributed to external, environmental characteristics such as difficulty of the task, bad luck, and other situational factors. Further, a similar pattern is present in group situations. Individuals who are members of successful groups have a greater tendency to assume major responsibility for the group's performance than do members of unsuccessful groups. This profile might be best summed up as *I had a lot to do with the victory; I had very little to do with the loss* or *I played very well and we won; my teammates played very poorly and we lost.*

There is also a direct relationship between attributions made to internal versus external factors and the pride-shame and satisfaction-dissatisfaction experienced by the individual (Iso-Ahola, 1976; Nicholls, 1976; Weiner and Kukla, 1970). A participant who feels that success is a product of the internal factors of personal ability or effort experiences more pride and satisfaction with the outcome than does a participant who feels that external factors such as good luck or an easy opponent were the cause. Similarly, if the participant attributes a failure to low ability or inadequate effort, greater shame and dissatisfaction are experienced than when the loss is considered to result from the superior play of an opponent or from bad luck. In short, greater emotion is associated with the internal attributions than with the external ones.

Research also reveals that a participant's previous experiences and the present outcome both influence the use of stable versus unstable types of explanations (Iso-Ahola, 1975; Roberts, 1975; Spink, 1978). For example, if a failure is encountered after a string of successes or a success occurs after a series of failures, the participant perceives that unstable factors such as luck, effort, mood, officiating, and so on have had a major influence on the outcome. On the other hand, if the ouctome is a success within a long series of successes or a failure within a series of failures, the participant uses stable factors such as personal ability, level of training, and so on to account for that outcome.

There is an inherent reasonableness in this latter pattern of findings. A tennis player who has been consistently successful against an opponent or a student who has repetitively obtained an A standing in schoolwork would be inclined to view a failure as an isolated phenomenon, resulting from bad luck or a decline in personal effort (factors which are unstable, variable) — not too low ability or the difficulty of task (factors which are stable, not easily overcome). Similarly, these same two generally successful individuals would be inclined to attribute another success to personal ability and/or the relative simplicity of the task rather than extreme luck or exceptional effort.

There is also a direct relationship between attributions made along the stable-unstable dimension and the expectancies that the individual holds for future success/failure (Nicholls, 1976). In the case of failure, an attribution to the stable factors of low ability and/or the extreme difficulty of the task is usually associated with an expectancy for future failures. This is represented by the profile *I haven't been very successful in the past* (prior experience), *I wasn't very successful today* (present outcome), and *I probably won't be successful next time either* (future expectancy). A success ascribed to the stable attributes would be associated with an expectancy for future successes. The sequence in this instance would be *I've been successful in the past* (past experience). *I was successful today* (present outcome), and *I will probably be successful next time* (future expectancy).

In the same vein, when attributions are made to unstable factors, there is an awareness or understanding that the outcome could change in the future. For example, if a wrestler lost because of what he felt was a lack of effort, this could be rectified. Therefore, there would be a relatively high expectation that an increase in effort would lead to success — that failure could be avoided through effort.

PROPOSITION: Children develop stable opinions about the causes of events and these influence subsequent motivation.

a) **Mastery-oriented children — children who come to believe that the chief reason for their failure is some variable factor such as the amount of effort they have expanded — react to failure with renewed effort, greater persistence and continued involvement in the task.**

b) **Learned helplessness children — children who come to believe that the chief reason for their failure is some stable factor such as ability — react to failure with diminished effort, less persistence, and reduced involvement.**

In their research on children's responses in classrooms and problem-solving situations, Carol Dweck and her colleagues (Diener and Dweck, 1978, 1980; Dweck, 1975; Dweck and Goetz, 1978; Dweck and Reppucci, 1973) have observed that dramatic individual differences exist in responses to failure experiences, differences which have come to be referred to as *learned helplessness* and *mastery-oriented behavior*. Dweck and Goetz (1978) defined each of these as follows:

> "*Learned helplessness in achievement situations exists when an individual perceives the termination of failure to be independent of his responses. This perception of failure as insurmountable is associated with attributions of failure to invariant factors, such as lack of ability, and is accompanied by seriously impaired performance. In contrast, mastery-oriented behavior — increased persistence or improved performance in the face of failure — tends to be associated with attributions of failure to variable factors, particularly to a lack of effort*" (p. 157).

In short, when failure occurs, learned helplessness children assume that they do not have the resources to overcome the difficulty — their ability is perceived to be inadequate for the task. Consequently, they lose interest and motivation. Mastery-oriented children, on the other hand, attribute the source of their problem to a lack of effort and, therefore, they respond to failures with greater vigour and persistence.

Having less ability is not, in fact, the actual problem in the learned helplessness child. In the studies carried out by Dweck and her colleagues, the different reactions to failure by the mastery-oriented and learned helplessness-oriented children occurred in spite of equivalent performance success prior to the introduction of failure and equivalent performance on measures of ability (e.g., IQ and reading comprehension).

Diener and Dweck (1980) did find, however, that there are important differences between learned helplessness and mastery-oriented children in their perceptions of success. In comparison to mastery-oriented children, learned helplessness children underestimate the number of previous successes they have experienced, overestimate the number of their failures, do not view any success as a true indication of their ability, and do not expect successful experiences to continue. As Diener and Dweck (1980) noted

> "*Overall, the results show that if there is a way to devalue one's present performance or to be pessimistic about one's future performance, the helpless children are likely to make use of it. Indeed, they do not even have to experience a negative outcome for this tendency to display itself. In sharp contrast, the mastery-oriented are realistically optimistic when they are succeeding and are surprisingly undaunted by failure*" (p. 950).

As the name implies, learned helplessness is an acquired belief — children come to believe that they are not competent (and, therefore, failure must be a result of their insufficient ability). Further, this belief develops as a result of negative (failure) feedback received from important people in the child's life. Interestingly, if the important person is generally negative (negative about a number of different aspects), there is less likelihood that learned helplessness will develop than if the important person is continually negative about one aspect only. Apparently, in the first instance, the child comes to discount the feedback ("Oh, that teacher's always criticizing me") but in the second instance, the specific feedback is perceived to be a true judgment on ability.

PROPOSITION: There are age and sex differences in the way attributions are used.

a) Males and females differ in the type of attributions they endorse following success and failure, the pride and shame they experience, and the expectancies they hold for subsequent performance.

b) Young children cannot or do not readily distinguish between the contributions of their personal ability and effort to their success and failure.

One major difference between the sexes is in the perception of personal ability. In comparison to males, females tend to evaluate their personal ability much lower prior to an event and, as a consequence, have much lower expectations for success. In addition, effort is viewed by females as the most important factor for performance success. Thus, prior to an event, the female begins with a lower perception of her ability and a strong belief in the need for effort (McHugh, Duquin, and Frieze, 1978).

Following the outcome — regardless of whether it was successful or unsuccessful — women most frequently endorse the importance of task difficulty and luck. That is, women tend to rate all tasks easier than males which leads to a reduction in the value attached to success and an increase in the stigma associated with failure. Similarly, in contrast to men, women strongly endorse luck for all outcomes — successes and failures. As a consequence, there is less responsibility (and satisfaction) attached to a positive outcome but less responsibility (and dissatisfaction) attached to a negative outcome (McHugh, Duquin, and Frieze, 1978).

The profiles associated with the above can be summarized and illustrated (see Table 4.3). Relative to the female, the male typically enters an achievement situation with a high expectancy. If he is successful, this success is attributed to ability or other stable internal factors. As a consequence, there is maximum pride and satisfaction associated with the successful outcome and an expectation is developed for subsequent success in future performance.

If the male enters the achievement situation with a high expectancy and is unsuccessful, a self-serving pattern of analysis usually occurs with the outcome being viewed as a result of bad luck or a strong opponent. This pattern of attribution is associated with minimum shame and dissatisfaction and the individual retains a high expectation for subsequent success.

On the other hand, the female who enters an achievement situation with a low perception of personal ability has a low expectancy for success. When the outcome is successful, the perceived reasons used tend to be good luck, special effort or the relative ease of the task. The profile associated with this is *I won because I tried especially hard, I had good luck, and, besides, my opponent wasn't that difficult.*

Only minimum pride and satisfaction are associated with a perception that success resulted from external factors (good luck, task ease). As Table 4.3 illustrates, this would then be the case with this specific profile.

Further, the endorsement of unstable factors (luck, effort) and task ease would not have any positive impact upon expectancy for subsequent performances — it would remain low. Again, as Table 4.3 illustrates, this would be the case with this profile.

The final option in Table 4.3 reflects a self-fulfilling prophecy. The expectation is low, the outcome is consistent with that expectation and the result is an even lower expectancy for subsequent performance. This profile would undoubtedly characterize the potential sport drop out.

Table 4.3 The interaction of initial expectancy, outcome, causal attributions and resultant affective reaction and expectancy
(Adapted from McHugh, Duquin, and Frieze, 1978).

INITIAL EXPECTANCY	PERFORMANCE LEVEL	CAUSAL ATTRIBUTION	EMOTIONAL (AFFECTIVE) REACTION	EXPECTANCY
High[1]	High	Ability, or other stable, internal factors	Maximum pride and satisfaction	Higher
High	Low	Bad luck, difficult task, or lack of effort or other unstable factors	Minimum shame and dissatisfaction	High
Low[2]	High	Good luck, special effort, or the relative ease of the task	Minimum pride and satisfaction	Low
Low	Low	Lack of ability, difficulty of the task, or stable internal factors	Maximum shame and dissatisfaction	Lower

[1]Associated with males
[2]Associated with females

The general pattern for female attribution presented in Table 4.3 is probably most characteristic of the young athlete or women engaged in recreational-leisure pursuits. Since women in competitive athletics are high achievers, this is probably not a pattern which characterizes their perception of causality (McHugh, Duquin, and Frieze, 1978).

The attribution process also apparently changes with age (Roberts, 1980). That is, prior to approximately 10 years of age, children cannot or do not readily distinguish between effort and ability as the primary cause for good performance. Ability is assumed to be highly similar among all participants. The significant implication from this, of course, is that young children do not readily recognize personal deficiencies in ability and the effort that they put into sport and physical activity is generally high. Further, they continue to maintain their involvement and to put out a maximum effort — often in spite of evidence of relatively low ability levels.

It is only at 12 to 13 years of age and older that children become sensitive to the role that their ability plays in outcomes. This increasing self awareness of high versus low ability does not arise simply because the child has success or failure — coaches, parents and peers also provide the child with information on competence. This information serves to affect the initial expectancy aspect of the attribution process which was illustrated in Table 4.3. Thus, the top two profiles of Table 4.3 would be typical of the competent child while the lower two profiles would be characteristic of the less competent child. Children with a high expectancy are much more positive about sport than children with a low expectancy.

If the expectancy of children is toward low competence, they might begin to lose motivation and interest in the activity. They can also develop *sports learned helplessness* (Roberts, 1980). The child develops a belief that he or she is not very good in sports, that no amount of effort or practice can change this, and, so, a loss of interest and motivation results. Ultimately, if this cycle continues, the child drops out of sport and physical activity.

PROPOSITION: The tendency to attribute the cause of an event to ability varies with the sport task.

The type of task the participant is engaged in also appears to influence the attributions made. In intellectual tasks and competitive sports situations, ability is viewed as the predominant contributing factor in successful outcomes. However, in unsuccessful outcomes, ability is not typically considered to be a major reason. As indicated previously, the profile here is *I was successful because of my ability and other personal factors; I was unsuccessful because of factors outside of my personal control.*

This is not the case with either strength or fitness-related skills (Rejeski and Lowe, 1980). When tasks involving cardiovascular endurance or strength are used, individuals attribute their successful performances to both ability and effort whereas unsuccessful performances are attributed to a lack of ability only. This pattern of attribution occurs *regardless* of the person's level of ability. In short, even individuals with good cardiovascular endurance and/or good strength readily perceive a lack of success in a fitness-related task to be a result of inadequate endurance or strength.

Unlike intellectual ability (or athletic ability in sport), fitness-related ability is probably viewed as relatively unstable (Rejeski and Lowe, 1980). As a consequence, participants are less defensive about assigning the cause of a poor performance to themselves. A familiar profile here is *Sure, I'm in poor shape but I'm going to quit smoking, go on a diet and start exercising so things will get better.* On the other hand, an unfamiliar, unexpected profile would certainly be a person with the attitude *Sure, I'm dumb but I plan to start working on it so things will get better.*

Another factor is that in fitness-related tasks, effort is not something that is vague and unquantifiable. The individual is aware that he or she exerted a certain degree of effort. Thus, there may be good reasons for the tendency in cardiovascular and strength tasks to avoid blaming a lack of effort when the outcome is unsuccessful. The individual knows (and can feel) that he or she tried.

Implications for the Coach and Teacher

A rather specific process was laid out in Figure 4.2. This sequence has a number of implications for the coach and teacher. One implication is that if motivation and subsequent performance are to be influenced directly by the teacher and coach, then the most promising place for manipulation in this sequence is at the attribution phase. It is inevitable that events occur and outcomes occur — sport and physical activity are achievement activities and every participant inevitably experiences both successes and failures. The analysis phase is also inevitable. And, when the participant arrives at a reason why the outcome occurred, feelings of satisfaction, dissatisfaction and expectancies for the future inevitably follow. Thus, for example, if a learned helplessness child could be taught to attribute failure in gymnastics to a lack of effort (as the mastery-oriented child would) rather than to the absence of ability, then any setbacks would be met with renewed vigour and persistence.

Dweck (1975) has carried out this type of program with some degree of success in an experimental setting. A group of extreme learned helplessness children were identified and subjected to either of two long-term treatment programs involving problem-solving experiences in a laboratory setting. One half of the group was provided with constant success during the 25-day period. It was felt that this might provide them with an increase in confidence in their ability. For the second half of the group, successful outcomes were predominant but a number of failure trials were programmed in each day. When the failure occurred, the experimenter very directly contrasted the child's failure performance to an earlier successful trial and then attributed the failure for the child to a lack of effort. In short, the children in this latter situation were directly shown how to interpret the cause of their failures.

At the end of the treatment period, failure experiences were provided for both groups. The learned helplessness children who had experienced attribution retraining now reacted in a manner identical to mastery-oriented children; they attributed their failure to a lack of effort. However, the group that had received constant success experiences showed no improvement over their pre-treatment reactions. Once failure was introduced, performance suffered, motivation decreased and failure was attributed to a lack of ability. In short, a history of success is not sufficient to offset the negative impact of failure for learned helplessness children. What is critical is attribution retraining; learning to interpret failures differently.

A second implication arises from the fact that the greatest satisfaction after success and the greatest dissatisfaction after failure are experienced when personal, internal factors are thought to be the primary reason for the outcome. Since this is the case, it might be tempting when a setback occurs for coaches and teachers to encourage participants to attribute the outcome to external factors to spare the participants any unnecessary discomfort or threats to their self-esteem. This is represented by the profile *You have nothing to be ashamed of. We had a great deal of bad luck and the refereeing was atrocious.* There is less shame or dissatisfaction if the cause is perceived to be out of the participant's direct control. However, it could be a serious mistake to encourage participants to emphasize external factors after a setback (even if the coach or teacher also believed that external factors such as bad luck were the primary cause!)

Learned helplessness can develop in situations where the individual repetitively attempts an achievement task, fails, and then perceives the cause of that failure to be external — out of personal control. Certainly, anyone who has coached is familiar with the athlete (or coach!) who consistently blames external factors following a loss. The learned helplessness which develops and becomes associated with this perspective removes the need to reexamine such factors as training, effort, practice habits, and ability. As a consequence, the athlete (or coach) maintains the same established training habits, and continues to put out the same effort when what is really needed is personal improvement, reorientation, and change.

A third implication concerns the attributions found to be characteristic of female performers. It was pointed out that the third profile in Table 4.3 is characteristic of young female participants. Since coaches and teachers have a responsibility to aid their athletes in the development of potential, attributional retraining may be necessary to insure that effort and ability are emphasized and luck and task difficulty deemphasized. For example, athletes who use effort as an explanation obtain maximum pride after a success and are motivated to increase their effort and training after a failure. Also, it is particularly important for the female participant who lacks confidence in her own ability to learn to attribute successes to personal ability and not to luck or task ease. By internalizing the cause of success, the participant develops an increased expectancy for future success.

The final implication arises from the fact that the attribution process changes with age. Since organized competition for children (with its intensive social comparison experience) is an integral part of our culture, the child must be helped to cope with it in order to provide the maximum quality experience possible. Thus, coaches and teachers must become sensitized to the competitive process as it pertains to children. Children are not miniature adults and, therefore, do not perceive competition (and the causes and effects of outcomes) in the same way as adults. Thus, the young child who has lost but is reasonably satisfied with his/her effort does not benefit from a harangue based upon an adult's perception of the cause (Roberts, 1980).

It has been noted earlier that personal expectancy has a very direct bearing on outcome. But, also, the expectancy others have for the participant also strongly influences the outcome. Rosenthal and Jacobson (1968) clearly documented this with their *Pygmalion effect* or *self-fulfilling prophecy* (this is discussed in a subsequent section). They found that when teachers held an expectation for superior or inferior performance for their students, the students' performances closely matched these expectations. Since the teachers' expectations were manipulated on the basis of randomly assigned information (and not actual ability or potential), the implications for coaches and teachers are obvious. The young participant must be helped to develop positive expectation and to feel good about personal performance — to fit into the first profile illustrated in Table 4.3. In this way, the motivations and beliefs of participants in themselves is increased. Whether these participants actually do perform better is another issue, but psychologically the coach and teacher has done his or her best for the child. This is particularly true of individuals with low self-confidence and low self-esteem (Roberts, 1980).

INTRINSIC INTEREST AS A MOTIVATOR

> *Human beings like to feel competent and self determining and this is one of the reasons they seek out challenges to overcome. Great satisfaction comes from the actual experience of being (or feeling) competent and in control.*
>
> Terry Orlick

It has been emphasized in other sections of this book that there are a number of highly dissimilar reasons why people participate in sport and physical activity — to be with friends, to improve personal fitness, to develop physical skills, to please parents, friends, or teachers, to obtain a scholarship, to earn a living. These reasons are sometimes categorized according to whether they are *intrinsic* (internal) or *extrinsic* (external) to the task.

The distinction between the two categories of reasons (or motives) is a fundamentally important one. Garvie (1981) highlighted this distinction when he provided the following definition:

"*Intrinsic motivation may be thought of as task motivation or task reasons for engagement. A person intrinsically motivated would perform for the rewards inherent in the doing — attention on the task. A person extrinsically motivated would perform for rewards external to the doing — attention on gaining some associated return but not the task action itself*'' (p. 5).

In short, intrinsic interest is represented by a motivation to participate in an activity or task for its own sake — for the enjoyment, excitement, and challenges which are an integral part of involvement in the activity. On the other hand, extrinsic interest is represented by a motivation to participate because of the external (tangible) rewards which have become associated with involvement in the activity or task.

It has been repeatedly demonstrated in research experiments that intrinsic interest (intrinsic motivation) is the more powerful of the two. But, both are generally present in sport and physical activity. In fact, it has also been assumed traditionally by coaches and teachers that when both intrinsic and extrinsic motivation are present together, the participant will be most strongly motivated. So, for example, a parent or coach could decide that if a child was playing soccer because of the interest, excitement, and challenge that that sport provides (which are intrinsic reasons, intrinsic interests, intrinsic motives) offering to provide a team jacket for continued involvement (which is an extrinsic reward) should only serve to increase overall motivation. In short, the view endorsed in this example would be that the two motives are *additive* — that extrinsic rewards add to intrinsic interest.

This viewpoint is accurate under some circumstances. However, recent research (Deci, 1975; Lepper and Greene, 1975; Lepper, Greene, Nisbett, 1973) has also revealed that introducing extrinsic rewards can serve to decrease intrinsic motivation in many situations. The classic study by Lepper, Greene, and Nisbett (1973) clearly illustrates this.

Felt-tip pens (magic markers) were introduced into a nursery school playroom by the investigators and the amount of time each child spent drawing and using the markers was then recorded. Following this basic initial observation period, the children were randomly divided into three experimental groups: 1) a group that was asked to draw with the magic marker pens and promised a reward for doing so (an *expected reward condition*); 2) a group that was asked to draw with the magic marker pens but no reward was mentioned or given (a *no reward condition*); and 3) a group that was asked to draw with the magic marker pens and then was given a reward unexpectedly afterwards (an *unexpected reward condition*). The no reward condition, of course, was used to provide a base line — a measure of the reactions the investigators might typically expect from a group of children, under normal circumstances.

A week after the initial test period, the magic marker pens were again placed on the tables in the nursery school. No mention was made of rewards to any of the children. The investigators observed the children and recorded the amount of time spent with the pens. (Amount of free-time spent playing with the magic markers was used as a measure of the children's intrinsic interest.) Lepper, Greene, and Nisbett found that the mean percentage of free-time spent with the magic markers was substantially less for children in the expected reward condition (8.6%) than in either the no reward (16.7%) or the unexpected reward (18.1%) conditions.

The interpretation that can be put on these findings is that children who are offered a bribe for doing something they find interesting (the expected reward condition) will show a decrease in interest. Conversely, children who are surprised by a reward after doing something interesting (the unexpected reward condition) will show an increase in interest. Why? What is it about the way the reward is perceived that produces these contrasting responses? The answer to these two questions lies within discussion of the first set of propositions which follow.

PROPOSITION: Extrinsic (tangible) rewards influence the participant's level of intrinsic motivation to carry out a task or activity.

a) **An extrinsic reward which helps to convey information to its recipient that he or she is more competent increases intrinsic motivation.**
b) **An extrinsic reward which helps to convey information to its recipient that he or she is incompetent or less competent decreases intrinsic motivation.**
c) **An extrinsic reward which helps to convey information to its recipient that he or she does not have direct control or responsibility over personal behavior and actions serves to decrease intrinsic motivation.**

Edward Deci, one of the foremost authorities on intrinsically motivated behavior, has defined it as behavior motivated by a need to feel competent and self-determining in dealing with different situations (Deci, 1975). Thus, Deci has suggested that extrinsic (tangible) rewards like jackets, letters, and trips can serve two different functions and both of these can influence the level of intrinsic motivation.

One of these is a *controlling function* while the other is an *informational function* (see Figure 4.3). Their impact on the recipient's self perceptions (and intrinsic motivation) is quite different as the propositions above would indicate.

A reward serves a controlling function when its introduction into an activity that an individual finds naturally interesting, challenging, or exciting alters the performer's perception of personal responsibility and self determination. In turn, when perceptions of personal responsibility and self determination decrease, intrinsic motivation decreases. A story presented by Casady (1974) illustrates how this might occur.

"[An] *old man lived alone on a street where boys played noisily every afternoon. One day the din became too much, and he called the boys into his house. He told them he*

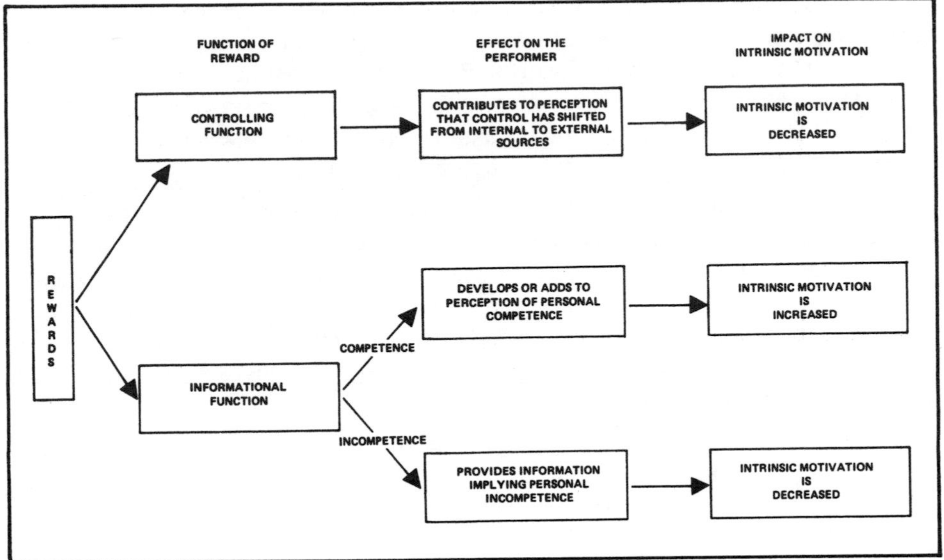

Figure 4.3
The functions of rewards and their impact on intrinsic motivation.

> *liked to listen to them play, but his hearing was failing and he could no longer hear their games. He asked them to come around each day and play noisily in front of his house. If they did, he would give them each a quarter. The youngsters raced back the following day, and made a tremendous racket in front of the house. The old man paid them, and asked them to return the next day. Again, they made noise, and again the old man paid them for it. But this time he gave each boy only 20 cents, explaining that he was running out of money. On the following day, they got only 15 cents each. Furthermore, the old man told them, he would have to reduce the fee to five cents on the 4th day. The boys became angry, and told the old man they would not be back. It was not worth the effort, they said, to make noise for only five cents a day*" (p. 52).

Initially, the boys played because they wanted to; it was their decision; they initiated it, controlled its amount, intensity, and so on. When the old man began to pay them, however, he became the person in charge. Thus, to use Deci's terminology, the locus of control shifted in the boy's perspective from an internal to an external focus. Similarly, in the Lepper, Greene, and Nisbett study introduced earlier, this interpretation is also a reasonable one to account for the decreased intrinsic motivation exhibited by the children in the expected reward group. The children lost some of their initial interest in the magic marker pens because they felt they were not totally in charge of their own play; the investigators held this responsibility by virtue of the rewards they had offered to the children for agreeing to use the pens.

As indicated above, rewards also have an informational function — they convey information to the recipient about personal competence in a task or activity. Thus, rewards which contribute to the performer's perception that he or she is competent serve to increase intrinsic motivation. On the other hand, rewards which serve to convey information that the person is incompetent or less competent than he or she previously believed, lead to a decrease in intrinsic motivation.

It seems likely that the performance of the children in the unexpected reward group in the Lepper, Greene, and Nisbett study can be accounted for by this explanation. That is, the children played with the magic marker pens and then unexpectedly received a "Good Player Award" (which was the reward in that study). Their interpretation would probably be that they had done something well, that they were competent and skillful with the magic markers. In turn, this new information on competence served to increase their intrinsic interest in the activity.

There is considerable research support for the general propositions presented at the beginning of this section and the Deci viewpoint that intrinsic motivation is associated with a need to feel competent and personally responsible. For example, the research project carried out by Richard De Charms (1968, 1976) in a school environment highlights the interrelationships between self determination, perception of control, and intrinsic motivation.

De Charms aptly noted that in a traditional school situation, classroom teachers can be viewed as "Origins" — they control the situation, dictate the content, set the learning pace, assignments, grading scheme, and seating arrangements. In the same context, students can be viewed as "Pawns" in that they have little personal responsibility or control. De Charms reasoned that if this could be changed, if the school situation could be modified so that students could have more say in the "origins" of their school behavior, intrinsic motivation would increase and school performance would benefit. A research project was initiated to test this proposition.

A motivation training workshop was set up for a group of teachers, The Origin-Pawn concept was introduced, the impact on behavior of being an Origin was discussed, and teaching techniques which highlighted student versus teacher control were set out. Then, in a program which extended over a four-year period, students were directly taught how to become Origins for their own education — to set realistic, attainable goals, and assume personal control, responsibility, and accountability. The results were highly positive. School grades improved dramatically (and stayed high even after the termination of the project), and the students expressed greater enjoyment and satisfaction with school.

Studies by Deci, Cascio, and Krusell (1973) and Vallerand, Reid, and Marisi (1980) serve to highlight the interrelationships between information feedback, perceptions of competence, and intrinsic motivation. In both the Deci et al. and Vallerand et al. studies, it was found that negative verbal feedback about performance decreased the intrinsic motivation of the participants whereas positive verbal feedback increased it.

In summary then, all people have a need to feel competent and personally responsible (self-determining) for decisions in their life. A marked preference is shown and intrinsic interest is highest in activities and situations which contribute to this feeling. When extrinsic rewards contribute to the development and maintenance of the individual's perception of competence and personal responsibility, they also serve to increase intrinsic motivation. When extrinsic rewards serve to decrease the feeling of personal control and competence, they also decrease intrinsic motivation (Kruglanski, 1975; Lepper and Greene, 1975; Ross, 1976; Swann and Pittman, 1977).

PROPOSITION: The sex of the recipient has an influence on the interpretation of the extrinsic reward and its resulting impact on intrinsic motivation.

Ryan (1977, 1980) has reported results from a sport context which contribute to a suggestion that males and females may interpret the same tangible extrinsic reward in a different way. He was interested in the impact of athletic scholarships on male and female athletes. Ryan reasoned that male athletes on scholarship would show a reduced level of intrinsic motivation because their scholarship would be viewed as "pay for play". The result would be a reduction in the athlete's sense of control, personal responsibility, and self-determination. On the other hand, Ryan also felt that female athletes on scholarship would show an increased level of intrinsic motivation from their scholarship because the award would be viewed as a measure of competence. (When the study was conducted athletic scholarships for females were relatively new, few women received them, and, therefore, a scholarship provided information about superior ability.) The results supported both of Ryan's prediction. Compared to male nonscholarship athletes, the male scholarship athletes enjoyed their daily practices less, found college athletics less enjoyable than they had expected, and less enjoyable than high school athletics. On the other hand, the opposite pattern was found in the female athletes.

Iso-Ahola (1977a, 1978) has also found that males and females differ in their perception of what conditions are essential for free-time pursuits to be perceived as "leisure time" activities (i.e., to be considered "play" as opposed to "work"). With males, the important element was having freedom of choice. That is, it is not important to a male if an activity is related to work as long as he has the freedom to participate or not to participate. So, for example, physical conditioning is essential for a professional ice hockey player to be successful. Thus, a player might jog and lift weights during the summer to prepare for the coming season. If that conditioning program is completely voluntary, it will likely be viewed as a leisure-time activity. On the other hand, if that program is largely the result of a mandatory, enforceable team policy, it will likely be considered as work and not as play.

A different reaction was found for the females in the Iso-Ahola study. With females, the important element contributing to the perception that free-time activities are leisure was whether or not the activity was work related. Freedom of choice to engage or not engage in the activity was not an important consideration. Thus, the female physician who reads medical journals in her spare time (and of her own volition) will probably perceive this as work and not as play or a leisure-time activity.

PROPOSITION: The age of the recipient has an influence on the interpretation of the extrinsic reward and its resulting impact on intrinsic motivation.

An extrinsic reward can be viewed by the recipient as a bribe or a bonus. The tendency to settle on one or the other of these options changes with age. That is, research (Halliwell, 1978a; Karniol and Ross, 1976; Smith, 1975) has shown that when an extrinsic reward is given to children who are engaged in an activity which they find intrinsically interesting, the tendency to view that reward as a bribe increases with age. Very young (i.e., kindergarten and pre-school) children have a tendency to consider the reward as a bonus which adds incentive value to the task or activity. As age increases, however, there is also an increase in the perception that the reward has been offered as a bribe — a bribe to insure continued involvement.

For example, Halliwell (1978a) developed a videotape in which two scenes were presented. In one, a boy was rewarded for playing on a trampoline; in the other, no reward was given. This videotape was shown to seven groups of students — children from kindergarten, first, second, third, fourth, fifth and tenth grades. The younger children (kindergarten and first grade) perceived that the reward was given as a bonus and that the rewarded actor was the most intrinsically motivated. On the other hand, second grade and older children considered the reward as a bribe and judged the nonrewarded actor as the most intrinsically motivated.

PROPOSITION: The intrinsic satisfaction associated with sport and physical activity is at its highest when the participant has a sense of control over clear and challenging goals, has no distractions, anxieties, or worries, and the activity is carried out for its own sake.

Not only can extrinsic rewards fail to contribute to overall motivation if they are improperly administered, they can also change a situation from play to work. That is, preoccupation with the attainment of tangible rewards such as jackets, trophies, trips, and so on can produce feelings of "stress, forceful attempts to win at all costs, less spontaneity, complaint, pressure and frustration. This straight line may lead to dropout since extrinsic rewards may not satisfy and intrinsic rewards may have gone unnoticed" (Garvie, 1981, p. 5).

Because extrinsic rewards are associated with work and intrinsic rewards are associated with play, a number of writers have been interested in determining what form intrinsic rewards take, what they are like. For example, Garvie (1978, 1981) had high school athletes complete a battery of 22 tests which included, amongst others, measures of basic needs, locus of control, self-esteem, personal orientation, and sport incentive motivation. The intrinsic rewards in sport and physical activity were identified by Garvie as:

- an enjoyment which develops through the use of physical skills,
- a sense of accomplishment which results from improvement and skill acquisition, and
- a feeling of excitement and stimulation which is associated with the challenges present.

The focus in each of these is the activity or task itself, its practice and execution. By concentrating on these intrinsic rewards, the feeling of work is avoided. Instead, a circular relationship is established whereby the athlete initially enjoys the activity, is stimulated and challenged by it, and, therefore, practices to improve. Practice, in turn, leads to improvements which produce more enjoyment and, thus, the cycle continues.

Another writer interested in the relationship of play and intrinsic rewards has been Mihaly Csikszentmihalyi (Csikszentmihalyi and Bennett, 1971; Csikszentmihalyi, 1975). He interviewed 175 people involved in a wide cross-section of activities — rock climbing, chess, dance, basketball, and music composition — in order to determine if the participants experienced similar kinds of satisfaction. It was found that when the respondents reported that they had had "fun", had experienced a feeling of "enjoyment", had had what Csikszentmihalyi termed the *flow experience,* a specific group of conditions were generally present. These included:

- a merging of action and awareness; the person was totally involved in the task.
- a centering of attention; the individual had to concentrate on only a limited number of options.
- a loss of ego (or self-forgetfulness); the individual did not worry about personal adequacy, embarrassment, self-consciousness.
- a control of action and environment; the individual had a feeling of control over his or her actions and things occurring in the situation itself.
- clear demands and clear feedback; the task demands were clear to the individual and feedback provided an accurate, non-ambiguous picture of what was happening.
- there were no extrinsic goals or rewards; the activity's rewards were in the performance itself.

According to Csikszentmihalyi, when the participant's skills are equal to the task demands (the challenges) and the previous six conditions are present, the individual has a flow experience; the intrinsic satisfaction from the activity is at its highest (see Figure 4.4).

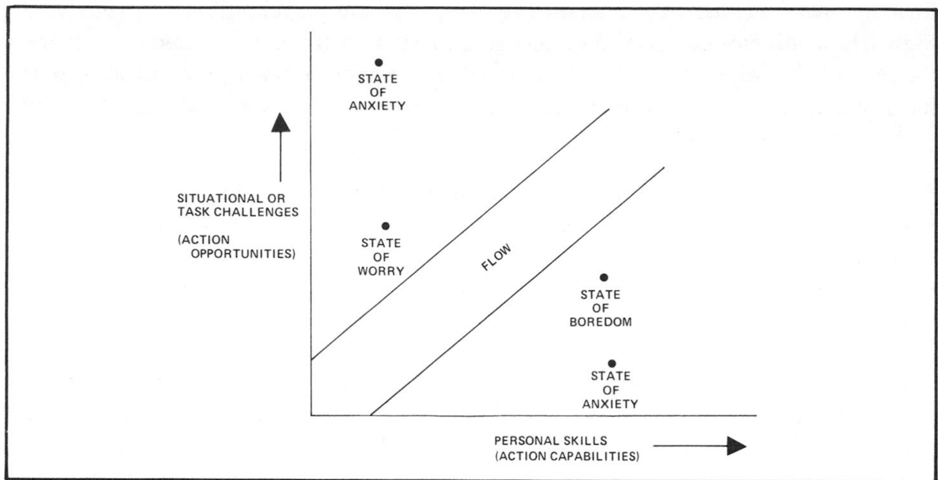

Figure 4.4
The flow state (Adapted from Csikszenthmihalyi, 1975).

If the challenge is somewhat greater than the participant's capabilities, a state of worry results. This turns into anxiety if the challenge becomes even greater. As the lower portion of Figure 4.4 shows, when the participant's skills are greater than the challenges offered by the activity, boredom can arise. It is also replaced by anxiety if the challenge (the activity) is excessively simple relative to the person's capabilities.

Implications for the Coach and Teacher

Possibly the most important implication to be drawn from the information on intrinsic motivation is that providing extrinsic rewards to children does not automatically insure that they will be more motivated and enjoy the activity more. As Halliwell (1978a) pointed out in a summary of his research:

> *"Because the findings...revealed that children as young as 7 years of age appear to interpret the receipt of rewards for participation in intrinsically attractive activities as a bribe, it is suggested that coaches and administrators of youth sports programs exercise caution in administering overly sufficient external rewards. Although most age-group athletic activities are intrinsically desirable in and of themselves, adults frequently continue to conspicuously reward young athletes with trophies, jackets, trips, and the like. A knowledge of the potential undermining effects of rewards upon intrinsic motivation may help responsible adults to determine the appropriateness of using extrinsic reinforcers in youth sports programs. Instead of the present heavy reliance upon external rewards to motivate young athletes, attention should be directed toward enhancing the attractiveness of the athletic activities themselves"* (p. 417).

In short, a great deal of care must be taken to insure that the rewards do not produce the exact opposite effect to that desired.

It should also be emphasized, however, that the results from the research on intrinsic motivation — the results that have shown that extrinsic rewards decrease intrinsic motivation — do not in any way support a conclusion that coaches and teachers should not use extrinsic, tangible incentives. Such an interpretation would be incorrect (Siedentop and Ramey, 1977). Also, it would be in direct contradiction to the conclusion drawn about the use of token rewards in an earlier section in this book (see Chapter 2; Token Rewards as a Motivator). Rewards given under the right circumstances will positively influence behavior and performance. But, what are those right circumstances?

The most important single consideration is that the rewards should be provided for competence. Thus, when a token reward system is introduced, the coach or teacher outlines the target behavior in measurable observable terms: "I want the members of this class/team to stop being late". The contingency is then set out: "When you are on time, I will put a star beside your name on this wall chart". And, finally, the reward is awarded for correct behavior, for competence.

A second consideration is that the tokens used in a token reward system should be small. As was pointed out in Chapter 2, the rewards should be things like stars, points, public recognition, and candy, and not major items such as T-shirts, plaques, and medals. The token rewards are symbolic, reflecting accomplishment and achievement.

A second implication to be drawn from the information on intrinsic motivation is that participants should be provided with opportunities for input, responsibility, and self-determination — for an opportunity to serve as an Origin rather than as a Pawn. Halliwell (1978b) has provided a number of examples:

- Consult participants for suggestions on the establishment of a code of behavior for the team or classroom; e.g., dress code, interpersonal behavior, reactions to officiating decisions.
- Have participants lead one segment of the practice or class, develop an innovative drill weekly, and/or provide suggestions for strategy in practices and classroom competitions.
- Use the participants themselves to monitor any behavior code or token economy system which is set up.
- Heighten each participant's feelings of competence and self-worth by highlighting performance improvements rather than absolute standards of accomplishment.

What each of these techniques represent, of course, is an attempt on the part of the coach or teacher to insure that the participant gains a feeling of personal worth, personal responsibility, and personal competence.

THE EXPECTATIONS OF OTHERS AS A MOTIVATOR

Trust men and they will be true to you; treat them greatly and they will show themselves great.

Emerson

All of us would like to view ourselves as objective in our dealings with others — as the type of person who withholds judgments and decisions until all of the evidence is in. At the same time, it is also inevitable that in dealing with new, unfamiliar situations or people, we use any cues available — information from others, past experiences, and physical appearnce. These cues help us to predict or prophesize what the unfamiliar will be like. In turn, these cues also lead to the development of expectations.

One source of our expectations in social situations is information obtained from others. So, for example, we may be led to expect that the person we are about to meet is extremely pleasant. This expectation will influence our perceptions of that person and behavior towards him/her. Certainly, we will be more open, more pleasant, and less guarded about what we say and do than if we had heard that the person was extremely unpleasant.

Physical characteristics such as hair colouring, skin colouring, clothing worn, an accent, wrinkles, and so on are another source of cues from which we make predictions and develop expectations. Allport's (1961) research carried in the 1950's provides a good illustration of this. He showed people a series of pictures and asked them to comment on the person in the photo. A number of stereotypical judgments or expectations were held by the respondents including:

- faces with wrinkles around the eyes were associated with friendliness, a sense of humour, and an easy going personality;
- women with thicker lips than average were judged as sexy; women with thinner lips as asexual;
- people with blond, fair complexions were given more favourable attributes; people with dark skin were described as unfriendly, hostile, and lacking a sense of humour;
- older men were viewed as distinguished, responsible, and refined while older women were viewed as motherly;
- smiling faces were seen as more intelligent;
- individuals wearing glasses were judged to be more intelligent, dependable, and industrious.

Not surprisingly, the use of predictions and prophecies and the development of expectations for behavior and performance is also a characteristic of coaching, teaching, and officiating in sport and physical activity. And, as is the case in social situations, these predictions and expectations develop quite naturally from information received from others, physical cues, and past experiences. And, again, any expectation that develops will influence the coach's, teacher's or official's perceptions and behavior. Thus, for example, a teacher or coach might be told that one athlete is outstanding and either have no information on a second or have an expectation that he/she is not as proficient. Inevitably, that first athlete initially will be evaluated more positively no matter what differences (or lack of differences) are present in ability level (Carron, 1980).

An example of how information about ability can influence expectations (and subsequent judgments) about performance is provided in an experiment carried out by Hatfield and Landers (1978). Observers were brought into the laboratory to watch the balancing performance of two individuals who were described as having superior and inferior ability. In reality, these two performers were accomplices of the experimenters who possessed identical ability levels on the balancing task. In the experiment itself, their performances were identical. When the observers were asked to evaluate these performances, however, the high expectancy (superior) performer was judged to have had greater time in balance and made fewer performance errors.

Preperformance information also can have a dramatic impact upon the perceptions and expectations of officials in sports such as gymnastics, diving, synchronized swimming, and figure skating. In a gymnastics competitions, for example, those athletes on a team who have lesser ability usually compete first. Thus, gymnastic coaches must rank-order their gymnasts from poorest to best and then use these ratings to set out the order of appearance during competition. But, judges are also familiar with this procedure and they can develop expectations about the magnitude of the scores which should be awarded.

A series of experiments by Ansorge, Scheer, and their colleagues (Ansorge, Scheer, Laub, and Howard, 1978; Scheer and Ansorge, 1975, 1979) serves to illustrate how preperformance expectations can influence the perceptions and judgments of officials. The performances of teams of gymnasts were recorded on videotape and presented to groups of officials to judge. However, the order of appearance on the videotape was rotated systematically so that the same gymnast was shown first, second, third, fourth, and fifth. It was discovered that the scores awarded for performance also varied systematically with the order of appearance. In other words, if a gymnast appeared first in the rotation (and, therefore, the judges held an expectation that the performance they were viewing was from the weakest gymnast on the team), the scores awarded were less than when the same routine appeared second. Similarly, if the routine appeared second, the points awarded were less than when it appeared third, and so on.

Coaches and teachers also develop expectations from physical cues and characteristics such as size, body type, and sex. For example, Brawley, Landers, Miller, and Kearns (1979) brought male and female observers into a laboratory setting to judge the muscular endurance performance of a male and female performer. The two performers were accomplices of the experimenters, they were of similar size, and during the experiment itself, their performances were identical. The male and female observers, judged that the male performer was superior in terms of the length of time the muscle contraction was maintained.

The prophecies and predictions that a teacher or coach makes and the expectations that they hold for a performer can be a positive asset in some instances. For example, any experienced coach or teacher has developed different performance expectations for individuals of different ages and sex, physical size, and level of maturity. And, as Rejeski and Hutslar (1980) have pointed out:

> "*These ideas guide the coach and teacher in structuring individualized learning centers, identifying performers with unique potential, and structuring the sport socialization process*" (p. 91).

On the other hand, the coach's and teacher's preconceived ideas could be highly detrimental to the performer. Again, Rejeski and Hutslar (1980) have commented upon this aspect of the expectations held by teachers and coaches:

> "*These preconceived ideas are not without drawbacks. Specifically, a tendency exists for observers to prejudge performer potential, to expect certain outcomes. These expected outcomes may bias the quality of a teacher's or coach's interactions with the performer and may significantly influence both the achievement behavior and emotional state of the performer*" (p. 91).

While preconceived ideas may be good or bad because of the way in which they influence the teacher's or coach's behavior toward the student or athlete, there is yet another important consideration. Rosenthal and Jacobson (1968) highlighted this consideration in their book *Pygmalion in the Classroom.*

> "*Our predicition or prophecy may in itself be a factor in determining the behavior of other people. When we are led to expect that we are about to meet a pleasant person, our treatment of him at first meeting may, in fact, make him a more pleasant person. If we are led to expect that we shall encounter an unpleasant person, we may approach him so defensively that we make him into an unpleasant person ... one person's expectation for another person's behavior can quite unwittingly become a more accurate prediction simply for its having been made*" (p. vii).

If the student or athlete is the object of a preconceived evaluation which is negative or detrimental, he or she may begin to behave in a manner which is consistent with that evaluation. A son or daughter who is unfairly perceived and then repeatedly accused of skipping school, using drugs, engaging in premarital sex, may finally adopt these behaviors. This is known as a *self-fulfilling prophecy* — an expectation or prediction which serves to initiate a series of actions that eventually cause the original expectation or prediction to come true. In short, individuals will often behave as they are expected to behave. The self-fulfilling prophecy forms the basis for the propositions which follow:

PROPOSITION: The expectations held by teachers and coaches regarding the level of ability of an individual influence their subsequent social relationship with that individual

PROPOSITION: The expectations held by teachers and coaches regarding the level of ability of an individual have an influence on that individual's motivation and performance.

The classic work on the impact of expectations upon performance is the Rosenthal and Jacobson (1968) study which was referred to earlier. As a point of interest, the title chosen by Rosenthal and Jacobson for their book was suggested by George Bernard Shaw's (1941) work, *Pygmalion.* In that story, Eliza Doolittle muses over her state:

> "*You see, really and truly, apart from the things anyone can pick up (the dressing and the proper way of speaking, and so on), the difference between a lady and a flower girl is not how she behaves, but how she's treated. I shall always be a flower girl to Professor Higgins, because he always treats me as a flower girl, and always will; but I know I can be a lady to you, because you always treat me as a lady, and always will*" (p. 127).

In the Rosenthal and Jacobson study, experimenters went into an elementary school at the end of one academic year and administered a general intelligence test referred to as the *Harvard Test of Inflected Acquisition.* This test was purported to be a predictor of the tendency to show spurts in intelligence and ability following a dormant period.

Just prior to a new academic year, 20 percent of the children in the school (grades one through six) were identified for their teachers as potential "late intellectual bloomers." That is, the teachers were led to believe that this group of students had scored well on the *Harvard Test of Inflected Acquisition* and, therefore, would probably show substantial improvements in their school performance over the course of the year.

The important point, however, is that there was no academic or intellectual basis for this claim. The late intellectual bloomers "had been selected by means of a table of random numbers. The difference between the children was in the mind of the teacher" (Rosenthal and Jacobson, 1968, p. 70).

The results showed evidence of a self-fulfilling prophecy — the late intellectual bloomers began to behave as they were expected to behave. Tests administered at the end of the year revealed that the special group showed dramatic improvements in comparison to their undesignated classmates — particularly the students in the younger grades and students from disadvantaged socioeconomic backgrounds. Forty-seven percent of the late intellectual bloomers in grades one and two showed IQ gains of 20 points or more.

Not surprisingly, the Rosenthal and Jacobson study generated a tremendous amount of interest among psychologists and educators. Numerous attempts were undertaken to further examine the impact of positive and negative expectations in other contexts such as laboratory and social situations and research in educational situations was continued. Not all of these were successful which led to a questioning of the reliability and validity of the self-fulfilling prophecy.

In 1976, Rosenthal (1976) analyzed the results of over 300 studies from laboratory, classroom, and industrial settings using a statistical technique referred to as meta-analysis. According to Rosenthal, significant results consistent with the self-fulfilling prophecy were obtained in 37 percent of the studies. Also, the great majority of results which were not significant were in a direction consistent with a self-fulfilling prophecy prediction. And, finally none of the classroom studies showed results which were in the opposite direction to that predicted by a self-fulfilling prophecy (i.e., a high expectation producing a *poorer* performance).

Another comprehensive review of the research has also been carried out by Brophy (1982). He concluded that, in general, the studies support three generalizations.

1. There is a great deal of evidence to support the notion that expectations can serve as a self-fulfilling prophecy;
2. The evidence from classroom settings on the impact of teacher expectations on student achievement has not been positively consistent; and
3. Although there is always a potential opportunity for teachers' expectations to function as a self-fulfilling prophecy, the extent to which this actually has an effect is only 5 to 10 percent.

Brophy (1982) then pointed out that "these conclusions clearly imply that even ideal teacher education related to the topic of teacher expectations will not work miracles in our schools, but they do *not* imply that the topic is unimportant. Even a five percent difference in educational outcomes is an important difference, the moreso as it is compounded across school years" (p. 9-10).

If teachers' expectations do have an impact on student achievement and this impact is important, what are the factors which contribute to this impact? This question has been the object of close scrutiny by a number of researchers who focused on the relative effects of both high and low expectations. High expectations seem to have a positive effect because of four principal factors (Rosenthal, 1974). First, they help to create a good climate in the teaching-coaching situation by improving social-emotional relationships between teachers-coaches and students-athletes. Second, high expectation individuals are given more attention generally as well as more specific feedback about their performance. Third, high expectation individuals are presented with greater challenges because a greater amount of (and more difficult) material is presented to them. Finally, high expectation individuals are offered more opportunities to respond and demonstrate their skills.

The results of low expectations, on the other hand, are even more complex. A list of 17 consequences of low teacher expectations was compiled by Brophy (1982) and Brophy and Good (1974) on the basis of available research findings. They found that teachers are guilty of the following in their dealings with students for whom they have a low expectation:

1. Waiting less time for an answer (e.g., Allington, 1980; Rowe, 1974; Taylor, 1979).
2. Giving them answer or calling on someone else instead of trying to improve their answer through repeated questioning, providing clues, or asking rephrased questions (e.g., Brophy and Good, 1970; Jeter and Davis, 1973).
3. Rewarding inappropriate behavior or incorrect responses; in short, expecting less (e.g., Kleinfeld, 1975).
4. Being more critical following any failures (Brophy and Good, 1970).
5. Providing less praise following success (e.g., Cooper and Baron, 1977; Page, 1971).
6. Failing to give feedback to public responses (e.g., Good, Cooper, and Blakey, 1980; Jeter and Davis, 1973).
7. Generally paying less attention to them and interacting with them less frequently (e.g., Adams and Cohen, 1974).
8. Calling on them less frequently to respond to a question (e.g., Rubovits and Maehr, 1971).
9. Seating them farther away (e.g., Rist, 1970).
10. Being less demanding of them (e.g., Beez, 1968).
11. Interacting more privately than publicly with them and monitoring and structuring their activities more closely (see Brophy and Good, 1974).
12. Using a different (less stringent) standard of grading on their tests and assignments (e.g., Finn, 1972).
13. Being less friendly in interactions with them including less smiling (e.g., Page, 1971).
14. Providing briefer, and less informative feedback to their questions (e.g., Cooper, 1979).
15. Providing less non-verbal communication signifying attentiveness and responsiveness to them e.g., forward lean, positive head nodding during interactions (e.g., Chaikin, Sigler, and Derlega, 1974).
16. Being less intrusive in terms of providing instructions while they are practising; allowing them more opportunity to practice independently (e.g., Anderson and Rosenthal, 1968; Beeze, 1968).
17. Using effective but time-consuming instructional methods to a lesser extent with them when time is limited (e.g., Swann and Snyder, 1980).

Are the different expectations that teachers and coaches have for students and athletes in sport and physical activity also associated with different patterns of interaction — the positive and negative interactions just listed? The answer to this question seems to depend upon whether the focus is physical education classes or organized youth sport. Research with physical education classes showed the same pattern as that found in other classes in educational settings; research in an organized youth sport situation showed a markedly different pattern.

Martinek and Johnson (1979) had five elementary school teachers rate their students on how they expected each to perform in terms of physical achievement. The top versus bottom ranked 10 percent were considered to be students for whom high versus low expectations were held. The teacher-student interactions were then observed during standard physical education classes.

It was found that the teachers approached the expected high achievers more frequently than the expected low achievers thus providing the high expectations students with greater opportunities to interact. Also, the teachers gave the expected high achievers more praise and supportive encouragement and showed a greater acceptance and use of their ideas. Martinek and Johnson (1979) concluded:

> "*In summary, it is feasible to assume that within a physical education setting high achievers have all the advantages — more attention, more praise, more acceptance, more intellectual stimulation and better self-concept. It follows, then, that the physical education teacher should become sensitized to those behavioral mechanisms that mediate expectations which perpetuate success and failure in children* (p. 69).

In a study with youth basketball players (ages 8 to 12 years), the generally negative pattern represented in the list of 17 differences in teachers' approaches to low versus high expectation students was not present. Rejeski, Darracott and Hutslar (1974) tested a sample of 14 coaches and 71 male athletes. At the beginning of the experiment, the coaches were asked to rank order their players according to ability level. It was then assumed that the coaches held high expectations for the higher ranking players; low expectations for the lower ranking. During the course of the season, the behavior of the coaches to each of these groups of athletes was recorded using the *Coaching Behavior Assessment System* (see Table 2.2).

The results showed that the high expectancy athletes did receive more positive reinforcement. But, this is probably not surprising, however, because in the *Coaching Behavior Assessment System,* positive reinforcement refers to a coaching response to *desirable* performance on the part of the athlete. Since the high expectancy athletes were the best performers, it seems reasonable to assume that they also had more correct responses than did the low expectancy athletes — there were quite simply more positive things to reinforce or reward.

Rejeski et al. also found that correct responses were not ignored as frequently when they were performed by low expectancy as opposed to high expectancy athletes. If something positive occurred, the coaches tended to notice it and comment upon it. This is contrary, of course, to the 17 points raised above where it was indicated that low expectation students in the classroom received less of the teacher's attention.

It was also noted that the coaches provided more general technical instruction to low expectation athletes. In short, the coaches spent the most instructional time with the poorest athletes. Again, this is a point which is in opposition to the general theme contained in the 17 points listed above.

Finally, there was no difference in coaching interactions with low and high expectation athletes in terms of general communications (conversations and communications unrelated to basketball), general encouragement, encouragement following mistakes, or corrective instructions following mistakes. Certainly, there was no evidence supporting the 17 negative consequences of low expectancy detailed above.

Rejeski et al proposed three possibilities to account for why their results were different from those in educational settings. One reason suggested was that because the league rules dictated that all children were to receive equivalent playing time, it was to the coaches' advantage to work with the lower skilled (low expectation) players to insure team success. A second reason suggested was that the coaches might have perceived that youth basketball was being played for fun and enjoyment and not high achievement and competition. As a consequence, their interactions would have been evenly distributed among all the players; not just the high achievement (high expectation) group. A final possibility suggested was that in the youth basketball situation, unlike the typical classroom, all the children were active participants. Thus, the gifted did not possess the same distinct advantage as they might have in a classroom where the better students could dominate a teacher's time and attention.

Implications for the Coach and Teacher

An important consideration concerning the expectations held for participant's achievement which must be kept in mind is that, in the main, these expectations are reasonable; they are the product of frequent interactions between students-athletes and their teachers-coaches. Brophy (1982) emphasized this point when he pointed out that

> *"Discussions of teacher expectations sometimes imply or even state that these expectations are based on dubious inferences from irrelevant information or are impervious to input or change. Similarly, discussions of differential patterns of teacher-student interaction often imply that equality should be the expected norm, and that any differential patterns observed are evidence of teacher favouritism of some students and bias against others. These notions represent invalid generalizations from laboratory experiments to the naturalistic classroom setting ... Studies of inservice teachers' expectations for their actual students reveal that most teacher perceptions of students are accurate and based on the best available information, and that most of the inaccurate ones are corrected when more dependable information becomes available ... Several implications follow from this ... First, teachers' expectations are generally accurate, reality based, and open to corrective feedback. This limits the degree to which they are likely to accept and act upon information*

supplied by an experimenter who is trying to mislead them. Furthermore, even those teachers who accept such information initially would likely come to discount it before long, because they would remain open to newer and better information" (p. 10-12).

Individual participants have different ability levels and coaches and teachers rapidly become aware of these and develop different expectations based on these different abilities. Thus, it is unreasonable to suggest that all individuals must be treated identically. Realistic goals should be set for each individual based upon his or her present ability and rate of development. If the differences in ability and capability among individuals are ignored and unrealistically high expectations are set out for some students or athletes, the ultimate result will be frustration and a loss of motivation. The most effective approach to be used with all participants involves some degree of individualization. This also means that the approach taken with lesser skilled individuals (the low expectation performers) must differ from that used with better skilled (high expectation) individuals (Brophy 1982).

Brophy (1982), in a discussion of research on the self-fulfilling prophecy, developed a set of guidelines to assist teachers in their attempts to minimize negative expectation effects and maximize positive expectation effects in the skills instruction aspects of their teaching. These guidelines can also be adapted to sport and physical activity. According to Brophy, teachers and coaches should:

- Concentrate on how to effectively teach (and where necessary reteach) sport skills and strategies to the class, team, or group as a whole rather than worry too much about individual differences.
- Monitor individual participants' progress closely in order to keep expectations current; stress present performances rather than past accomplishments.
- Set realistic group and individual goals. These should be expressed in terms of minimal goal levels (Rotter 1954) rather than as ceilings.
- Use each participant's own personal previous level of performance as their reference point when providing individualized instruction and feedback; avoid normative comparisons such as, for example, "the group's level of performance is X units, your level of performance is Y units."
- Provide objective feedback rather than merely providing an evaluation of success or failure.
- Think through the activity or skill so that when participants do not understand an explanation or demonstration, it can be retaught in a different way. Without proper skill diagnosis, the teacher or coach may merely repeat the same instructions or give up in frustration.
- Challenge every participant; encourage them to work towards personal bests whether the targeted performance is goals against, fouls, time, weight, temper control, or free shooting percentage.

Although individualization makes a great deal of sense for *skills instruction* purposes, it is not defensible if it creeps into the *social interactions* that occur between coaches and teachers and their participants. But, this does seem to occur. It may be recalled that one of the significant differences in the way in which teachers treated highly skilled (high expectation) and lesser skilled (low expectation) students related to the social-emotional climate they developed. It has been observed repeatedly that high expectancy individuals are given more attention, less criticism for failure, more praise following success, and more non-verbal communications (i.e., smiles, head nodding) which signify responsiveness and attentiveness.

But, research has also shown that coaches and teachers "do not intentionally bias their interpersonal interactions with students. Thus, merely an awareness of expectancies and their possible effects may assist teachers and coaches in detecting the 'hidden intentions' of their own interpersonal styles. Presenting such information in pre-service and in-service programs should not prove difficult. In pre-service education this material could be included in any one of several theory or methods courses in the professional preparation curriculum. For the practicing teacher/ coach, workshops would be more functional. These could be organized within the context of either school or community based programs." (Rejeski and Hutslar, 1980, p. 93).

Coaches and teachers should also arrange to have a colleague monitor their behaviors — tabulate the number of times they communicate positively and negatively and, more importantly, compile a list of the frequency with which various students or athletes are the objects of these communications. It could prove enlightening. Certainly, most teachers and coaches are unaware of their ineffective mannerisms and/or the degree to which they use positive and negative reinforcement and provide encouragement. Thus, it also seems unlikely that they are aware of any differences in the way in which they treat different participants for whom they have either high or low expectations.

SELF-CONFIDENCE AS A MOTIVATOR

Serenity is knowing that your worst golf shot is still going to be pretty good.

Johnny Miller

It has been repeatedly pointed out that motivation is a term (a concept, a theoretical construct) which is used to represent the selectivity, the intensity, and the persistence which is present in behavior. And, since this is the case, self-confidence should be viewed as a major component of motivation. Certainly, a diver faced with a choice between two dives which are rated as equally difficult, will select the one in which she has the most confidence. Similarly, a basketball player will be less tentative, less hesitant, less cautious, and will play with greater intensity if he is confident about his abilities. And, finally, all athletes will persist in their efforts to learn a new and difficult skill or cope with a new situation if they have the confidence that they will eventually master it. In other words, self-confidence is exhibited by participants in the selectivity, intensity, and persistence they exhibit in sport and physical activity.

Recently, clinical and experimental psychologists and educators have begun to show an increased research interest in self-confidence because of its importance in any individual's attempts to cope with situations that are anxiety-producing. If a person has a fear of driving, learning to swim, meeting new people, or competing in front of crowds, the key for successfully coping with these is increased self-confidence.

The major impetus for this increase is scholarly interest came from work carried out by Albert Bandura on what he called *self-efficacy* (Bandura 1977). As Bandura (1977) pointed out

> *"Expectations of personal mastery affect both initiation and persistence of coping behavior. The strength of people's convictions in their own effectiveness is likely to affect whether they will even try to cope with given situations. At this initial level, perceived self-efficacy influences choice of behavioral settings ... Not only can perceived self-efficacy have directive influence on choice of activities and settings, but, through expectations of eventual success, it can affect coping efforts once they are initiated. Efficacy expectations determine how much effort people will expend and how long they will persist in the face of obstacles and aversive experiences. The stronger the perceived self-efficacy, the more active the efforts"* (pp. 193-194).

Self-efficacy, which is defined as the strength of a person's conviction that he or she can successfully execute a behavior, carry out a task, or handle the responsibilities necessary to produce a desired outcome, is a situationally specific form of self-confidence. How does self-efficacy differ from self-confidence? Self-confidence, which is a more general, global belief, is usually treated as a trait of personality. Thus, if you have the trait of self-confidence, you should possess the conviction that you will be successful in *all situations* — athletic, academic, social, and business. Because most individuals are typically confident in some situations but less confident in others, researchers have felt that it is more precise to use the term self-efficacy when discussing self-confidence for specific situations. In this book, however, self-efficacy and self-confidence are used interchangeably to represent a situationally specific form of confidence.

Feelings of self-confidence arise from four principal sources: performance accomplishments, vicarious experiences, verbal persuasions, and emotional arousal (Bandura 1977). This is illustrated in Figure 4.5.

Self-confidence which arises because of *performance accomplishments* is especially powerful because it is based upon personal experiences which have been successful. Obviously, performance exposure — actually doing the skill — which leads to success is the best method for instilling confidence. However, there are also other effective ways (see Figure 4.5). With *participant modeling,* for example, the participant initially practices the skill in a less-threatening situation. Thus, swimmers can gain confidence by imitating (modeling) the instructor's surface dive, drownproofing strokes or rescue techniques on the deck prior to trying them in the water. In *performance desensitization,* the individual is gradually introduced into threatening or anxiety

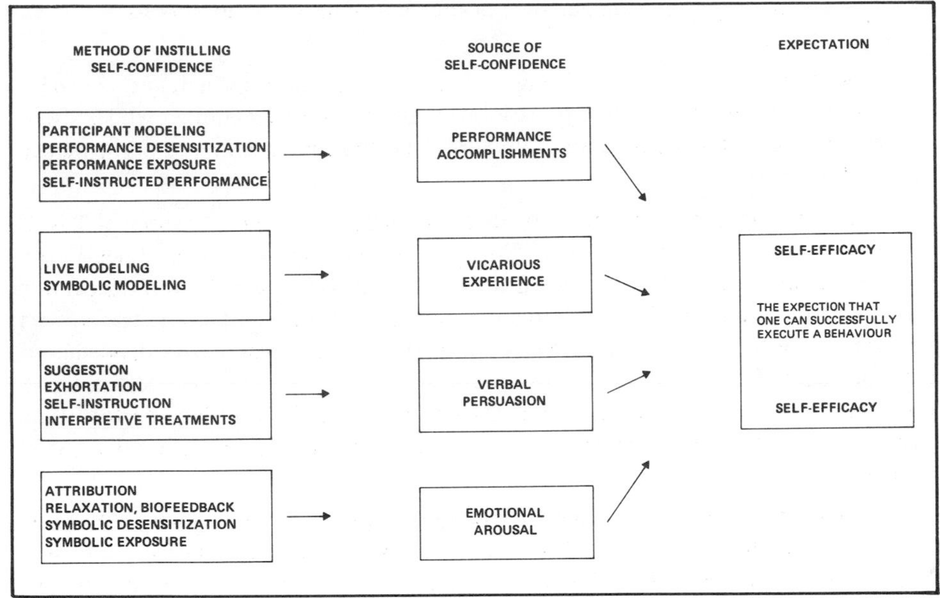

Figure 4.5
Factors contributing to self-confidence (Adapted from Bandura, 1977).

producing situations. Thus, a freshman basketball player could be given brief, but progressively increasing amounts of game exposure in the initial games in the season. Finally, confidence can be gained through *self-instruction,* by verbally rehearsing the steps necessary for effective performance.

The *vicarious experience* of seeing someone else perform a difficult or threatening activity without harmful consequences also can contribute to an expectation that improvement will come through more effort. (See Figure 4.5). The model could be live or symbolic. *Modeling* is most effective when:

- the actor is seen overcoming obstacles and making improvements with difficulty; a highly competent model who carries out the task with extreme ease has very little in common with the nervous, inexperienced beginner;
- the actor is similar to the observer in characteristics such as age, sex, height, weight, body type;
- the target behavior is demonstrated by a number of models in a variety of ways (although the previous two points are valid, watching a number of different actors with widely differing characteristics also leads the observer to reasonably conclude that he or she also has a chance for success);
- there is a clear outcome to the performance; it is more meaningful for an observer watching a model demonstrate free throw shooting to see both the

shooting technique and the outcome of the shot than to see the shooting technique only.

The third method of instilling self-confidence in a participant is *verbal persusasion.* This approach has definite limitations. A younger swimmer who is afraid of water will gain less confidence from verbal persuasions than from performance accomplishments.

The fourth factor associated with self-confidence is *emotional arousal* which is an index of the person's anxiety or fear. Physiological arousal — increased heart rate, sweating, respiratory rate — is not simply just a contributor to self-confidence; it is also an effect of self-confidence. Thus, because high arousal usually detracts from performance effectiveness, participants are likely to have greater confidence about their prospects for success when they are not weighted down by extreme anxiety or fear. But, also, as self-confidence increases through acclimatization, performance success, vicarious experiences, and/or verbal persuasion, emotional arousal decreases.

Much of the research carried out by Bandura and others which formed the basis for Bandura's (1977) theory of self-efficacy was carried out with phobics — people hampered by a variety of fears and inhibitions (e.g., deep water, snakes, height, crowded places). More recently, however, a number of researchers, recognizing the natural application of self-confidence to sport and physical activity, have broadened the focus of research.

PROPOSITION: Self-confidence influences degree of effort and persistence (motivation) as well as performance.

Self-confidence does have a positive effect on motivation and performance but the adage "you can't make a purse out of a sow's ear" does have some relevance. Confidence on its own, without capability, cannot produce success. But, self-confidence and the expectation of a successful outcome do lead to greater persistence and effort in the face of adversity. Bandura (1977) emphasized this point when he stated that the fact that self-confidence

> "*influences performance is not meant to imply that expectation is the sole determinant of behavior. Expectation alone will not produce desired performance if the component capabilities are lacking. Moreover, there are many things that people can do with certainty of success that they do not perform because they have no incentives to do so. Given appropriate skills and adequate incentives, however, efficacy* [confidence] *expectations are a major determinant of people's choice of activities, how much effort they will expend, and how long they will sustain effort in dealing with stressful situations*" (p. 194).

This was clearly illustrated in a laboratory experiment carried out by Weinberg, Gould, and Jackson (1979). A muscular endurance task was used which required experimental subjects to hold their leg in an extended position in competition against another person, a person who was actually a confederate of the experimenters. Self-confidence was manipulated by having the confederates state prior to the competition that they were either a varsity track athlete who lifted weights for leg strength (thereby producing low confidence about the prospects for success in the experimental subject) or that they were an individual who had recently suffered strained knee ligaments (thereby producing high confidence in the experimental subjects). In order to test the prediction that high self-confidence leads to greater effort and persistence when difficult, adverse and negative circumstances are encountered, the experiment was rigged so that the experimental subject lost the leg strength competition on two successive trials.

The results were completely consistent with the preexperimental predictions. On the first trial, the subjects with high self-confidence maintained their contraction significantly longer than the low self-confident subjects. Moreover, on the second trial, after being told that they had lost the first competition, performance of the high self-confidence group improved in comparison to trial one while the low self-confidence group became even poorer. In short, the performance differences which were present between the high confident and low confident subjects were maximized by the negative consequences of failure.

It does seem reasonable to assume that self-confidence is both a cause and an effect of performance. Thus, high self-confidence will lead to better effort, persistence and performance but, in turn, effective performance will lead to greater self-confidence. Support for this viewpoint was obtained by Feltz (1982, 1983) in a comprehensive study concerned with the approach-avoidance behavior of female college students who were attempting to learn a modified back dive.

The dive consisted of holding the arms overhead, extending the head back as far as possible, arching backwards, and falling into the water. The degree of difficulty could be varied by the diver by adjusting the height of the diving board above the deck. Four predetermined heights were possible. Performance assessment was based on a combination of the board's height and an "approach" rating. This approach rating took into account whether the diver refused to approach the end of the board; got on the end of the board but refused to enter the water; jumped rather than dived; back flopped or twisted during the dive; or, made a correct dive. Self-confidence ratings were obtained by having the subjects indicate the strength of their belief (on a 10-point scale) that they could execute the dive successfully.

Feltz found a circular cause and effect relationship between self-confidence and performance but the strengths of the relationships were not equal. That is, after the first dive, performance had a greater impact on self-confidence than self-confidence had on performance. "Regardless of what subjects thought they were capable of performing after the first diving attempt, once they stepped up to [the end of] the board, their next performance was determined more by what they did on the previous trial. If a subject avoided the dive on the first attempt, it was likely that she would avoid it again. If she was successful on the first attempt, she was more likely to try the dive again, possibly at a greater height" (Feltz 1982, p. 780).

PROPOSITION: The observation of others (models) engaging in high-avoidance (threatening) activities without experiencing adverse consequences increases self-confidence and reduces inhibitions.

PROPOSITION: Participant modeling has a stronger positive impact on a participant's confidence for participation in high-avoidance (threatening) activities than a live-model or a videotape demonstration.

Many physical activities contain elements of danger or risk and, thus, can be referred to as high-avoidance skills. Gymnastics, swimming, and diving represent only a few examples. Participants often perceive these situations as unpleasant or even potentially dangerous when they are first exposed to them, and, therefore, try to withdraw if it is possible. The task of the coach or teacher is to overcome this avoidance/withdrawal reaction. Modeling — observing others engaging in the threatening activity — has proven to be a particularly effective technique (Bandura 1977).

Generally, three approaches to modeling have been used in sport and physical activity: live modeling, videotape modeling, and participant modeling. With live modeling, the student (observer) is provided with a demonstration by the instructor or another performer. A similar approach is taken with videotape modeling except that, as the name suggests, the demonstration is provided on videotape. The third approach, participant modeling, consists of, first, watching a model demonstrate the threatening task, and, second, practicing that task either jointly with the model or with guided support. Thus, an essential feature of participant modeling is that the performer actually experiences the task and has some performance success.

As Feltz, Landers, and Raeder (1979) suggested:

"Both videotape modeling and live modeling alone may be effective and efficient techniques in physical education when the skills to be learned are considered low in avoidance (e.g., dancing, bowling, golf), and the individuals do not doubt their own capabilities. However, when skills to be learned are fear-provoking (e.g., swimming, springboard diving, aerial tumbling), modeling alone is a less dependable source of information about one's own capabilities than the direct evidence of personal accomplishment. Modeling, therefore, may not be as effective as participant modeling in enhancing self-efficacy and reducing avoidance behavior" (p. 114).

Feltz et al. examined this proposition with female divers using the modified back dive task previously discussed. In the pretest session, which consisted of four practice dives, each diver in the videotape and live-model group was provided with a demonstration by a model prior to their dive. Divers in the participant modeling group were given a demonstration and then were supported through each dive.

In the test session (which also consisted of four dives), the participant modeling group produced more successful dives and expressed greater self-confidence than either the live-modeling group or the videotape modeling group. There was no difference between these latter two groups. Similar results were reported by McAuley (1983) with subjects learning a complex gymnastics skill.

Implications for the Coach and Teacher

Elite athletes possess more self-confidence than lesser-skilled athletes. This may be the scientific equivalent of concluding that birds can fly but it does bear repetition. Even at the very highest levels of ability in a sport, there are differences in self-confidence which favor the best performers. For example, Mahoney and Avener (1977), in a field study which focused on the psychological factors affecting finalists for the 1976 U.S. Olympic Gymnastics Team, found that those athletes who reported experiencing occasional self-doubts (a lack of confidence in their abilities) showed a tendency to perform poorly during the qualifying meet. Similarly, Highlen and Bennett (1979) tested elite wrestlers prior to competition for positions on three Canadian World Wrestling teams and found that self-confidence (an absence of self-doubts) was the single most important factor which distinguished the qualifiers from the non-qualifiers.

There is no basis in these two studies for suggesting a cause-effect relationship, of course. Confidence leads to success and success leads to confidence and there is no way of determining what was the most predominant relationship in either the Mahoney and Avener gymnasts or the Highlen and Bennett wrestlers. But, this question seems relatively unimportant. There is no doubt that self-confidence is related to persistence and effort. And, ultimately persistence and effort by a skillful athlete will show up in performance benefits. Thus, the task of the teacher and coach is to improve self-confidence in the participant.

Lack of confidence is relative, of course. The beginner may have doubts about his or her capability to learn a sport skill; the elite participant may have doubts about his or her capability to move off a performance plateau. Their respective obstacles (or psychological barriers as they are also called) are equally limiting.

Because success (mastery experiences) are so closely related to the development of self-confidence, care must be taken to structure the coaching/teaching environment to ensure that the beginner experiences some successes. After self-confidence and positive "expectations are developed through repeated success, the negative impact of occasional failures is likely to be reduced. Indeed, occasional failures that are later overcome by determined effort can strengthen self-motivated persistence if one finds through experience that even the most difficult obstacles can be mastered by sustained effort" (Bandura 1977, p. 195).

Thus, it is important that children of the same developmental age and experience compete together, that the environment (e.g., field size, net size, basket size, ball size) be scaled down appropriately, that activities be introduced in increasing order of difficulty (e.g., T-ball before slow pitch and slow pitch before fastball or baseball), and that children be introduced into a recreational, relatively non-competitive situation initially.

In activities which are considered to be threatening or dangerous by the child, desensitization (which involves having the person engage in less threatening activities until confidence is gained) has been shown to be highly successful. And, as we observed in the previous section, participant modeling is more effective than simply watching a demonstration either from a live model or on videotape. In turn, all three of these techniques are better than verbal persuasion alone.

With elite performers, the problem is even more complex. The improvements with practice that are characteristic of the early stages of skill acquisition are no longer experienced. Months of practice may bring only small, almost inperceptible improvements. Consequently, the athlete may begin to feel that physical or genetic factors have imposed a ceiling and that there is little chance to improve to the next level — "I just don't have the height," or "I'm just not strong enough" or "I learned this skill too late in life to get any better now".

While this may be the case, it is also possible that any barrier to further improvements is psychological, and not physical or genetic. For example, Ness and Patton (1977) tested subjects in a weight lifting experiment in which the lifters were either unaware of the amount they were asked to lift, believed the weight to be less than it actually was, or believed the weight to be more than it actually was.

The subjects were able to bench press a significantly greater amount of weight when they were operating under the belief that the weight was less than its actual value. This technique is frequently used by competitive weight lifters to help each other gain confidence and improve beyond performance plateaus (Feltz 1982).

As another example, Nelson and Furst (1972) tested male subjects on arm strength and then asked them to provide an estimate of their strength relative to their peers. The subjects were then paired for an arm wrestling competition. One of the individuals was clearly superior to the other but in every pairing both individuals were led to believe that the stronger person was weaker. In the competition, the person who was objectively weaker won 83 percent of the time. Thus, as the Ness and Patton and Nelson and Furst studies clearly show, expectations for success can directly influence performance.

Imagery, where the participant mentally rehearses successful outcomes, has been used with success to help elite performers overcome psychological barriers (Nideffer and Sharpe 1978; Suinn 1980). Feltz (1982) discussed another innovative technique:

> *"Perceived ability can also be changed in other ways. An example in the popular media has been the Soviets use of imagery to break performance barriers of their Olympic athletes. Films of these athletes performing at their maximum have been modified to show them performing better. They have the athlete then actually observe him/ or herself performing better in hopes of changing their performance beliefs"* (p. 780).

It was also pointed out in the introduction to this section that extreme emotional arousal detracts from feelings of self-confidence and ultimately performance. A number of techniques or coping strategies are now being used to help athletes control the excessive stress associated with high level competition. Included among these techniques are self-hypnosis (Pulos 1979), attention control training (Nideffer 1979), progressive relaxation training (Nideffer 1981), and visuo-motor imagery (Suinn 1976). Each of these has been implemented successfully with high level performers. A brief discussion of attention control training and progressive relaxation training is given in the next chapter.

SUMMARY

The participant brings his or her own motives to sport and physical activity. In the present chapter those factors within the athlete which the coach or teacher have the potential to manipulate were discussed. These included incentive motivation, the perception of causality, intrinsic motivation, the expectations of others, and self-confidence. On the basis of the research evidence which is available, a number of general propositions can be supported:

1. The majority of young participants have multiple motives for their involvement in sport and physical activity.
   a) The most dominant, consistently endorsed reasons for participation are affiliation, skill development, excitement, success and status, fitness, and energy release.
   b) A need for independence, power, aggression, and the influence of significant others (such as parents) are relatively minor factors for participation.
   c) There are no sex differences in the motives for involvement in sport and physical activity.
   d) There are no age differences in the motives for involvement in sport and physical activity.
   e) There are no major differences across different cultures in the motives for involvement in sport and physical activity.
2. The reasons for discontinuing involvement in sport and physical activity are diverse and complex.

a) The most dominant, consistently stated reason for discontinuing involvement in a sport or physical activity is the development of an interest in other activities.
b) Among the negative reasons for discontinuing involvement in a sport and physical activity are lack of playing time, lack of success, lack of skill improvement, lack of fun, boredom, injury, and lack of encouragement from significant others
c) The negative reasons for discontinuing involvement play a more important role with younger participants.

3. A participant's perception of the causes for an outcome influence subsequent motivation.
   a) Positive outcomes which are perceived to be the result of internal, personal factors (e.g., ability, effort, training) rather than external environmental factors (e.g., good luck, ease of the task, officiating decisions) are associated with the greatest amount of pride and satisfaction.
   b) Negative outcomes which are perceived to be the result of internal, personal factors (e.g., poor ability, low effort, inadequate training) rather than external environment factors (e.g., bad luck, difficulty of the task, officiating bias) are associated with the greatest amount of shame and dissatisfaction.
   c) Positive outcomes which are perceived to be the result of stable factors (e.g., high ability, ease of the task) rather than unstable factors (e.g., exceptional effort, good luck) are associated with the greatest expectancy for subsequent success.
   d) Negative outcomes which are perceived to be the result of stable factors (e.g., poor ability, difficulty of the task) rather than unstable factors (e.g., poor effort, bad luck) are associated with the lowest expectancy for subsequent success.
4. Children develop stable opinions about the causes of events and these influence subsequent motivation.
   a) Mastery-oriented children — children who come to believe that the chief reason for their failure is some variable factor such as the amount of effort they have expended — react to failure with renewed effort, greater persistence, and continued involvement in the task.
   b) Learned helplessness children — children who come to believe that the chief reason for their failure is some stable factor such as ability — react to failure with diminished effort, less persistence, and reduced involvement.
5. There are age and sex differences in the way attributions are used.
   a) Males and females differ in the type of attributions they endorse following success and failure, the pride and shame they experience, and the expectancies they hold for subsequent performance.
   b) Young children cannot or do not readily distinguish between the contributions of their personal ability and their effort to their success and failure.
6. The tendency to attribute the cause of an event to ability varies with the sport

task.

7. Extrinsic (tangible) rewards influence the participant's level of intrinsic motivation to carry out a task or activity.
   a) An extrinsic reward which helps to convey information to its recipient that he or she is more competent increases intrinsic motivation.
   b) An extrinsic reward which helps to convey information to its recipient that he or she is incompetent or less competent decreases intrinsic motivation.
   c) An extrinsic reward which helps to convey information to its recipient that he or she does not have direct control or responsibility over personal behavior and actions serves to decrease intrinsic motivation.
8. The sex of the recipient has an influence on the interpretation of the extrinsic reward and its resulting impact on intrinsic motivation.
9. The age of the recipient has an influence on the interpretation of the extrinsic reward and its resulting impact on intrinsic motivation.
10. The intrinsic satisfaction associated with sport and physical activity is at its highest when the participant has a sense of control over clear and challenging goals, has no distractions, anxieties, or worries, and the activity is carried out for its own sake.
11. The expectations held by teachers and coaches regarding the level of ability of an individual influence their subsequent social relationship with that individual.
12. The expectations held by teachers and coaches regarding the level of ability of an individual have an influence on that individual's motivation and performance.
13. Self-confidence influences degree of effort and persistence (motivation) as well as performance.
14. The observation of others (models) engaging in high-avoidance (threatening) activities without experiencing adverse consequences increases self-confidence and reduces inhibitions.
15. Participant modeling has a stronger positive impact on a participant's confidence for participation in high-avoidance (threatening) activities than a live-model or a videotape demonstration.

It is probably unwise to attempt to sum up a total chapter in a few paragraphs. However, it does seem that the teaching and coaching approach which is necessary to incorporate most of the motivational factors discussed in the present chapter is *humanistic.* If the principal concern is the participant, then teaching/coaching strategies can be implemented to develop feelings of competence and self-determination (intrinsic motivation, self-confidence), to instill a positive expectation in every participant (self-fulfilling prophecy, self-confidence), and to ensure that some of the more important reasons for participating in sport and physical activity (incentive motivation) are satisfied. Research on learned helplessness and self-efficacy/self-confidence also points to the need to provide every participant with successful (mastery) experiences. This research also highlights the need to emphasize the contributions of effort and persistence to any outcome.

SUGGESTED READINGS

Alderman, R.B. Strategies for motivating young athletes. In W.F. Straub (Ed.), *Sport psychology: An analysis of athlete behavior.* Ithaca, N.Y.: Mouvement, 1978.

Bandura, A. Self-efficacy: Toward a unifying theory of behavioral change. *Psychological Review,* 1977, *84,* 191-215.

Brawley, L.R. and Roberts, G., C. An introduction to attribution research in sport: Explaining the cause of winning and losing. In J.M. Silva and R.S. Weinberg (Eds.), *Psychological foundations of sport.* Champaign, Ill.: Human Kinetics, 1984.

Brophy, J. and Good, T. *Teacher - student relationships.* New York: Holt, Rinehart & Winston, 1974.

Deci, E. *Intrinsic motivation.* New York: Plenum, 1975.

Halliwell, W. Intrinsic motivation in sport. In. W.F. Straub (Ed.), *Sport psychology: An analysis of athlete behavior.* Ithaca, N.Y.: Mouvement, 1978.

Rejeski, W.J. and Hutslar, S. The mediational role of teacher expectancies on the acquisition and performance of sport skills. *Motor Skills: Theory into Practice,* 1980, *4,* 91-94.

Rosenthal, R. and Jacobson, L.R. Teacher expectations of the disadvantaged. *Scientific American,* 1968, *218,* 19.

CHAPTER 5

Personal Factors Not Readily Subject to Change

Two personality theorists have suggested that each person is like all others, like some others, and like no others (Kluckhohn and Murray, 1949). At first glance this statement seems to be so general that it says nothing. But, this isn't the case. In fact, the statement is actually a very good definition of personality.

The first component of that statement — the phrase that each person is like all others — is an acknowledgement that all human beings have a great many physical and psychological characteristics in common. For example, all humans share the same physiological needs for food and water and for sleep. In addition, there are a number of general, nonphysiological drives which are present in all adults and children. These include the drive for bodily activity, the curiosity drive, and the drive for affection. And, all individuals possess the same personality traits, although, and this is important, in different degrees. Thus, in many important ways, all humans are alike.

The second component of the statement — the phrase that each person is like some other person — is a reference to the fact that every individual possesses some of the identical physical and psychological characteristics as some other person. Thus, it is not unusual to hear statements like "He has his dad's curly hair"; "She has her mother's temperment"; "All of the children in that family are the same size"; "He and his uncle are like two peas in a pod". A combination of our genetic makeup and the situation in which we are raised helps to contribute to the presence of some close similarities among different people.

The fact that "every individual is like all other individuals" and that "every individual is like some other individuals" is the reason why it is possible for coaches and teachers to have a generalized impact upon the motivation levels of their athletes and students. In short, because people are alike, the motivational techniques outlined in previous chapters will have a generally positive impact on the overwhelming majority of participants. But, the extent of this impact will also vary from one person to another because each individual brings a different personality to the athletic situation — each individual is unique.

This uniqueness was acknowledged in the last component of the introductory statement where it was pointed out that each person is like no other. Thus, while we may possess many general characteristics and even share one or two specific traits with someone else, our total personality, the combination of our physical and psychological traits, makes us unique.

The origin of this uniqueness in personality among individuals is a combination of the *genetic* blueprint which is passed on from parents to their children and the specific *situational* experiences encountered during the process of growth and development. Thus, two children might have the same genetic potential for intellectual growth but one might be encouraged to develop this potential by parents and teachers while the other might not. Or two individuals might be born with an equal tendency to be aggressive. However, through cultural and family influences, one might learn self control while the other might not.

Researchers have disagreed about the extent to which heredity and environment contribute to the uniqueness that characterizes every individual. But, they do agree on three points. The first is that whatever the relative influence of heredity and environment, both are important in the development of personality. Second, there is also agreement on the fact that personality is relatively stable and enduring — it does not change very much over time. And, finally, there is also agreement that personality serves to set broad limits around the range of possible behaviors an individual might exhibit.

An example serves to illustrate what is meant by these three points. Automobile manufacturers create different kinds of cars which contain engines with differing amounts of horsepower. The small and mid-sized cars provide better gas mileage than the larger cars but they have less power. In addition, through constant everyday use, every car loses some of its efficiency and effectiveness. Thus, all automobiles should profit from a periodic tune-up. But, even with a tune-up, a small-sized engine cannot achieve the power and acceleration of a large-sized engine. There are constraints or limits placed on performance by the physical size of the engine.

A parallel can be drawn from this example to sport and physical activity. A coach or teacher could use a variety of motivational and psychological techniques in an effort to help a participant improve performance. But, the participant's basic personality will also have an influence upon the impact or effectiveness of these techniques.

Thus, for example, every person possesses a desire to achieve success and a desire to avoid failure. These are personality dispositions which are referred to as the *need for achievement* (achievement motivation) and the *fear of failure*. Every individual possesses these dispositions (or traits as they are also called) to a greater or lesser degree. Also, they are independent. Consequently, it is possible to be high in one, low in the other, high in both, or even low in both. The specific combination which is present in a sport participant places constraints or limits upon his/her response to a competitive situation. This is illustrated in Figure 5.1

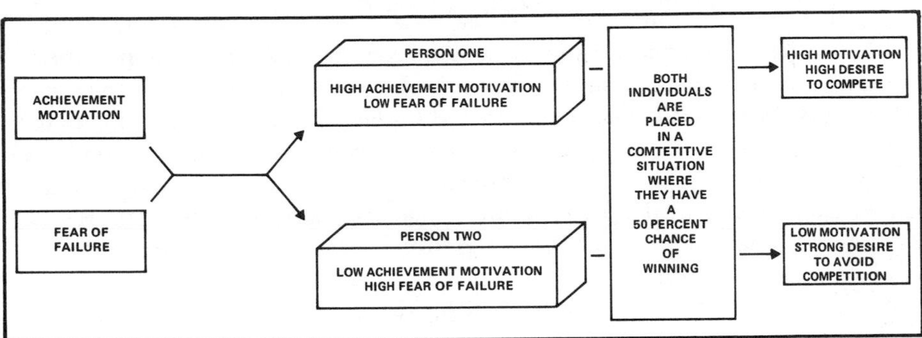

Figure 5.1
The interaction of two personality traits.

An individual with the personality traits of high fear of failure and low achievement motivation feels very uncomfortable and anxious when the chances of winning or losing are equal. On the other hand, an individual with the personality traits of low fear of failure and high achievement motivation is most highly motivated by this challenging type of situation. Consequently, the coach or teacher who places a participant in this situation would receive two different responses from the two different people. The person with high achievement motivation and a low fear of failure would be highly motivated whereas the person with low achievement motivation and a high fear of failure would have a strong desire to avoid the situation. And, because personality is relatively stable and enduring — it changes very minimally and gradually over time — there is little that a coach or teacher could do to change this situation.

In the present chapter, propositions are presented which are related to three important personality characteristics which influence motivation and performance —anxiety, achievement motivation and attentional style.

ANXIETY AS A MOTIVATOR

Anxiety is the interest paid on trouble before it is due.
Dean Inge

The interest in anxiety as an important component of personality can be traced to Sigmund Freud and the development of psychology as a science. Following Freud's initial discussions, anxiety remained a focal point in psychological theorizing. But, as Endler and Hunt (1973) pointed out, there has been a great deal of confusion about the nature of anxiety. "It has been viewed sometimes as a reaction to situations in which the person has encountered pain (Freud, 1932; Hull, 1943; Miller and Dollard, 1941). It has been viewed also as a chronic characteristic of persons which is relatively constant across both situations and occasions, and this view has been implicit for most of those who have constructed instruments for assessing individual differences in anxiousness as a trait" (Endler and Hunt, 1973, p. 53).

In an attempt to eliminate some of the confusion which has prevailed and to bring more precision to the measurement of anxiety, Charles Spielberger and his colleagues (Spielberger, 1966; Spielberger, Gorsuch and Lushene, 1970) drew attention to the distinction between *state anxiety* and *trait anxiety.* State anxiety is considered to be a changing emotional state which is characterized by feelings of tension and apprehension and increased activity in the autonomic nervous system (heart rate, respiratory rate, adrenaline in the blood, and so on). On the other hand, trait anxiety is considered to be a personality trait — a relatively stable tendency or disposition to perceive a wide variety of objectively nondangerous situations as threatening.

Although they are different, trait and state anxiety are also considered to be related since it is believed that individuals with greater trait anxiety (A-trait, the personality disposition) will respond to threatening situations with more intense state anxiety (A-state, the stress reaction).

Subsequently, Rainer Martens (Martens, 1977) extended Spielberger's work by developing a questionnaire — *Sport Competition Anxiety Test (SCAT)* — to assess the degree to which athletes possess the personality trait of anxiety in the specific context of sport and physical activity. As Martens (1977) pointed out:

> *"One person may become quite anxious when taking a math test, sitting in the dentist's chair, or delivering a speech but not become anxious when competing in a hockey game, performing at a piano recital, or taking a driver's examination. Thus, we can better predict behavior when we have more knowledge of the specific situation and how persons tend to respond to these types of situations ... After reviewing some of the research using situation specific A-trait instruments, Spielberger (1972b) concluded that in general, situation specific trait anxiety measures are better predictors of elevations in A-state for a particular class of stress situations than are general A-trait measures"* (p. 26-27).

Numerous studies have now been carried out to assess whether athletes differ from nonathletes in the general personality trait of anxiety and the specific personality trait of sport competition anxiety. In addition, there has been an interest in determining whether sport participants who differ in the personality trait of anxiety (either sport competition anxiety or general anxiety) differ in either the degree to which they experience stress (state anxiety)[1] before, during, and after competition or

[1]Although a distinction is sometimes made between *state anxiety* and *stress* (e.g., Martens, 1977; McGrath, 1970; Spielberger, 1972), these two terms are used interchangeably here. They represent an emotional state which is characterized by feelings of apprehension and tension and an increased level of arousal.

the degree to which their actual performance is influenced during competition. These issues are dealt with in the propositions which follow.

PROPOSITION: Anxiety, as a personality trait, does not have any special relationship to excellence in sport.

a) **Sport performers do not differ from nonparticipants on the personality trait of anxiety.**
b) **Outstanding sport participants do not differ from average, or lesser skilled participants in either the general personality trait of anxiety or the specific personality trait of sport competition anxiety.**
c) **The degree to which sport participants possess the specific personality trait of sport competition anxiety gradually decreases with age and experience.**

Much of the early research in sport psychology was concerned with personality. As a result, various groups — athletes and nonathletes, male and female athletes, individual and team sport athletes, contact and noncontact sport athletes — have been compared on different personality inventories. Although the interest was on personality generally, not surprisingly, the personality trait of anxiety (or A-trait) attracted special attention; many people had a "hunch" that good performers would differ from poor performers in anxiety. This hunch has never been borne out.

In some of the studies carried out, differences were found between groups and in others, no differences were obtained. In addition, in some of the studies where differences were found, the athletic groups showed higher levels of trait anxiety while in other studies, they showed lower levels (see Carron, 1980, for a more complete discussion of this research). Martens (1977) summarized this area of research very well then he stated that:

> *"It is clear then that reliable differences in A-trait among athletes when compared to other athletes or nonathletes have not been obtained using the inventory approach. This is not only true for the personality disposition of A-trait, but other personality traits as well. It is also clear that researchers have not been able to find a reliable relationship between A-trait and the athlete's skill level"* (p. 13).

There is evidence, however, that with age and experience, there are decreases in the degree to which any sport participant possesses the trait of anxiety. For example, when Griffin (1972) tested 682 females from eight competitive sports, it was found that the average general trait anxiety score decreased systematically in three groups ages 12-13 years, 16-17 years, and 19 years and over. Also, Gould, Horn, and Spreeman (1983) found a similar result for the specific personality trait of sport competition anxiety when they assessed 464 elite young wrestlers aged 13 to 19 years. After the total sample was subdivided into two groups on the basis of age (athletes 13 to 16 years and athletes 17 to 19 years), it was observed that the younger athletes possessed higher trait anxiety scores. Similarly, when the total sample was subdivided into two groups on the basis of experience (1-4 years and 5 or more years of wrestling experience), the more experienced wrestlers had lower trait anxiety scores. No differences were found when the athletes were subdivided into winners (placed in the top six in the tournament) and nonplacers (finished below sixth).

PROPOSITION: Performers who differ on the personality trait of sport competition anxiety show differences in degree of stress (state anxiety) associated with competition.

a) **High trait anxious individuals experience high feelings of stress or state anxiety prior to the start of competition.**
b) **High trait anxious individuals experience high feelings of stress or state anxiety during competition.**
c) **High trait anxious individuals experience high feelings of stress or state anxiety after competition.**

There are obviously a large number of factors which produce feelings of nervousness, stress, or state anxiety in young competitors. Passer (1981) in his summary of the research on children's sport, provided a list which included (1) whether the activity is an individual or team sport (individual sports are more stressful), (2) the degree of importance of the game or competition, (3) the outcome (winning decreases stress; losing or tying increases it), (4) the level of self-esteem possessed (stress is greatest in children with low self-esteem), (5) the expectations held for success (children with lower expectations possess greater stress), and (6) the level of sport competition anxiety (see Figure 5.2). Because this is the case, it would be incorrect to overemphasize the impact of any one variable such as the personality trait of sport competition anxiety. Nonetheless, numerous studies (e.g., Gill and Martens, 1977; Martens, 1977; Martens and Gill, 1976; Scanlan and Passer, 1978, 1979) have consistently shown that trait anxiety has a major impact on how competition is perceived. "Prior to competition, high competitive-trait-anxious children evidence more state anxiety than low competitive-trait-anxious children. A similar but slightly weaker relationship is obtained during competition, where it appears that competitive trait anxiety and ongoing success-failure outcomes are equally good predictors of children's state anxiety. After competition is over, state anxiety exhibits a weak relationship with competitive trait anxiety." (Passer, 1981, p. 236).

A typical study examining this issue was undertaken by Gould, Horn, and Spreeman (1983) with 464 junior elite wrestlers participating in a national tournament in the United States. (This study was also discussed in the previous section.) Gould et al. found major differences in the degree of competitive stress reported by the wrestlers. In comparison to the high-trait anxious wrestlers, the low-trait anxious wrestlers experiences less stress (1) 24 hours prior to competition, (2) 1 hour prior to

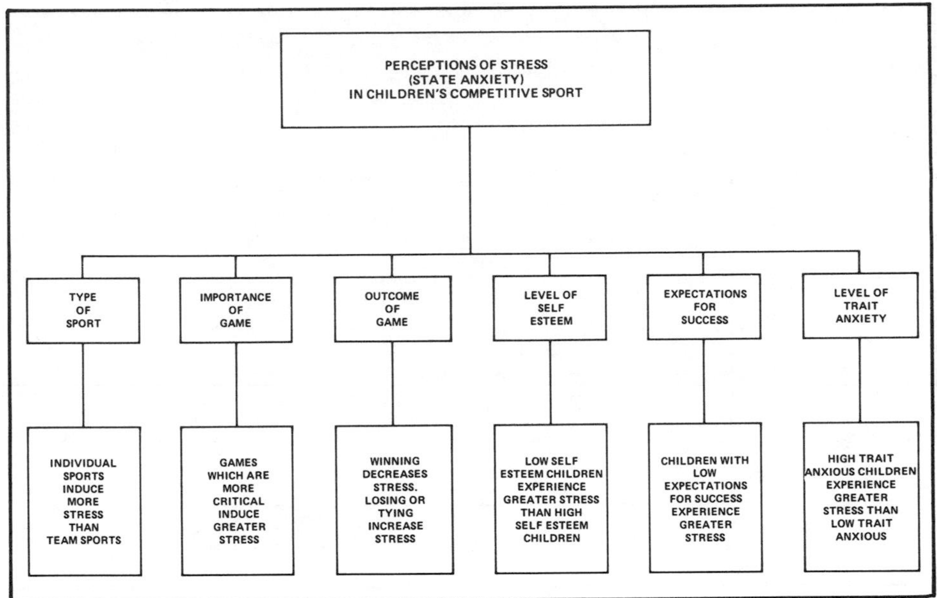

Figure 5.2
Factors influencing perceptions of stress in children's competitive sport (Adapted from Passer, 1981).

competition, (3) 2 minutes prior to competition, and (4) in the actual competition against the individual perceived to be their toughest opponent (see Figure 5.3). The low trait-anxious wrestlers were also superior in terms of (1) their perception of personal ability, (2) their pretournament confidence, (3) the percentage of all matches in which they did not worry, and (4) the trouble (or, rather, lack of difficulty) they had sleeping.

Implications for Coaches and Teachers

Three important conclusions which follow from the preceeding discussion are that

- the personality trait of anxiety is *stable* and only changes slowly as the individual gains experience;
- individuals who differ in the personality trait of anxiety also differs in the degree of *stress* or *state anxiety* they experience prior to, during, and after competition; and;
- the degree to which a performer possesses the personality trait of anxiety has no influence on ultimate ability level.

The fact that individuals are different and that one of the areas in which this difference is most apparent is in their general perception and reaction to competition

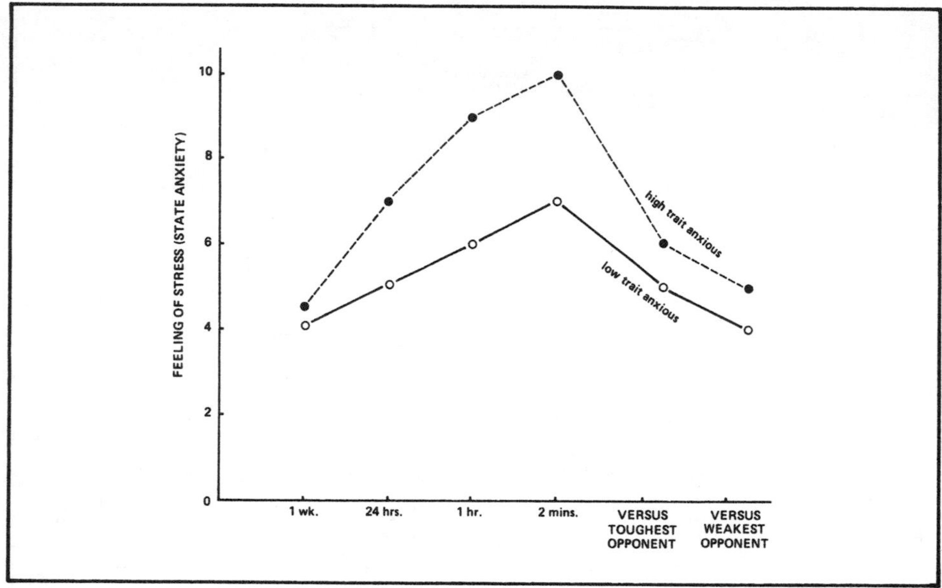

Figure 5.3
Degree of stress (state anxiety) reported by wrestlers who differ in the personality trait of sport competition anxiety (Adapted from Gould, Horn, and Spreeman, 1983).

is not a surprise. This simply "confirms what coaches have already known from their experience; namely, that there are basically two kinds of athletes: the first kind are the calm, low strung, relaxed, composed players. The other kind are the nervous, high strung, excitable, anxious players" (Klavora, 1979, p. 162).

Coaches and teachers also recognize that an individual can become an outstanding performer with either high or low levels of trait anxiety. Personality differences in anxiety do not have any influence upon performance potential and achievement. Consequently, from a basic performance point-of-view, knowledge of a competitor's trait anxiety level is not overly important for the coach or teacher.

On the other hand, the degree to which an athlete finds the whole competitive experience enjoyable is strongly related to his/her trait anxiety level. It was pointed out previously that performers who are high in sport competition anxiety feel higher levels of stress before, during, and even after competition. They also have less confidence and a lower perception of their own ability. And, finally, they also have greater difficulty sleeping prior to competition. Thus, coaches or teachers who become aware by direct measurement or by observation that one of their competitors has a personality characterized by high anxiety, must try to help that athlete learn to cope with the anxiousness; to learn to *relax*.

Two simple techniques which have been used with success are *meditation* and *progressive relaxation.* Essentially both of these techniques involve dissociation — changing the athlete's focus of attention from some stressful situation or stimulus such as the impending game or competition to some neutral situation or stimulus such as personal breathing rate.

Robert Nideffer (1981) has described these procedures extensively in his textbook, *The Ethics and Practice of Applied Sport Psychology.* Insofar as meditation is concerned, the following suggestions were advanced. First, the technique must be practiced regularly — 15 to 20 minutes once or twice daily. The ability to meditate is a skill which improves with practice and decreases with lack of practice. Second, the technique should be practiced with eyes closed in a quiet place that is free of distraction. Third, the actual technique consists of sitting quietly, with eyes closed, and counting (silently) each time a breath is exhaled. Breathing is carried out normally and all that the individual does is focus attention on counting on each exhalation. Fourth, the whole approach should be as *passive* as possible. "This means that individuals do not fight to force attention. If they lose count, find themselves distracted, their mind wanders, that is all right. They simply react to each distraction by gently and unemotionally bringing their attention back to counting one on each exhale. It is very important that the individual learn to react in this rather passive unemotional way to distractions. In fact, that is one of the major benefits of medition for athletes, because the negative spiral is broken by a passive attentional focus" (Nideffer, 1981, p. 171).

The techniques involved in meditation are quite simple and each athlete assumes personal control and responsibility for his/her program. The coach or teacher is not involved as the athlete finds a quiet place, and then with eyes closed concentrates passively on counting breaths. For those individuals who are extremely high in anxiety and/or low in self-confidence and self-esteem, a more structured program such as progressive relaxation which involves the assistance and support of some other person (like a coach or teacher) is more effective (Nideffer, 1981).

Progressive relaxation is an active attempt to relieve tension and anxiety. This is done by systematically relaxing each of the main muscle groups of the body — the neck, the shoulders, the arms, the stomach. The actual procedure advocated by Nideffer is somewhat like self-hypnosis but hypnosis is never mentioned. The athletes are simply instructed on when and how to relax. The actual technique for initiating, proceeding through, and ending a relaxation program is described by Nideffer (1981) as follows:[2]

> *"I would like you to begin by sitting down and making yourself as comfortable as possible. Most people find that the procedure works best if they have their feet flat on the floor, and their hands and arms resting in their lap. If you feel that you would be more capable of relaxing in some other position, however, that's fine. Just make*

[2]Used with permission, Mouvement Publications.

yourself as comfortable as you can. Now I would like you to close your eyes and begin by inhaling deeply from down in your abdomen, and exhaling slowly. That's fine, now as you exhale, I want you to relax all of the muscles in your right arm. Relax the muscles in your right hand, in the wrist, forearm, and upper arm. Notice that as you relax those muscles and as you exhale, your arm becomes heavier, sinking down against the chair, or against your body. Notice that as you exhale and as you relax the muscles in your right arm it becomes heavier, sinking down. That's fine! Now I want you to relax all of the muscles in your left arm. Relax the muscles in the fingers ... hand ... wrist ... forearm ... upperarm. Again notice that as you relax those muscles and as you exhale, your left arm becomes heavier ... sinking down against your body, or against the chair. As you exhale, and as you relax the muscles in both arms, they become heavier ... sinking down against your body or against the chair. Now, I want you to relax the muscles in your right leg ... Relax the muscles in the foot ... ankle ... calf ... and thigh ... Just completely relax all of the muscles in your right leg and as you do, notice that as you exhale ... your leg becomes heavier ... pushing down against the chair ... and against the floor ... That's fine! Now, relax all of the muscles in your left leg ... Relax the muscles in the foot ... ankle ... calf ... and thigh ... Just completely relax all of the muscles in both legs and as you do notice that as you exhale your legs become heavier. It's a very pleasant heaviness as you feel your arms and legs relaxing and pressing down against the chair. Feeling very comfortable and very relaxed ... Relaxing all of the muscles in both arms ... and both legs.

Now, I want you to relax all of the muscles in your neck and shoulders. Just completely relax ... let yourself go ... You will always be able to hear the things that I say and you will be able to enjoy the very pleasant feelings of being completely relaxed ... Now, relax the muscles in your face ... and jaw. Relax the muscle around your eyes ... As you relax the muscles in your jaw, just let your mouth open slightly ... That's fine ... Just completely relax, relaxing all of the muscles in your arms ... legs ... neck ... shoulders ... face ... and jaw ... Notice as you relax and exhale how much heavier your body feels as you sink down into the chair ... always able to hear the things that I say. Now, relax the muscles in your chest ... stomach ... and back ... Just completely relax and let yourself go ... In a moment, I am going to count from one to twenty. With each count you will find yourself drifting down ... becoming more comfortable ... more relaxed ... always able to hear the things that I say ... With each count you will find yourself drifting ... floating ... becoming more and more relaxed ... One ... relaxing all of the muscles in your right arm ... in the fingers ... hand ... forearm ... and upperarm ... Noticing that as you relax and as you exhale ... your arm becomes heavier ... drifting down ... Two ... relaxing all of the muscles in the left arm ... in the fingers ... wrist ... hand ... forearm ... and upperarm. Completely relaxing all of the muscles in both arms. Three ... breathing deeply and slowing from the abdomen ... relaxing all of the muscles in your right leg ... Four, relaxing the muscles in your left leg ... Five ...

Six ... Seven ... becoming more and more relaxed ... relaxing all of the muscles in both arms and both legs ... Very comfortable, very relaxed ... Eight ... relaxing the muscles in your neck ... and shoulders ... Nine ... relaxing the muscles in your face ... and your jaw ... Just letting yourself go ... becoming completely relaxed ... always able to hear the things that I say ... Ten ... halfway ... drifting down ... becoming heavier ... and more relaxed ... drifting ... floating ... in a very pleasant ... relaxed state. Eleven ... Twelve ... Thirteen ... Fourteen ... down ... down ... down ... Becoming more and more relaxed. Fifteen ... relaxing all of the muscles in your entire body ... in your arms ... legs ... neck ... shoulders ... face ... jaw ... chest ... back ... stomach ... Completely relaxed ... very comfortable ... Noticing that as you relax your muscles and as you exhale, you drift down deeper ... deeper ... still deeper. Sixteen ... seventeen ... eighteen ... nineteen ... twenty ... very comfortable ... completely relaxed ...

Alright, just continue to relax ... while I talk to you for a minute ... I want you to continue relaxing until you are ready to get up and to go back to preparing for the competition ... When you get ready to get up, it will be important to do so in a very systematic way .. You have been able to get very relaxed and as a result could get slightly dizzy or disoriented if you jumped up suddenly. To prevent this, just count three to yourself when you are ready to get up. On the count of one ... inhale deeply ... On the count of two, stretch your arms and legs ... and on the count of three ... open your eyes. Whenever you are ready, ... count one ... inhale deeply ... count two ... stretch your arms and legs ... and count three ... and open your eyes ..." (pp. 176-177).

Although progressive relaxation is used to help athletes relax and concentrate just prior to competition, it is also extremely effective for helping athletes get to sleep on nights preceeding an important competition. For this latter purpose, the individual must either learn the technique and apply it personally or have the relaxation directions put on a tape.

Obviously, neither meditation nor progressive relaxation could be used during a game or competition. A technique which has been developed that is very effective for helping an athlete cope with stress and/or focus attention on performance is called *centering.* It is discussed in the section entitled "Focus of Attention as a Motivator".

NEED FOR ACHIEVEMENT AS A MOTIVATOR

Experience shows that success is due less to ability than to zeal. The winner is he who gives himself to his work, body and soul.
Charles Buxton

The earliest, comprehensive work concerned with exploring the origins of achievement-related behavior was carried out by David McClelland and John Atkinson in the 1950s and 1960s (e.g., Atkinson, 1964; McClelland, 1961). Atkinson and McClelland felt that the competitiveness or need to achieve which is a characteristic of behavior in business, school, athletics, and a wide variety of other situations is the result of two personality dispositions[3] which operate simultaneously within the individual. One of these, the *motive for success* (or need for achievement as it is also called) is a disposition to get involved in achievement situations. The other, the *motive to avoid failure* (or fear of failure as it is also called) is a disposition to avoid entering into achievement situations. In other words, in any achievement situation, the opportunity for success and its accompanying rewards and satisfactions contributes positively to an overall desire to get involved. At the same time, concerns about possible failure and its accompanying embarrassment and dissastisfaction produces reluctance on the part of the individual to do so.

Each of these two dispositions are thought to develop as a result of early childhood experiences. In addition, because they are personality dispositions, they are also thought to be stable (after they have developed, they change very little over time), universal (they influence need for achievement in all achievement situations), and independent (it is possible for any one individual to be high in both, low in both or high in one and low in the other). Thus, if an individual possesses a high need for achievement and a low fear of failure for example — which is the top profile presented in Figure 5.1 — that person could be expected to have the same high motivation and high desire to achieve in school situations, in business situations, in social situations, and in sport situations.

In their writings on achievement behavior, Atkinson and McClelland also emphasized how important the situation is in determining achievement behavior. For example, the rewards associated with success and/or the embarrassment associated with failure vary from one achievement situation to another. Thus, beating a higher ranked tennis opponent would produce an increase in prestige. Consequently, there would be large rewards associated with this situation. On the other hand, losing to a lower ranked player would lead to a loss of prestige and, therefore, would represent a situation with minimal rewards. Similarly, the probability for success also varies from one situation to another. In the two examples presented above, the probability for success would be quite different; it would be lower against the higher ranked opponent than it would be against the lower ranked one.

The two situational factors (the probability for success-failure and the incentives attached to success-failure) were combined by Atkinson and McClelland with the two personality dispositions (need for achievement and fear of failure) to form an overall model or theoretical framework to examine achievement behavior. Essentially, in this model, it is proposed that the personality dispositions and the situational factors jointly influence achievement motivation. Some propositions arising from the research which has been carried out to test this theoretical model are presented in the discussions which follow.

[3]In the science of personology, the terms trait, motive, need, and disposition are used interchangeably to represent stable qualities in human personality.

PROPOSITION: The competitive drive in achievement situations is influenced by the personality traits of need for achievement and fear of failure.

a) **The competitive drive of individuals with a personality profile characterized by a high need for achievement and low fear of failure is most strongly aroused in tasks of intermediate difficulty.**

b) **The competitive drive of individuals with a personality profile characterized by a high fear of failure and a low need for achievement is most strongly aroused in tasks which are either extremely difficult or extremely easy.**

In Chapter 3 in the section dealing with the competitor as a motivator, it was pointed out that, in general, the competitive drive is most strongly aroused when the two participants feel that they are equal in ability. There is an exception, however, for individuals who possess a high fear of failure relative to their need for achievement.

For example, individuals who have a very high need for achievement and a very low fear of failure are most strongly motivated by competitive situations where the possibility for success is about 50 percent. There is an equal chance of winning or losing and the competitive drive becomes strongly aroused as a result (see Figure 5.1). On the other hand, those individuals who have a very high fear of failure and a very low need for achievement are most strongly motivated in situations where the probability for success is extremely high or extremely low; e.g., a 90-percent chance of success or a 10 percent chance of success (Atkinson and Litwin, 1960; Roberts, 1974). In both of these instances, the individual is in a "can't lose" type of situation. When the odds or chances for success are extremely high, the individual is almost guaranteed a victory. And, when the odds or chances for success are almost insurmountable, the individual also can't lose from a psychological point of view because any loss is to be expected. Therefore, there is no shame associated with it.

Ryan and Lakie (1965) have found that the performance of individuals with high anxiety (which is often considered in research to be synonymous with fear of failure) and low need for achievement was most effective in noncompetitive situations. On the other hand, individuals with a high need for achievement and low anxiety performed best under competitive conditions.

PROPOSITION: Differences in social histories and social experiences contribute to differences in achievement motivation.

a) **Achievement motivation varies in individuals from different cultures.**

b) **Achievement motivation varies in males and females.**

It has been argued by Maehr (1974) and Duda (1981) that achievement motivation is similar to anxiety in that it is specific to specific situations. That is, in the earlier discussion on trait anxiety, it was pointed out by way of illustration that some individuals perceive public speaking as their most threatening, anxiety producing situation while for others, competing in sport, or taking an exam is the most threatening. In a similar fashion, according to Maehr and Duda, the need to achieve is most highly aroused in some individuals when they are in academic situations while for others it is most highly stimulated in sport situations. As Duda (1981) pointed out:

> *"According to this viewpoint, then, an athlete's behavior in a sport setting is a product of his/her past social history and the immediate social context. Athletes from different backgrounds may respond to various competitive environments in different ways. Certain situations might optimize achievement motivation in some groups more than others ... with respect to Maehr's viewpoint (1974), athletes are not more or less motivated — athletes are motivated in different ways, toward different ends, in different contexts".* (pp. 25-26)

Because males and females and people from different cultures have quite different social experiences as they go through childhood, and consequently acquire different attitudes and beliefs, it might be expected that they would also possess different amounts and kinds of achievement motivation. For example, having fun, playing well, or developing good friends might be the most important criteria for success for participants from one culture whereas participants from another culture might consider winning as either the most important or as even the only criterion for success.

Coaches and teachers of minority groups are familiar with the fact that the perceptions of success and achievement vary from one culture to another. Take for example, the experiences of Norman Neil, the team coach for the Northwest Territories cross-country ski team. In commenting on his work in the sparsely populated, 1,304,903 square mile region of northern Canada, Neil observed that "the natives, especially the elders, have too many issues to deal with ... social and economic ones. Their concept of sport varies greatly from that of the whites" (Newman, 1978, p. 23). Later he also added that "up there you can make all the schedules you want, but chances are you won't be on schedule. Things don't move as fast. If people are late, people don't get uptight. There are less ulcers per capita. I was used to a faster pace before" (Newman, 1983, p. 23).

Neil also found that the definitions for success and failure in sport were different in Northern Canada, an observation which was also echoed by Duda (1980) on the basis of her research with Navajo Indian high school students. Success in track and field for the Navajo children was equated with effort, trying hard, practicing a lot and having ability. The outcomes typically emphasized by society-in-general as measures of success — the setting of records, winning, beating opponents — were not as important to these Navajo students.

In a follow-up study, Duda and Allison (1982) compared the attitudes of black and white males and females toward various classroom, sport, and general life situations. They found that the perceptions of what constitutes success (achievement) varied from one situation to the next as well as according to the race and the sex of the respondents. Some of the more interesting similarities and differences found by Duda and Allison were that:

- Blacks and Whites held the same perceptions for success in sport but possessed quite different orientations for achievement in the classroom and life in general;
- in sport situations both Blacks and Whites considered trying hard, having good ability, and winning as the most important measures of success;
- in classroom situations and life in general, Blacks tended to define success (achievement) according to external factors such as how others perceived them (e.g., popularity, membership in the most important groups, and having money) whereas Whites tended to define success according to internal factors such as how they perceived themselves (e.g., possessing feelings of self respect, having control over themselves);
- males and females held the same perceptions for what constituted success in the classroom but differed on their definitions for success in sport and for life in general;
- females defined success and failure in sport situations according to whether or not they practiced a great deal and tried hard whereas males saw success and failure in terms of whether they won or lost and did or did not possess ability;
- in situations characteristics of life in general, males associated success with gaining self awareness, self-respect, and knowledge, and working well with others.

The pattern of sex and cultural differences found by Duda is by no means unique. A number of other studies have also reported that males and females attach a different personal meaning to success and failure (e.g., Deaux, 1977; Ewing, 1981; Reis and Jelsma, 1978). Similarly, race and cultural differences have been found in numerous studies (e.g., Duda, 1981, 1982; Madsen and Shapira, 1970; McNally and Orlick, 1975; Shapira and Madsen, 1969).

Implications for the Coach and Teacher

One of the most important implications from the work on achievement motivation concerns the need for the coach and teacher to view and treat each individual as an individual. As Atkinson (1974) pointed out:

> *"The same treatment may have dramatically opposite effects on different individuals. This ... is one of the most important implications of contemporary research on human motivation — the challenge it poses for those who think there may be some single method of instruction or treatment which will produce optimal motivation for learning in all students irrespective of personality"* (p. 37).

Because of the large numbers that they must deal with, there may be a tendency for coaches and teachers to deal with their athletes and students as a whole group, team, or class. But, the student or athlete who has an exceptionally high fear of failure may need substantially more praise and encouragement, and be unable to tolerate as much criticism as a participant who has a low fear of failure and high need achievement.

Second, the coach and teacher must work with their athletes and students to establish realistic goals and objectives. It was pointed out that individuals high in fear of failure and low in achievement motivation have a tendency to seek out situations which are inordinately difficult or easy. This insures that either they won't fail because their opponent is easy or, if they do (against an impossibly difficult opponent), there will be minimal embarrassment. Consequently, coaches and teachers have to become sensitive to their athlete's goals to insure that they are appropriate.

An effective goal setting program for a group of males and females must take into account the relative differences between the sexes in order to maximize the opportunities for all participants to achieve their potential. For a goal setting program to be successful, it must (1) take into account individual differences in *capacity* and *potential,* and (2) focus on *effort* (striving for mastery) rather than on an absolute criterion of success. Reis and Jelsma (1978) emphasized these two points when they observed that

> "*Obviously, performance must be referred to same sex standards, since physiological differences in the sexes' physical capacities makes direct comparison unreasonable* ... [Absolute] *success at competition is available only to a small handful of participants and is always challenged, usually by more and more skilled competitors. A personally skillful performance, exceeding one's previous levels is, however, virtually always accessible to all athletes. The Mastery-oriented athlete therefore stands a considerably better chance to come away from a performance satisfied*" (p. 282).

A third implication (which is related to the previous two points) stems from the fact that each individual possesses a different amount of the traits fear of failure and desire for success, the negative and positive motives which are stimulated in achievement situations. As a consequence, there are also wide differences in the degree to which each member of a team can tolerate criticism and negative feedback, or be comfortable when placed in challenging competition situations. The sensitive coach or teacher must try to adapt his/her comments to the individual.

Another important implication, one suggested by Donnelly and Birrell (1978), is that coaches and teachers can use sport and physical activity to help participants develop or nurture higher levels of achievement motivation. "Although achievement motivation generally is believed to be a personality disposition developed at an early age, McClelland and Winter (1969) have had some success in increasing the level of motivation in Indian businessmen. The development programme they devised included teaching the trainees to exhibit behaviors characteristic of individuals with high achievement motivation, such as producing achievement imagery in response to the Thematic Apperception Test; encouraging them to reflect on the significance of achievement in their lives; and helping them to set realistic goals for themselves. McClelland and Winter (1969) report significant changes in entrepreneurial activity for individuals enrolled in their courses. It seems feasible to suggest that a modified form of such a programme could be instigated in sport settings, either informally or formally, providing an accessible and generally enjoyable setting for developing achievement motivation." (Donnelly and Birrell, 1978, p. 75).

FOCUS OF ATTENTION AS A MOTIVATOR

When I'm totally tuned it, it's like I'm looking down a tunnel where there's nothing else but the pitcher.

Don Baylor

Attentional style is not a motivator in the strict sense that the term has been used in this textbook. Nonetheless, it is highly associated with motivation because increased arousal — which is a natural consequence of all competition — directly influences attention and the ability to concentrate. And, of course, the ability to concentrate and to focus attention on the requirements of the task are tied in with performance success. The pass receiver who is worried about dropping the ball as it approaches in the air, the basketball player who is preoccupied with a previously missed free throw, the golfer who is distracted by the noises of the crowd, and the coach who has difficulty making decisions during extremely important games all show problems in concentrating and focusing their attention on the requirements of their tasks. And, as a result, they are less effective then they could or should be.

Recently, a great deal of interest has been directed toward the role that mental processes (such as attention) play in successful and unsuccessful athletic performance. For example, in an article in *Time,* writer John Leo (1983), discussed specific problems faced by a number of different major league baseball players. The case of Steve Sax is typical:

> *"In the second inning of this season's All-Star game, Los Angeles Dodger Second Baseman Steve Sax fielded an easy grounder, straightened up for the lob to first, and bounced the ball past First Baseman Al Oliver, who was less than 40 ft. away. It was a startling error even for an All-Star game studded with bush-league mishaps. But, hard-core baseball fans knew it was one more manifestation of a leading mystery of the 1983 season. Sax, 23, last year's National League Rookie of the Year, cannot seem to make routine throws to first base. (Of his first 27 errors this season, 22 stem from bad throws). Sax is not alone. Over the years, a number of major league baseball players have developed odd mental blocks and sent psychologists scurrying for explanations"* (p. 54).

In Sax's case, the problem obviously was not due to wandering attention or a lack of concentration. As Leo (1983) went on to relate in his article, the problem probably resided in being overly preoccupied with the task:

"The coaches are telling him 'Don't think about a bad throw, just throw the ball.' That, of course, usually makes matters worse. Says Sax: 'It's like if somebody comes up to you and says 'Don't think about an elephant for the next five seconds'. The first thing you're going to think about is an elephant' " (p. 54).

It doesn't really matter whether the athlete's performance suffers because of poor concentration or over-concentration — in the final analysis, the important point is that attentional problems have interefered with performance effectiveness. Because mental processes are so closely associated with performance, sport scientists have begun to show an increasing interest in this issue. One of the most comprehensive, most significant contributions has been made by Robert Nideffer in his work on *attention control training.* Nideffer (1981) has proposed a conceptual framework or foundation within which to consider attention. He has also developed a psychological test, *Test of Interpersonal and Attentional Style (T.A.I.S.),* which is used to determine each individual's attentional strengths and limitations.

As a basis for his conceptual framework, Nideffer has proposed that there are at least three aspects of attention which must be taken into account: *width* of attention, *direction* of attentional focus, and *ability to shift* from one type of attention to another.

The width of attention refers to the amount of information a person can attend to at any point in time. In this regard, a distinction is made between *broad* and *narrow.* For example, in the last minutes of a closely played basketball game, good coaches must have a broad focus of attention in order to concentrate on all the possible strategies that they and their opponents might use. On the other hand, a golfer about to attempt a difficult putt or a basketball player about to take a foul shot must have a very narrow, sharply concentrated focus of attention.

The direction of attention refers to the fact that at any given moment in time, it is possible for us to focus our attention inwardly on our own thoughts, and ideas or outwardly on events going on around us. Thus, the direction of attentional focus can also be either *internal* or *external.* Both the basketball player preoccupied with a previously missed shot and the coach preoccupied with strategy are focusing their attention internally. On the other hand, a quarterback looking for pass receivers and a goaltender studying the changing flow of the other team's offense are using an external focus.

Direction and width combine to form four types of attention: broad-external, narrow-external, broad-internal, and narrow-internal. The description and characteristics of each of these is summarized in Table 5.1

All of us use all four of these in sport and in general life situations — we shift back and forth constantly. However, it is assumed that different people tend to have different strengths and preferred attentional styles. Some individuals, for example, are extremely effective at analyzing, interpreting, and providing overviews or summaries; this involves a broad-internal attentional style. Other individuals are most effective at concentrating on a single task no matter how many distracting events are going on around them — a narrow-internal attentional style.

Table 5.1 Description of the attentional styles used in sport and physical activity (Adapted from Nideffer, 1981).

WIDTH OF ATTENTIONAL FOCUS		DIRECTION OF ATTENTIONAL FOCUS: EXTERNAL	DIRECTION OF ATTENTIONAL FOCUS: INTERNAL
	NARROW	**NARROW EXTERNAL** Required when an overt response is made. Attention is narrow and focused externally on an opponent, the ball, a target	**NARROW INTERNAL** Required for mental rehearsal. Attention is narrow and focused internally on a single idea, thought, plan
	BROAD	**BROAD EXTERNAL** Required for reading or analyzing complex situations. Attention is external and broadly focused to view the total field	**BROAD INTERNAL** Required for analysis and overall planning. Attention is internal and broad in order to consider all possible courses-of-action

Although it is possible (and every person does) shift back and forth from one attentional focus to another in general-life, everyday situations, this ability to shift is dramatically influenced in situations characterized by pressure, stress, and increased arousal. Three things happen in these types of situations. First, the ability to shift back and forth from one type of attention to another breaks down and, the person begins to rely most heavily on his/her strength (the most effective or dominant attentional style). In some cases, this could be advantageous but others not. For example, an individual who has a narrow-external focus might be an excellent archer in pressure situations but would likely be a poor coach. The tendency to narrow and focus attention would be good for participating but poor for analyzing the total situation. Thus, what is a strength in one situation is a limitation in another. The limitations or attentional errors associated with each style are summarized in Table 5.2.

A second thing that occurs in stressful situations is that with increasing arousal, attention narrows. This occurs involuntarily. "Whether or not this narrowing of attention will help or hinder performance depends on several factors including: 1) How complex the performance is. That is, how great the attentional demands are; 2) The base level ability of the athlete to begin with ... Some athletes seem more capable than others of developing a broad focus of attention. Those who can attend to more things to begin with have greater capacity to deal with increasing pressure — they have more room to move" (Nideffer, 1981, p. 29).

Table 5.2 Description of the limitations and errors associated with each attentional style (Adapted from Nideffer, 1981).

WIDTH OF ATTENTIONAL FOCUS	DIRECTION OF ATTENTIONAL FOCUS: EXTERNAL	DIRECTION OF ATTENTIONAL FOCUS: INTERNAL
	NARROW EXTERNAL	**NARROW INTERNAL**
NARROW	Lack flexibility and ability to adjust to changing situations. Problems with staying too long with original plans or responses	Become too locked into own ideas, and feelings and don't react or function
	BROAD EXTERNAL	**BROAD INTERNAL**
BROAD	Don't think because too busy reading and reacting to situations. Problems with making same mistake over and over because of lack of analysis	Problems with over analysis. May out-think themselves because of the tendency to explore all options. Paraliysis of analysis

The final effect of increased arousal is that attention becomes more internally focused — the athlete becomes more aware of the normal physical changes that occur in the body. These, of course, include increased muscle tension, elevated heart rate, respiratory rate, and blood pressure.

A number of studies have examined the impact of attentional focus upon performance. The generalizations evolving from that research are contained in the propositions which follow:

PROPOSITION: Concentration and ability to focus attention are necessary for performance effectiveness.

a) **There are wide individual differences in attentional styles.**
b) **There are differences in the attentional style most appropriate for different sport tasks.**

It was pointed out earlier that individuals differ in their ability to concentrate and direct attention. Some sport performers tend to be highly analytical — they show an exceptional ability to analyze their sport, the skills they need to work on, and their opponent's strengths and weaknesses. Other performers lack this ability but, instead, are able to shut out every distraction and concentrate on the task-at-hand.

In addition, sport tasks vary in the degree to which specific attentional styles are beneficial. A simple example is provided by the sport of basketball. When a player is at the free-throw line, an outward, narrow, highly concentrated focus of attention directed toward the basket is required. When that same player is bringing the ball up the court, however, an outward, broad attentional scope is required in order to determine what other offensive players and the defence are doing. And, finally, when that same player is discussing strategic possibilities with the coach during a time-out, a broad, internal, analytical approach is required.

It has been reported in a number of studies that the ability to effectively use a specific attentional style is related to performance success in different tasks. For example, Nettleton (1982) had subjects practice a coincident anticipation task in the laboratory. The subjects were asked to anticipate (and then respond) when a target moving along a trackway arrived at a certain point. Nettleton found a high relationship between a narrow attentional focus (the top two cells of Table 5.1) and coincident-anticipation performance.

In another laboratory experiment, Reis and Bird (1982) had subjects track a rotary target with a probe. During tracking performance each of four lights adjacent to the tracking apparatus became illuminated and the subject then had to respond as quickly as possible to those lights by pressing a reaction key. Reis and Bird hypothesized that broad external attenders (the bottom left cell of Table 5.1) would perform better than narrow attenders. Their results supported this hypothesis.

Attentional style has also been linked to performance in non-laboratory studies. For example, Van Schoyck and Grasha (1981) ranked 90 male and female tennis players into three skill categories: beginner, intermediate, and advanced. They found that the ability to use a broad attentional style (the bottom two cells in Table 5.1) was associated with a higher skill level. A similar finding was also reported by Nakagawa (1982) with rugby football players who were required to recognize the weaknesses in specific game situations and outline how the weakness could be attacked. The better the player's skill level, the better the recognition and the more accurate the response.

It has also been observed in some studies that lesser skilled athletes have difficulty because they are unable to shift from one style of attention to another. Thus, their specific attentional style becomes a liability. For example, consider Table 5.2 again. If an athlete narrows attention too much (a condition referred to by Nideffer as *reduced attentional focus, RED*), he/she would lack the flexibility and adaptability required in many sports. (This situation is represented by the top two cells of Table 5.2). It is also possible for athletes either to be distressed by the events going on around them (which is referred to as *overload by external stimuli, OET)* or be distracted by personal thoughts and ideas (which is referred to as *overload by internal stimuli, OIT*).

Landers, Furst, and Daniels (1981) tested open skill shooters (skeet/trap) and closed skill shooters (rifle/pistol) and found that the better performers were less likely to have a reduced attentional focus (RED) or to be overloaded by external stimuli (OET). Similarly, Nideffer (1976) found that when compared to consistent swimmers, inconsistent swimmers were more overloaded by external (OET) and internal (OIT) distractions.

Implications for the Coach and Teacher

The ability to effectively control, direct, and adjust attention underlies all successful performance. This is equally true for the coach who is responsible for strategic decisions, for the athlete who is trying to ignore pain, the "psyching" efforts of opponents, a previous error, or an upcoming event, and for the referee who must block out the crowd, coaches, or athletes.

Orlick (1980) summarized this very well when he stated that:

> "*Focusing your attention involves becoming aware of one thing (or one important area of focus), to the exclusion of others. In sports, frequently a very narrow focus of attention is required, such as in archery, when focusing all attention on the center of a single target. At other times a broader focus of attention is necessary, such as when a quarterback is scanning the field for a defensive play pattern or an open receiver. Very often there is a shifting back and forth from narrow to broad to narrow ... Concentration in sport must be adjustable, like a zoom lens on a camera, capable of zooming in and zooming out. It can be likened to an adjustable garden hose or light beam which can be very intense and narrow or more spread out and broadened in scope*" (p. 115-116).

In many instances, the transition from one attentional style to another occurs naturally. The quarterback learns to scan the total field and then zoom in on a primary receiver. And, the coach learns to weigh all options, select the best one and then effectively concentrate on transmitting that one to the competitor or team.

But, there are also many instances where effective concentration or the ability to shift back and forth is broken. Nideffer (1981) emphasized this point when he stated that "there are a tremendous number of situations in sport where the individual must either recover from a distraction to prevent a problem to begin with, or where he/she must recover from a mistake in order to prevent additional problems" (p. 193).

How does an athlete do this? How does an athlete recover from distractions or mistakes? One approach that we know definitely doesn't work is to tell the athlete to forget it or ignore it. As Steve Sax pointed out in the quote used at the beginning of this section "It's like if somebody comes up to you and says, 'Don't think about an elephant for the next five seconds.' The first thing you're going to think about is an elephant" (Leo, 1983, p. 54).

A specific technique which has been used effectively involves teaching the individual to shift his/her attentional focus from distractions, mistakes, or negative and destructive thoughts and ideas to something neutral. This technique has been referred to as *centering* because it involves concentrating on a point in the body just below and behind the navel. This, of course, is where the centre of gravity lies and, thus, it is the center of the body (Nideffer, 1981). Essentially the athlete eliminates negative thoughts through self distraction.

The specific procedure, as outlined by Nideffer and Sharpe (1978), is as follows:

- Stand with feet shoulder width apart, weight evenly balanced, and knees slightly bent;
- Consciously relax the neck and shoulder muscles and open the mouth slightly to reduce tension in the jaw muscles;
- Breathe in slowly from the diaphragm while concentrating on the action of the stomach, maintain relaxation in the chest and shoulders; and the midpoint of the body;
- Exhale slowly while concentrating on feelings in the abdomen (the stomach muscles relaxing) and the feelings of heaviness that develop during exhalation.
- Repeat this process three times.

The centering technique can be used in any sport situation where negative thoughts and ideas can take hold. In diving, wrestling and figure skating, the most difficult period may be prior to the start of the event. In sports such as tennis, archery, bowling, and the high jump where there is a continuous sequence of action-no action, the centering technique may be useful during the no-action phases. Or, centering can be used after any unsuccessful performance. Because each individual and each sport is different, it is up to the coach-teacher and athlete-student to determine jointly how and when centering might be most beneficial.

SUMMARY

Every participant brings a unique set of personality traits, dispositions, and attitudes to sport and physical activity. And, the participant's personality influences his/her motivation and performance. Thus, the coach and teacher must be sensitive to the broad differences among participants in order to most effectively teach and coach. In this chapter, three important personality traits that influence athletic performance were discussed: anxiety, need for achievement, and attentional style. On the basis of available research, a number of propositions pertaining to these three were presented.

1. Anxiety, as a personality trait, does not have any special relationships to excellence in sport performance.
   a) Sport performers do not differ from nonparticipants on the personality trait of anxiety.
   b) Outstanding sport participants do not differ from average or lesser skilled participants in either the general personality trait of anxiety or the specific personality trait of sport competition anxiety.
   c) The degree to which sport participants possess the specific personality trait of sport competition anxiety gradually decreases with age and experience.
2. Performers who differ on the personality trait of sport competition anxiety show differences in degree of stress (state anxiety) associated with competition.
   a) High trait anxious individuals experience high feelings of stress or state anxiety prior to the start of competition.
   b) High trait anxious individuals experience high feelings of stress or state anxiety during competition.
   c) High trait anxious individuals experience high feelings of stress or state anxiety after competition.
3. The competitive drive in achievement situations is influenced by the personality trait of need for achievement and fear of failure.
   a) The competitive drive of individuals with a personality profile characterized by a high need for achievement and a low fear of failure is most strongly aroused in tasks of intermediate difficulty.
   b) The competitive drive of individuals with a personality profile characterized by a high fear of failure and a low need for achievement is most strongly aroused in tasks which are either extremely difficult or extremely easy.
4. Differences in social background and social experiences contribute to differences in achievement motivation.
   a) Achievement motivation varies in individuals from different cultures.
   b) Achievement motivation varies in males and females.
5. Concentration and ability to focus attention are necessary for performance effectiveness.
   a) There are wide individual differences in attentional styles.
   b) There are differences in the attentional style most appropriate for different sport tasks.

Because personality is stable and consistent and only changes very slowly over time, the coach or teacher must generally deal with each participant in light of the broad constraints and potential that his/her personality affords. Personality is a source of motivation within the participant over which the coach or teacher has little direct control. But, this fact notwithstanding, it is also possible to introduce techniques like centering, meditation, and/or progressive relaxation to participants in order to insure that they realize their potential and derive maximum enjoyment from their involvement in sport and physical activity.

SUGGESTED READINGS

Donnelly, P. and Birrell, S. *Motivation and sport involvement: The needs for stimulation and achievement.* Ottawa: CAHPER Sociology of Sport Monograph Series, 1978.

Martens, R. *Sport competition anxiety test.* Champaign, Ill.: Human Kinetics, 1977.

Nideffer, R.M. *The ethics and practice of applied sport psychology.* Ithaca, N.Y.: Mouvement, 1981.

CHAPTER 6

Motivation in Sport and Physical Activity

It has been suggested over and over that each of the motivational factors presented in this text is important. Consequently, a knowledge of each one is essential for the coach and teacher. But also, not surprisingly, many of these different motivational factors do have a relationship with each other; particularly the motivational factors which a coach or teacher can influence or manipulate (see Chapters 2 and 4). For example, the introduction of a goal setting program influences motivation and leads to performance improvement. In turn, this performance improvement contributes to the satisfaction of a participant's incentive for achieving excellence. Or, as another example, the use of positive social reinforcers contribute to the satisfaction of a participant's affiliation incentive, as well as to the level of intrinsic motivation present. And, as a final example, increasing self confidence in a participant is associated with a growing feeling of competence, satisfaction of the incentive for excellence, and intrinsic motivation.

This list of examples could go on. But, what is important, is the understanding that there is a relationship, a connecting thread which runs through many of the different motivational factors which the coach or teacher can influence. This connecting thread seems to be intrinsic motivation. As Garvie (1981) has emphasized, "*intrinsic reasons for participation* ... are the *central contingencies of sport continuance*" (p. 6).

This is not to say that each of the motivational constructs discussed in this text are a form of intrinsic motivation. This is simply not the case. But, most of the different motivational factors can influence intrinsic motivation and intrinsic motivation is the most powerful source of motivation. Consequently, if a coach or teacher wanted to focus on one area of motivation to the exclusion of others, intrinsic motivation would be the best place to start. In short, many of the other motivational factors, if used judiciously, contribute to intrinsic motivation.

It will be recalled that intrinsically motivated behavior is behavior which is motivated by a need to feel *competent* and *self-determining* (Deci, 1975). Thus, if coaches and teachers can contribute to participants' perceptions that they are competent and personally responsible, they will also contribute to the enhancement of the participants' intrinsic motivation. Figure 6.1 contains an overview of this general picture.

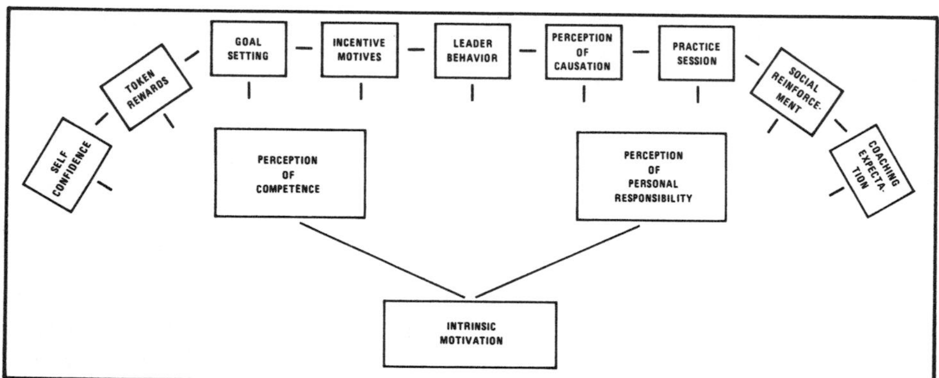

Figure 6.1
Motivation for sport and physical activity.

The perception of competence, one of the two major components of intrinsic motivation, can be directly enhanced by almost all of the motivational factors which have the potential to be manipulated or influenced by the coach or teacher (the factors discussed in Chapters 2 and 4). For example, consider the effects of goal setting, token rewards, coaching expectations, self confidence, social reinforcement, leadership behavior, the practice session, the perception of causation, and incentive motivation (see Figure 6.1).

A good goal setting program sets out difficult but attainable goals. Consequently, a perception of increasing competence should result as the successive targets or objectives are achieved. Similarly, the token rewards which are provided for desirable behavior or performance in a contingency management program can become tangible evidence of competency in the goal setting program.

Our perceptions of ourselves — whether it is the perception of competency or some other characteristic — are strongly influenced by the way others interact with us. Consequently, positive coaching expectations and the frequent use of positive social reinforcement also contribute to feelings of self-worth and personal competency.

Self confidence and the perception of competency are perhaps synonomous.

And, in turn, they interact in a circular fashion with performance success; self confidence and the perception of competency contribute to performance success which subsequently contributes to the perceptions of competency and self-confidence.

It will be recalled that one of the strongest incentives in sport and physical activity is excellence — the mastery of skills and techniques. Obviously, coaching behaviors which emphasize training and instruction (see Table 2.3 for a discussion of the characteristic behaviors of coaches-as-leaders) are most closely allied to the achievement of excellence. And, training and instruction behavior becomes much more effective when it is carried out in conjunction with a good goal setting program supplemented by the careful use of token rewards introduced into practice sessions that are stimulating, well planned, and characterized by variety.

Finally, the explanations people use to account for an outcome — their perceptions of causation — also have an impact on their perceptions of competency. For example, a perception of personal competency can only result if the participant attributes a success to personal internal factors such as personal ability and personal effort. A person who continually attributes success to luck or to the lack of difficulty of an opponent will never develop a perception of personal competency. Conversely, the participant who is often unsuccessful must be trained to regard the cause of those failures as a lack of effort rather than an absence of ability.

The perception of personal responsibility, the second major component of intrinsic motivation also can be directly influenced by the motivational factors outlined in Figure 6.1. Two of the more obvious examples are the impact of leader behaviors and the practice session. A participative (or democratic) decision style which allows for participant input obviously adds to the participant's perception of personal responsibility. Thus, for example, it is possible for participants to become involved in and monitor their own goal setting program, to direct the group or team token rewards program, and/or to have input into the nature and conduct of the practice session.

The factors which influence the participant's motivation do not operate independently but, rather, they interact to produce a total level of motivation. It is important, therefore, that the teacher and coach have information about all of the factors considered. Clearly, the teacher or coach cannot hope to appreciate the complexity of human motivation without some understanding of the person and the situation.

SUGGESTED READINGS

Alderman, R.B. Strategies for motivating young athletes. In W.F. Straub (Ed.), *Sport psychology: An analysis of athlete behavior.* Ithaca: Mouvement, 1978.

Carron, A.V. Motivating the athlete. In W.F. Straub (Ed.), *Sport psychology: An analysis of athlete behavior.* Ithaca: Mouvement, 1978.

REFERENCES

Adams, C., & Cohen, A. Children's physical and interpersonal characteristics that affect student-teacher interactions. *Journal of Experimental Education,* 1974, *43,* 1-5.

Alderman, R.B. Incentive motivation in sport: An interpretive speculation of research opportunities. In A.C. Fisher (Ed.), *Psychology of Sport: Issues & Insights.* Palo Alto, Calif.: Mayfield, 1976.

Alderman, R.B. Strategies for motivating young athletes. In W.F. Straub (Ed.), *Sport psychology: An analyses of athlete behavior.* Ithaca: Mouvement, 1978.

Alderman, R.B., & Wood, N.L. An analysis of incentive motivation in young Canadian athletes. *Canadian Journal of Applied Sport Sciences,* 1976, *1,* 169-176.

Allington, R. Teacher interruption behaviors during primary-grade oral reading. *Journal of Educational Psychology,* 1980, *72,* 371-377.

Allport, F.H. *Social psychology.* New York: Houghton-Mifflin, 1924.

Anderson, D., & Rosenthal, R. Some effects of interpersonal expectancy and social interaction on institutionalized retarded children. *Proceedings of the 76th Annual Convention of the American Psychological Association,* 1968, *3,* 479-480.

Ansorge, C.J., Scheer, J.K., Laub, J., & Howard, J. Bias in women's gymnastics induced by expectations of within-team order. *Research Quarterly,* 1978, *49,* 399-405.

Arnott, M. *Decision styles in coaching: Athletes' preferences.* Unpublished M.A. Thesis, University of Western Ontario, London, 1982.

Arwood, B., Williams, R.L., & Long, J.D. The effects of behavior contracts and behavior proclamations on social conduct and academic achievement in a ninth grade English class. *Adolescence,* 1974, *9,* 425-436.

Atkinson, J.W. *An introduction to motivation.* Princeton, N.J.: Van Nostrand, 1964.

Atkinson, J.W. The mainsprings of achievement-oriented activity. In J.S. Atkinson and J.O. Reynor (Eds.), *Motivation and Achievement.* New York: Halstead, 1974.

Atkinson, J.W., & Litwin, G.H. Achievement motivation and test anxiety as motive to approach success and motive to avoid failure. *Journal of Abnormal and Social Psychology,* 1960, *60,* 52-63.

Bandura, A. Self-efficacy: Toward a unifying theory of behavioral change. *Psychological Review,* 1977, *84,* 191-215.

Bandura, A., & Simon, K.M. The role of proximal intentions in self-regulation of refractory behavior. *Cognitive Theory and Research,* 1977, *1,* 177-193.

Becker, L.J. Joint effect of feedback and goal setting on performance: A field study of residential energy conservation. *Journal of Applied Psychology,* 1978, *63,* 428-433.

Beez, W. Influence of biased psychological reports on teacher behavior and pupil performance. *Proceedings of the 76th Annual Convention of the American Psychological Association,* 1968, *3,* 605-606.

Berlyne, D.E. Attention to change. *British Journal of Psychology,* 1951, *42,* 269-275.

Berlyne, D.E. The influence of albedo and complexity of stimuli on visual fixation of the human infant. *British Journal of Psychology,* 1958, *49,* 315-318.

Berlyne, D.E. *Conflict, arousal and curiosity.* New York: McGraw-Hill, 1960.

Berlyne, D.E. The reward value of indifferent stimulation. In J.T. Tapp (Ed.), *Reinforcement and behavior.* New York: Academic Press, 1969.

Bexton, W.H., Heron, W., & Scott, T.H. Effects of decreased variation in the sensory environment. *Canadian Journal of Psychology,* 1954, *8,* 70-76.

Birch, D., & Veroff, J. *Motivation: A study of action.* Belmont, Calif.: Brooks/Cole, 1966.

Bird, A.M. Cross sex effects of subject and audience during motor performance. *Research Quarterly,* 1975, *46,* 379-384.

Brawley, L.R., Landers, D.M., Miller, L., & Kearns, K.F. Sex bias in evaluating motor performance. *Journal of Sport Psychology,* 1979, *1,* 15-24.

Brawley, L.R., & Roberts, G.C. An introduction to attribution research in sport: Explaining the cause of winning and losing. In J.M. Silva & R.S. Weinberg (Eds.), *Psychological foundations of sport and exercise.* Champaign, Ill.: Human Kinetics, 1984.

Brenner, M. *Stagefright and Stevens Law.* Paper presented at the Eastern Psychological Association Meeting, 1974.

Brophy, J.E. *Research on the self-fulfilling prophecy and teacher expectations.* Educational Resources Information Center, National Institute of Education, U.S. Department of Education, Washington, D.C., July, 1982.

Brophy, J., & Good, T. Teachers' communication of differential expectations for children's classroom performance: Some behavioral data. *Journal of Educational Psychology,* 1970, *61,* 365-374.

Brophy, J., & Good, T. *Teacher-student relationships: Causes and consequences.* New York: Holt, Rinehart, and Winston, 1974.

Breyer, N.L., & Allen, G.J. Effects of implementing a token economy on teacher attending behavior. *Journal of Applied Behavior Analysis,* 1975, *8,* 373-380.

Brock, S., Brock, S., & Willis, J. The effect of tangible and token rewards on the pole vaulting behavior of high school students. *School Application of Learning Theory,* 1972, *43,* 32-37.

Broden, M., Hall, R.V., Dunlap, A., & Clark, R. Effect of teacher attention and a token reinforcement system in a junior high school special education class. *Exceptional Children,* 1970, *36,* 341-349.

Carron, A.V. Motivating the athlete. In W.F. Straub (Ed.), *Sport psychology: An analysis of athlete behavior.* Ithaca: Mouvement, 1978.

Carron, A.V. *Social psychology of sport.* Ithaca: Mouvement, 1980.

Carron, A.V. Sport psychology: Fact and fantasy. *Recreation Research Review,* 1980, *8,* 28-37.

Carron, A.V. *Social psychology of sport: An experiential approach.* Ithaca, N.Y.: Mouvement, 1981.

Carron, A.V. Processes of group interaction in sport teams. *Quest,* 1981, *33,* 245-270.

Carron, A.V., & Ball, J.R. Cause-effect characteristics of cohesiveness and participation motivation in intercollegiate hockey. *International Review of Sport Sociology,* 1977, *12,* 49-60.

Carron, A.V., & Chelladurai, P. Cohesiveness, coach-athlete compatibility, participation orientation, and their relationship to relative performance. *Psychology of Motor Behavior & Sport - 1982: Abstracts.* Maryland: North American Society for the Psychology of Sport and Physical Activity, 1982.

Carron, A.V., & Spink, K.S. The stability of causal attributions. *Canadian Journal of Applied Sport Sciences,* 1980, *5,* 19-24.

Casady, M. The tricky business of giving rewards. *Psychology Today,* 1974, *8,* 52.

Cattell, R.B., & Scheier, I.H. *The meaning and measurement of neuroticism and anxiety,* New York: Ronald, 1961.

Chadwick, B.A., & Day, R.C. Systematic reinforcement: Academic performance of under-achieving students. *Journal of Applied Behavior Analysis,* 1971, *4,* 311-317.

Chaikin, A., Sigler, E., & Derlega, V. Nonverbal mediators of teacher expectation effects. *Journal of Personality and Social Psychology.* 1974, *30,* 144-149.

Chelladurai, P. The coach as a motivator and chameleon of leadership styles. *Sports Sciences Periodical on Research and Technology in Sport Social Psychology (BU-2).* Ottawa: Coaching Association of Canada, 1981.

Chelladurai, P., & Carron, A.V. Appliability to youth sports of the Leadership Scale for Sports. *Perceptual and Motor Skills,* 1981, *53,* 361-362.

Chelladurai, P., & Carron, A.V. Task characteristics and individual differences and their relationship to preferred leadership in sports. *Psychology of Motor Behavior & Sport - 1982: Abstracts.* Maryland: North American Society for the Psychology of Sport and Physical Activity, 1982.

Chelladurai, P., & Carron, A.V. Athletic maturity and preferred leadership. *Journal of Sport Psychology,* In Press. 1984.

Chelladurai, P., & Saleh, S.D. Preferred leadership in sport. *Canadian Journal of Applied Sport Sciences,* 1978, *3,* 85-97.

Chelladurai, P., & Saleh, S.D. Dimensions of leader behavior in sports: Development of a leadership scale. *Journal of Sport Psychology,* 1980, *2,* 34-45.

Coaching Association of Canada. *National Coaching Certification Program: Level 2 Coaching Theory.* Ottawa: Coaching Association of Canada, 1979.

Cooper, H. Pygmalion grows up: A model for teacher expectation communication and performance influence. *Review of Educational Research,* 1979, *49,* 389-410.

Cooper, H., & Baron, R. Academic expectations and attributed responsibility as predictors of professional teachers' reinforcement behavior. *Journal of Educational Psychology,* 1977, *69,* 409-418.

Cottrell, N.B. Social facilitation. In C.G. McClintock (Ed.), *Experimental social psychology.* New York: Holt, Rinehart, Winston, 1972.

Cottrell, N.B., Wack, R.H., Sekerak, G.J., & Rittle, R.H. Social facilitation of dominant responses by the presences of an audience and the mere presence of others. *Journal of Personality and Social Psychology,* 1968, *9,* 245-250.

Cox, F.N. Some effects of test anxiety and presence or absence of other persons on boys' performance on a repetitive motor task. *Journal of Experimental Child Psychology,* 1966, *3,* 100-112.

Cratty, B.J. *The social dimensions of physical activity.* Englewood Cliffs, N.J.: Prentice-Hall, 1967.

Cratty, B.J. *Social psychology in athletics.* Englewood Cliffs, N.J.: Prentice-Hall, Inc., 1981.

Cratty, B.J. *Psychology in contemporary sport: Guidelines for coaches and athletes,* 2nd. ed, Englewood Cliffs, N.J.: Prentice-Hall, 1983.

Csikszentmihalyi, M. Play and intrinsic rewards. *Journal of Humanistic Psychology,* 1975, *15,* 41-63.

Csikszentmihalyi, M., & Bennett, S.H. An exploratory model of play. *American Anthropologist,* 1971, *73,* 45-58.

Curtis, B., Smith, R.E., & Smoll, F.L. Scrutinizing the skipper; A study of leadership and behavior in the dugout. *Journal of Applied Psychology,* 1979, *64,* 391-400.

Deaux, K. Sex differences. In T. Blass (Ed.), *Personality variables in behavior.* Hillsdale, N.J.: Erlbaum, 1977.

DeCharms, R. *Personal causation.* New York: Academic Press, 1968.

DeCharms, R. *Enhancing motivation: Change in the classroom.* New York: Halsted, 1976.

Deci, E.L. *Intrinsic motivation.* New York: Plenum Press, 1975.

Deci, E.L, Cascio, W.F., & Krusell, J. *Sex differences, positive feedback, and intrinsic motivation.* Paper presented at the meeting of the Eastern Psychological Association, Washington, D.C., 1973.

Dember, W.N. The new look in motivation. *American Scientist,* 1965, *53,* 409-427.

Dember, W.N., Earl, R.W., & Paradise, N. Response by rats to differential stimulus complexity. *Journal of Comparitive and Physiological Psychology,* 1957, *50,* 514-518.

Deutsch, M. A theory of cooperation and competition. *Human Relations,* 1949, *2,* 129-152. (a)

Deutsch, M. An experimental study of the effects of cooperation and competition upon group process. *Human Relations,* 1949, *2,* 199-231. (b)

Deutsch, M. The effects of cooperation and competition upon group process. In D. Cartwright & A. Zander (Eds.), *Group dynamics: Research and theory,* 3rd. ed. London: Tavistock Publications, 1968.

Dickie, D. Goof grief. *Coaching Review,* 1982, *5,* 17-19.

Dickinson, D.J. But what happens when you take that reinforcement away? *Psychology in the Schools,* 1974, *11,* 158-160.

Diener, C.I., & Dweck, C.S. An analysis of learned helplessness: Continuous changes in performance, strategy, and achievement cognitions following failure. *Journal of Personality and Social Psychology,* 1978, *36,* 451-462.

Diener, C.I., & Dweck, C.S. An analysis of learned helplessness: II The processing of success. *Journal of Personality and Social Psychology,* 1980, *39,* 940-952.

Donnelly, P., & Birrell, S. *Motivation and sport involvement: The needs for stimulation and achievement.* Ottawa: Cahper Sociology of Sport Monograph Series, 1978.

Duda, J.L. *Toward a phenomenology of children in sport: New directions in sport psychology research.* NAPEHE Proceedings, 1982.

Duda, J.L. Achievement motivation among Navajo Indians: A conceptual analysis with preliminary data. *Ethos,* 1980, *8,* 316-331.

Duda, J.L. *A cross-cultural analysis of achievement motivation in sport and the classroom.* Unpublished doctoral dissertation, University of Illinois, Urbana -Champaign, 1981.

Duda, J.L. Achievement motivation in sport: Minority considerations for coach. *Journal of Sport Behavior,* 1981, *4,* 24-31.

Duda, J.L. *Goals and achievement orientations of Anglo and Mexican-American adolescents in sport and the classroom.* Paper presented at the Tenth World Congress of Sociology, Mexico City, Mexico, 1982.

Duda, J.L., & Allison, M.T. Definitions of success and failure: Race, sex, and situational variables. *Journal of Research and Development in Education,* 1982.

Duffy, E. *Activation and behavior.* New York: Wiley, 1962.

Dweck, C.S. The role of expectations and attributions in the alleviation of learned helplessness. *Journal of Personality and Social Psychology,* 1975, *31,* 674-685.

Dweck, C.S., & Goetz, T.E. Attributions and learned helplessness. In J. Harvey, W. Ickes, & R. Kidd, (Eds.), *New directions in attribution research (Vol. II).* Hillsdale, N.J.: Erlbaum, 1978.

Dweck, C.S., & Reppucci, N.D. Learned helplessness and reinforcement responsibility in children. *Journal of Personality and Social Psychology,* 1973, *25,* 109-116.

Eitzen, D.S. The effect of group structure on the success of athletic teams. *International Review of Sport Sociology,* 1973, *8,* 7-17.

Endler, N.S., & Hunt, J.McV. Generalizability of contributions from sources of variance in the S-R Inventories of Anxiousness. In H.N. Mischel & W. Mischel (Eds.), *Readings in Personality.* New York: Holt, Rinehart & Winston, 1973.

Erez, M. Feedback: A necessary condition for the goal setting-performance relationship. *Journal of Applied Psychology,* 1977, *62,* 624-627.

Erle, F.J. *Leadership in competitive and recreational sport.* Unpublished M.A. Thesis, University of Western Ontario, London, 1981.

Ewing, M.F. *Achievement orientations and sport behavior of males and females.* Unpublished doctoral dissertation, University of Illinois, Urbana-Champaign, 1981.

Feltz, D.L. Path analysis of the causal elements in Bandura's theory of self-efficacy and on anxiety-based model of avoidance behavior. *Journal of Personality and Social Psychology,* 1982, *42,* 764-781.

Feltz, D.L. *Gender differences in the causal elements of Bandura's theory of self-efficacy on a high avoidance motor task.* Paper presented at the North American Society for the Psychology of Sport and Physical Activity Conference, East Lansing, Mich., 1983.

Feltz, D., Gould, D., Horn, T.S., & Weiss, M.R. *Perceived competence among youth swimmers and dropouts.* Paper presented at the annual meeting of the North American Society for the Psychology of Sport and Physical Activity, College Park, Maryland, June 1932.

Feltz, D., Landers, D.M., & Raeder, U. Enhancing self-efficacy in high-avoidance motor tasks: A comparison of modeling techniques. *Journal of Sport Psychology,* 1979, *1,* 112-222.

Fiedler, F.E. *A theory of leadership effectiveness.* New York: McGraw-Hill, 1967.

Finn, J. Expectations and the educational environment. *Review of Educational Research,* 1972, *42,* 387-410.

Foder, E.M. Group stress, authoritarian style of control and use of power. *Journal of Applied Psychology,* 1976, *61,* 313-318.

Forsythe, B., & Schlenker, B.R. Attributing the causes of group performance: Effects of performance quality, task importance and future testing. *Journal of Personality,* 1977, *45,* 220-236.

Forward, J., & Zander, A. Choice of unattainable group goals and effects on performance. *Organizational Behavior and Human Performance,* 1971, *6,* 184-199.

Frieze, I., & Weiner, B. Cue utilization and attributional judgments for success and failure. *Journal of Personality,* 1971, *39,* 591-605.

Freud, S. *New introductory lectures on psychoanalysis* (1932). (Trans. by W.J.H. Sprott). New York: Norton, 1933.

Fry, D.A.P., McClements, J.D., & Sefton, J.M. *A report on participation in the Saskatoon Hockey Association.* University of Saskatchewan, Saskatoon, Saskatchewan, Canada, 1981.

Garvie, G.T. *Focus of motivation: A principle factor in sport participation.* Unpublished doctoral dissertation, University of Alberta, Edmonton, Alberta, 1979.

Garvie, G.T. Adjusting your motivator intrinsically. In N.L. Woods (Ed.), *Coaching Science Update: 1980/81 Edition.* Ottawa: Coaching Association of Canada, 1981.

Gerwitz, J.L., & Baer, D.M. The effects of brief social deprivation on behaviors for a social reinforcer. *Journal of Abnormal Psychology,* 1958, *56,* 49-56.

Gill, D.L., Gross, J.B., & Huddleston, S. Participation motivation in youth sports. In: G.C. Roberts & D.M. Landers (Eds.), *Psychology of motor behavior and sport -1980.* Champaign, Ill.: Human Kinetics, 1981.

Gill, D.L., & Martens, R. The role of task type and success-failure in group competition. *International Journal of Sport Psychology,* 1977, *8,* 160-177.

Ginsburg, B., & Allee, W.C. Some effects of conditioning on social dominance and subordination in inbred strains of mice. *Physiological Zoology,* 1942, *15,* 485-506.

Glynn, E.L. Classroom applications of self-determined reinforcement. *Journal of Applied Behavior Analysis,* 1970, *3,* 123-132.

Good, T., Cooper, H., & Blakey, S. Classroom interaction as a function of teacher expectations, student sex, and time of year. *Journal of Educational Psychology,* 1980, *72,* 378-385.

Gould, D. Sport psychology in the 1980's: Status, direction and challenge in youth sports research. *Journal of Sport Psychology,* 1982, *4,* 203-218 (a).

Gould, D. *Future directions in youth sports participation motivation research.* Paper presented at Candian Psychomotor Learning and Sport Psychology Conference, Edmonton, Alberta, 1982 (b).

Gould, D., Feltz, D., Horn, T., & Weiss, M. Reasons for discontinuing involvement in competitive youth swimming. *Journal of Sport Behavior,* 1982, *5,* 155-165.

Gould, D., Feltz, D.L., Weiss, M., & Petlichkoff, L. Participation motives in competitive youth swimmers. *Proceedings Fifth World Congress of Sport Psychology.* Ottawa: Ontario, Canada, 1982.

Gould, D., & Horn, T. Participation motivation in youth athletes. In: J.M. Silva & R.S. Weinberg (Eds.), *Psychological foundations of sport and exercise.* Champaign, Ill.: Human Kinetics, 1984.

Gould, D., Horn, T., & Spreemann, J. Competitive anxiety in junior elite wrestlers. *Journal of Sport Psychology,* 1983, *5,* 58-71.

Gowen, G.R., Botterill, C.B., & Blimke, C.J.R. Bridging the gap between sport science and sport practice. In P. Klavora & J.V. Daniel (Eds.), *Coach, athlete, and the sport psychologist.* Champaign, Ill.: Human Kinetics, 1979.

Greenberg, P.T. Competition in children, an experimental study. *American Journal of Psychology* 1932, *44,* 221-248.

Griffin, L.E. *Why children participate in youth sports.* Paper presented at the American Association of Health, Physical Education and Recreation National Conference, Kansas City, Missouri, April 1978.

Griffin, M.R. A analysis of state and trait anxiety experienced in sports competition at different age levels. *Foil,* Spring, 1972, pp. 58-64.

Hass, J., & Roberts, G.C. Effect of evaluative others upon performance. In I.D. Williams & L.M. Wankel (Eds.), *Proceedings of the Fourth Canadian Psycho-Motor Learning and Sport Psychology Symposium.* Ottawa: Department of National Health & Welfare, 1972.

Hackman, J.R., & Lawler, E.E. Employee reactions in job characteristics. *Journal of Applied Psychology,* 1971, *55,* 259-286. (Monograph)

Halliwell, W.R. The effect of cognitive development on children's perceptions of intrinsically and extrinsically motivated behavior. In D.M. Landers & R.W. Christina (Eds.), *Psychology of Motor Behavior and Sport 1977.* Champaign, Ill.: Human Kinetics, 1978 (a).

Halliwwell, W. Intrinsic movitation in sport. In W.F. Straub (Ed.), *Sport Psychology: An analysis of athlete behavior.* Ithaca, N.Y.: Mouvement, 1978 (b).

Harney, D.M., & Parker, R. Effects of social reinforcement, subject sex, and experimenter sex on children's motor performance. *Research Quarterly,* 1972, *43,* 187-196.

Hatfield, B.C., & Landers, D.M. Observer expectancy effects upon appraisal of gross motor performance. *Research Quarterly,* 1978, *49,* 53-61.

Hebb, D.O. *The organization of behavior.* New York: Wiley, 1949.

Hemphill, J.K., & Coons, A.E. Development of the Leader Behavior Description Questionnaire. In R.M. Stogdill & A.E. Coons (Eds.), *Leader behavior: Its description and measurement.* Columbia: The Ohio State University, 1957.

Henchy, T., & Glass, D.C. Evaluation apprehension and social facilitation of dominant and subordinate responses. *Journal of Personality and Social Psychology,* 1968, *10,* 446-454.

Highlen, P.S., & Bennett, B.B. Psychological characteristics of successful and nonsuccessful elite wrestlers: An exploratory study. *Journal of Sport Psychology,* 1979, *1,* 123-137.

Hill, K.T., & Stevenson, H.W. The effects of social reinforcement versus nonreinforcement and sex of E on the performance of adolescent girls. *Journal of Personalty,* 1965, *33,* 30-36.

Hull, C.L. *Principles of behavior.* New York: Appleton & Century-Crofts, 1943.

Iso-Ahola, S. Determinants of evaluation of team performance. *Scandinavian Journal of Psychology,* 1976, *17,* 292-296.

Iso-Ahola, S. Effects of team outcome on children's self perception: Little League baseball. *Scandinavian Journal of Psychology,* 1977, *18,* 38-42. (a)

Iso-Ahola, S.E. *Social psychological determinants of perceptions of leisure.* Paper presented at the NRPA Research Symposium, Las Vegas, Nevada, 1977. (b)

Iso-Ahola, S.E. Basic dimensions of definitions of leisure. *Journal of Leisure Research,* 1978, *10.*

Ivancevich, J.M., & McMahon, J.T. Education as a moderator of goal setting effectiveness. *Journal of Vocational Behavior,* 1977, *11,* 83-94.

Jeter, J., & Davis, O. *Elementary school teachers' differential classroom interaction with children as a function of differential expectations of pupil achievements.* Paper presented at the Annual Meeting of the American Research Association, 1973.

Johnson, D.W., Marugama, G., Johnson, R., Nelson, D., & Skon, L. The effects of cooperative, competitive, and individualistic goal structures on achievement: A meta analysis. *Psychological Bulletin,* 1981, *89,* 47-62.

Jones, R. *A modified basketball game: The effects of contingency management on competitive game behavior of girls attending a basketball camp.* Paper presented at the Third Annual Convention of the Midwestern Association of Behavior Analysis, Chicago, Illinois, May, 1977.

Jones, R. A modified basketball game: *The effects of contingency management on competitive game behavior of girls attending a basketball camp.* Paper presented at the Fourth Annual Convention of the Midwestern Association of Behavior Analysis, Chicago, Illinois, May, 1978.

Julian, J.W., Bishop, D.W., & Fiedler, F.E. Quasi-therapeutic effects of intergroup competition. *Journal of Personality and Social Psychology,* 1966, *3,* 321-332.

Kahn, M. The effect of severe defeat at various age levels on the aggressive behavior of mice. *Journal of Genetic Psychology,* 1951, *79,* 117-130.

Kahneman, D. *Attention and effort.* Englewood Cliffs, N.J.: Prentice-Hall, 1975.

Karniol, R., & Ross, M. The development of causal attributions in social perception. *Journal of Personality and Social Psychology,* 1976, *34,* 455-464.

Kennedy, W.A., & Williatt, H.C. Praise and blame as incentives. *Psychological Bulletin,* 1964, *62,* 323-332.

Kerlinger, F.E. *Foundations of behavioral research,* 2nd. ed. New York: Holt, Rinehart and Winston, 1973.

Klavora, P. Customary arousal for peak athletic performance. In P. Klavora & J.V. Daniel (Eds.), *Coach, athlete, and the sport psychologist.* Champaign, Ill.: Human Kinetics, 1979.

Klein, M., & Christiansen, G. Group composition, group structure and group effectiveness of basketball teams. In J.W. Loy & G.S. Kenyon (Eds.), *Sport, Culture and Society.* New York: MacMillan, 1969.

Kleinfeld, J. Effective teachers of Eskimo and Indian Students. *School Review,* 1975, *83,* 301-344.

Kluckhohn, C., & Murray, H. *Personality in nature, society, and culture.* New York: Knopf, 1949.

Kohler, O. Uba den gruppenwirkungsgrad der menschlichen Korperarbeit und die bedingung optimaler kollektivkraftreaktion. *Indus Psychotech,* 1927, *4,* 209-226.

Komaki, J., & Barnett, F. A behavioral approach to coaching football: Improving the play execution of the offensive backfield on a youth football team. *Journal of Applied Behavior Analysis,* 1977, *10,* 657-664.

Klinger, E. Feedback effects and social facilitation of vigilance performance: Mere coaction versus potential evaluation. *Psychonomic Science*, 1969, *14*, 161-162.

Koppet, L. Homecourt: Winning edge. *New York Times*, January 9, 1972.

Korten, D.C. Situational determinents of leadership structure. *Journal of Conflict Resolution*, 1962, *6*, 222-235.

Kroll, W. The stress of high performance athletics. In P. Klavora and J.V. Daniel (Eds.), *Coach, athlete, and the sport psychologist*. Champaign, Ill.: Human Kinetics, 1979.

Kruglanski, A.W. The endogenous-exogenous partition. *Psychological Review*, 1975, *82*, 387-406.

Landers, D.M. Whatever happened to theory testing in sport psychology. *Journal of Sport Psychology*, 1983, *5*, 135-151.

Landers, D.M., Furst, D.M., & Daniels, F.S. *Anxiety/attention and shooting ability: Testing the predictive validity of the test of attentional and interpersonal style (TAIS)*. Paper presented at the meeting of the North American Society for the Psychology of Sport and Physical Activity, 1981.

Larose, R.S., & Carron, A.V. *Coach-athlete congruence of perception for the motivational basis for athlete participation*. Paper presented at North American Society for the Psychology of Sport & Physical Activity Conference, College Park, Maryland, 1982.

Latham, G.P., & Baldes, J.J. The "practical significance" of Locke's theory of goal setting. *Journal of Applied Psychology*, 1975, *60*, 122-124.

Latham, G.P., & Saari, L.M. Importance of supportive relationships in goal setting. *Journal of Applied Psychology*, 1979, *64*, 151-156.

Latham, G.P., & Yukl, G.A. Effects of assigned and participative goal setting on performance and job satisfaction. *Journal of Applied Psychology*, 1976, *61*, 166-171.

Lefebrve, L.M., & Passer, M.W. The effects of game location and importance on aggression in team sport. *International Journal of Sport Psychology*, 1974, *12*, 102-110.

Leo, J. Take me out of the ball game. *Time*, August, 1982.

Lepper, M.R., & Greene, D. Turning play into work: Effects of adult surveillance and extrinsic rewards on children's intrinsic motivation. *Journal of Personality and Social Psychology*, 1975, *31*, 479-486.

Lepper, M.R., Greene, D., & Nisbett, R.E. Undermining children's intrinsic interest with extrinsic rewards: A test of the "overjustification hypothesis." *Journal of Personality and Social Psychology*, 1973, *28*, 129-137.

Leuba, C. Toward some integration of learning theories: The concept of optimal stimulation. *Psychological Reports*, 1955, *1*, 27-33.

Lilly, J.C. Mental effects of reduction of ordinary levels of physical stimuli on intact healthy persons. *Psychiatric Research Reports*, 1956, *5*, 1-9.

Littman, R.A. Motives: History and causes. In M.R. Jones (Ed.), *Nebraska Symposium or Motivation*, (Vol. 6). Lincoln: Nebraska University Press, 1958.

Locke, E.A., & Bryan, J.F. The directing function of goals in task performance. *Organizational Behavior and Human Performance,* 1969, *4,* 32-42.

Locke, E.A., Feren, D.B., McCaleb, V.M., Shaw, K.N., & Denny, A.T. The relative effectiveness of four methods of motivating employee performance. In K. Duncan, M. Gruneberg, & D. Wallis (Eds.) *Changes in working life.* New York: Wiley, 1980.

Locke, E.A., & Schweiger, D.M. Participation in decision-making: One more look. In B.M. Staw (Ed.), *Research in organizational behavior* (Vol. 1). Greenwick, Conn.: JAL Press, 1979.

Locke, E.A., Shaw, K.N., Saari, L.M., & Latham, G.P. Goal setting and task performance: 1969-1980. *Psychological Bulletin,* 1981, *90,* 125-152.

Lopes, L.L. Individual strategies in goal-setting. *Organizational Behavior and Human Performance,* 1976, *15,* 268-277.

Lowin, A., & Craig, J. The influence of level of performance on managerial style: An experimental object-lesson in the ambiguity of correlational data. *Organizational Behavior and Human Performance,* 1968, *3,* 440-458.

Luschen, G. Cooperation, association, and contest. *Journal of Conflict Resolution,* 1970, *14,* 21-34.

Madsen, M., & Shapira, A. Cooperative and competitive behavior in urban Afro-American, Anglo-American, Mexican-American, and Mexican village children. *Development Psychology,* 1970, *3,* 16-20.

Maehr, M. *Sociocultural origins of achievement.* Belmont, California: Brooks/Cole, 1974.

Maehr, M.L., & Nicholls, J.G. Culture and achievement motivation: A second look. In N. Warren (Ed.), *Studies in cross-cultural psychology.* New York: Academic Press, 1980.

Mahoney, M.J., & Avener, M. Psychology of the elite athlete: An exploratory study. *Cognitive Therapy and Research,* 1977, *1,* 135-141.

Malmo, R.B. Activation: A neuropsychological dimension. *Psychological Review,* 1959, *66,* 367-386.

Mandelker, A.V., Brigham, T.A., & Bushell, D. The effects of token procedures on a teacher's social contacts with her students. *Journal of Applied Behavior Analysis,* 1970, *3,* 169-174.

Martens, R. Effects of an audience on learning and performance of a complex motor skill. *Journal of Personality and Social Psychology,* 1969, *12,* 252-260.

Martens, R. Influence of participation motivation on success and satisfaction in team performance. *Research Quarterly,* 1970, *41,* 520-528.

Martens, R. *Social psychology and physical activity.* New York: Harper & Row, 1975.

Martens, R., & Gill, D.L. State anxiety among successful and unsuccessful competitors who differ in competitive trait anxiety. *Research Quarterly,* 1976, *47,* 698-708.

Martens, R. *The sport competition anxiety test,* Champaign, Ill.: Human Kinetics, 1977.

Martens, R. From smocks to jocks: A new adventure for sport psychologists. In P. Klavora & J.V. Daniel (Eds.), *Coach, athlete, and the sport psychologist.* Champaign, Ill.: Human Kinetics, 1979.

Martens, R., & Landers, D.M. Evaluation potential as a determinand of coaction effects. *Journal of Experimental Social Psychology,* 1972, *8,* 347-359.

Martinek, T.J. Students' expectations as related to a teacher's expectations and self concepts of elementary age children. *Perceptual and Motor Skills,* 1980, *50,* 555-561. (a)

Martinek, T.J. Stability of teacher expectations for elementary school aged children. *Perceptual and Motor Skills,* 1980, *51,* 1269-1270. (b)

Martinek, T.J., & Johnson, A.B. Teacher expectations: Effects on dyadic interactions and self-concept in elementary age children. *Research Quarterly,* 1979, *50,* 60-70.

McAuley, E. *Modeling and self-efficacy. An examination of Bandura's model of behavioral change.* Paper presented at North American Society for the Psychology of Sport and Physical Activity Conference, East Lansing, Mich., 1983.

McClelland, D.C. Some social consequences of achievement motivation. In M.R. Jones (Ed.), *Nebraska symposium on motivation,* (Vol. 3). Lincoln: Univ. of Nebraska Press, 1955.

McClelland, D.C. *The achieving society.* Princeton, N.J.: Van Nostrand, 1961.

McClelland, D.C., & Winter, D.G. *Motivating economic achievement.* New York: Free Press, 1969.

McClements, J.D., & Botterill, C.B. Goal setting on shaping of future performance of athletes. In Klavora, P. & Daniel, J.V. (Eds.), *Coach, athlete, and the sport psychologist.* Champaign, Ill.: Human Kinetics, 1979.

McClements, J.D., & Laverty, W.H. A mathematical model of speedskating performance improvement for goal setting and program evaluation. *Canadian Journal of Applied Sport Sciences,* 1979, *4,* 116-122.

McCullagh, P.D., & Landers, D.M. Size of audience and social facilitation. *Perceptual and Motor Skills,* 1976, *42,* 1067-1070.

McGrath, J.E. A conceptual formulation for research on stress. In J.E. McGrath (Ed.), *Social and psychological factors in stress.* New York: Holt, Rinehart and Winston, 1970.

McHugh, M.C., Duquin, M.E., & Frieze, I.H. Beliefs about success and failure: Attribution and the female athlete. In C.A. Oglesby (Ed.), *Women and sport: From myth to reality.* Philadelphia: Lea & Febiger, 1978.

McKenzie, T. Token economy research: A review for the physical educator. *Motor Skills: Theory Into Practice,* 1979, *3,* 102-114.

McKenzie, T., & Rushall, B. Effects of self-recording on attendance and performance in a competitive swimming training environment. *Journal of Applied Behavior Analysis,* 1974, *7,* 199-206.

McLaughlin, T.F., & Malaby, J. Intrinsic reinforcers in a classroom token economy. *Journal of Applied Behavior Analysis,* 1972, *5,* 263-270. (a)

McLaughlin, T.F., & Malaby, J. Reducing and measuring inappropriate verbalizations in a token classroom. *Journal of Applied Behavior Analysis,* 1972, *5,* 329-333. (b)

McNally, J., & Orlick, T.D. Cooperative sport structures: A preliminary analysis. In J. Salmela, C. Bard, R. Desharnais, D. Drouin, & M. Fleury (Eds.), *Mouvement,* Quebec, 1975.

Miller, G.A. The magical number seven plus or minus two: Some limits on our capacity for processing information. *Psychological Review,* 1956, *63,* 81-97.

Miller, L.K., & Schneider, R. The use of a token system in project Head Start. *Journal of Applied Behavior Analysis,* 1970, *3,* 213-220.

Miller, N.E., & Dollard, J. *Social learning and imitation.* New Haven, Conn.: Yale University Press, 1941.

Morgan, C.T. *Introduction to psychology* (2nd ed.). New York: McGraw-Hill, 1961.

Morris, C.G. *Psychology: An introduction* (2nd ed.). Englewood Cliffs: Prentice-Hall, 1976.

Myers, A.E. Team competition, success, and adjustment of group members. *Journal of Abnormal and Social Psychology,* 1962, *65,* 325-332.

Nakagawa, A. A field experiment on recognition of game situations in ball games: The case of static situations in rugby football. *Japanese Journal of Physical Education,* 1982, *27,* 17-26.

Nelson, L.R., & Furst, M.L. An objective study of the effects of expectation on competitive performance. *Journal of Psychology,* 1972, *81,* 69-72.

Nemeroff, W.F., & Cosentino, J. Utilizing feedback and goal setting to increase performance appraisal interviewer skills of managers. *Academy of Management Journal,* 1979, *22,* 566-576.

Ness, R.G., & Patton, R.G. *The effect of external cue manipulation upon weight lifting performance.* Paper presented at the American Alliance of Health, Physical Education, and Recreation, Seattle, Wash., 1977.

Nettleton, B. Attentional style and performance in a coincident anticipation task. *Perceptual and Motor Skills,* 1982, *55,* 350.

Newman, S. Roger Neilson. *Coaching Review,* 1982, *5,* 6-12.

Newman, S. Coaching in Polar Bear Country. *Coaching Review,* 1983, *6,* 22-24.

Nicholls, J.G. Effort is virtuous, but it's better to have ability: Evaluative responses to perceptions of effort and ability. *Journal of Research in Personality,* 1976, *10,* 306-315.

Nideffer, R.M. Test of attentional and interpersonal style. *Journal of Personality and Social Psychology,* 1976, *34,* 397-404.

Nideffer, R.M. *Predicting human behavior: A theory and test of attentional and interpersonal style.* San Diego: Enhanced Performance Assoc., 1979.

Nideffer, R.M. *The ethics and practice of applied sport psychology.* Ithaca, N.Y.: Mouvement, 1981.

Nideffer, R.M., & Sharpe, R. *A.C.T.: Attention control training.* New York: Wyden Books, 1978.

O'Leary, K.D., & Becker, W.C. Behavior modification of an adjustment class: A token reinforcement program. *Exceptional Children,* 1967, *9,* 637-642.

O'Leary, K.D., Becker, W.C., Evans, M.B. & Saudargas, R.A. A token reinforcement program in a public school: A replication and systematic analysis. *Journal of Applied Behavior Analysis,* 1969, *2,* 3-13.

Orlick, T.D. The athletic dropout - a high price for inefficiency. *Canadian Association for Health, Physical Education and Recreation Journal,* 1974, Nov. - Dec. 21-27.

Orlick, T.D. *In pursuit of excellance.* Champaign, Ill.: Human Kinetics, 1980.

Orlick, T.D., & Botterill, C. *Every kid can win.* Chicago, Ill.: Nelson-Hall, 1975.

Orlick, T.D. *The cooperative sports & games book: Challenge without competition.* New York: Pantheon Books, 1978.

Page, S. Social interaction and experimenter effects in the verbal conditioning experiment. *Canadian Journal of Psychology,* 1971, *25,* 463-475.

Panda, K.C. Social reinforcement: Theoretical issues and research implications. *Psychological Studies,* 1971, *16,* 55-67.

Passer, M.W. Children in sport: Participation motives and psychological stress. *Quest,* 1981, *33,* 231-244.

Passer, M. *Participation motives of young athletes as a function of competitive trait anxiety, self-esteem, ability, and age.* Paper presented at the annual meeting of the North American Society for the Psychology of Sport and Physical Activity, College Park, Maryland, June, 1982.

Patterson, G.R., Littman, R.A., & Bricker, W. Assertive behavior in children: A step toward a theory of aggression. *Monographs of the Society for Research in Child Development,* 1967, *32,* No. 5., (Serial No. 113).

Petlichkoff, L.M. *Motives interscholastic athletes have for participation and reasons for discontinued involvement in school sponsored sport.* Unpublished master's thesis, Michigan State University, 1982.

Petlichkoff, L., & Gould, D. *Incentive motivation in interscholastic athletes.* Unpublished manuscript, 1982.

Piaget, J. *The moral judgment of the child.* New York: Harcourt Brace, 1932.

Pooley, J.V. *Drop-outs from sport: A case study of boys' age group soccer.* Paper presented at the American Alliance for Health, Physical Education, Recreation and Dance National Conference, Boston, Mass., April 1981.

Popper, K.R. *The logic of scientific discovery.* New York: Basic Books, 1959.

Porter, L.W., & Lawler, E.E. *Managerial attitudes and performance.* Homewood, Ill.: R.D. Irwin, 1968.

Pulos, L. Athletes and self-hypnosis. In P. Klavora J.V. Daniel (Eds.), *Coach, athlete, and the sports psycholgist.* Champaign, Ill.: Human Kinetics, 1978.

Rashad, A., & Deford, F. Journal of a plagued Year: Part II. *Sports Illustrated,* 1982, 57, 82-96.

Reiss, J. & Bird, A.M. Cue processing as a function of breadth of attention. *Journal of Sport Psychology,* 1982, *4,* 64-72.

Reiss, H.T. & Jelsma, B. A social psychology of sex differences in sport. In W.F. Straub (Ed.), *Sport psychology: An analysis of athlete behavior,* 2nd ed. Ithaca, N.Y., Mouvement, 1978.

Rejeski, W.J. & Brawley, L.R. Attribution theory in sport: Current status and new perspectives. *Journal of Sport Psychology,* 1983, *5,* 77-99.

Rejeski, W.J. Daracott, C., & Hutslar, S. Pygmalion in youth sports: A field study. *Journal of Sport Psychology,* 1979, *1,* 311-319.

Rejeski, W.J. & Hutslar, S. The mediational role of teacher expectancies on the acquisition and performance of sport skills. *Motor Skills: Theory Into Practice,* 1980, *4,* 91-94.

Rejeski, W.J. & Lowe, C.A. The role of ability and effort in attributions for sport achievement. *Journal of Personality,* 1960, *48,* 233-244.

Rikli, R. Effects of experimenter expectancy set and experimenter sex upon grip strength and hand steadiness scores. *Research Quarterly,* 1974, *45,* 416-423.

Ringer, V.M.J. The use of a "token helper" in the management of classroom behavior problems and in teacher training. *Journal of Applied Behavior Analysis,* 1973, *6,* 671-677.

Rist, R. Student social class and teacher expectation. The self-fulfilling prophecy in ghetto education. *Harvard Educational Review,* 1970, *40,* 411-451.

Roberts, G.C. Effect of achievement motivation and social environment on risk taking. *Research Quarterly,* 1974, *45,* 42-55.

Roberts, G.C. Win-loss attributions of Little League players. In J. Salmela, C. Bard, R. Desharnais, D. Drouin, & M. Fleury, Eds., *Mouvement.* Quebec: De L'Association des Professionels de l'Activate Physique du Quebec, 1975.

Roberts, G.C. Children in competition: A theoretical perspective and recommendation for practice. *Motor Skills: Theory into Practice,* 1980, *4,* 37-50.

Roberts, G.C., Kleiber, D.A. & Duda, J.L. An analysis of motivation in children's sport: The role of perceived competence in participation. *Journal of Sport Psychology,* 1981, *3,* 200-316.

Roberts, G.C. & Martens, R. Social reinforcement and complex motor performance. *Research Quarterly,* 1970, *41,* 175-181.

Robertson, I. *Children's perceived satisfactions and stresses in sport.* Paper presented at the Australian Conference on Health, Physical Education and Recreation, January 1981.

Robinson, T.T. & Carron, A.V. Personal and situational factors associated with dropping out versus maintaining participation in competitive sport. *Journal of Sport Psychology,* 1982, *4,* 364-378.

Reothlisberger. F.J. & Dickson, W.J. *Management and the worker.* Cambridge: Harvard University Press, 1939.

Rolider, A. *Effects of modeling, instructions and incentives on peer encouragement in a competitive basketball setting.* Paper presented at Midwest Applied Behavior Analysis Convention, Chicago, May, 1978.

Rosen, B. & D'Andrade, R.C. The psychological origins of achievement motivation. *Sociomentry,* 1959, *22,* 185-218.

Rosenbaum, L.L. & Rosenbaum, W.B. Morale and productivity consequences of group leadership style, stress, and type of task. *Journal of Applied Psychology,* 1971, *55,* 343-388.

Rosenthal, R. *On the social psychology of the self-fulfilling prophecy: Further evidence for Pygmalion effects and their mediating mechanics.* New York: MSS Modular Publications, 1974.

Rosenthal, R. *Experimenter effects in behavior research (2nd edition).* New York: Irvington, 1976.

Rosenthal, R. & Jacobson, L. *Pygmalion in the classroom: Teacher expectation and pupils' intellectual development.* New York: Holt, Rinehart, & Winston, 1968.

Rosenthal, R. & Jacobson, L. Teacher expectations of the disadvantaged. *Scientific American,* 1968, *218,* 19.

Ross, M. The self-perception of intrinsic motivation. In J.H. Harvey, W.J. Ickes, & R.F. Kidd, (Eds.), *New directions in attribution research* (Vol. I). Hillsdale, N.J.: Erlbaum, 1976.

Ross, M. Self-centered biases in attributions of responsibility: Antecedents and consequences. In E.T. Higgins, C.P. Herman, & M.P. Zanna (Eds.), *Social cognition: The Ontario Symposium.* Hillsdale, N.J.: Erlbaum, 1981.

Ross, R.C. & Vander Haag, E. *The fabric of society.* New York: Harcourt Brace, 1957.

Rotter, J.B. *Social learning and clinical psychology.* Englewood Cliffs, N.J.: Prentice-Hall, 1954.

Rowe, M. Wait-time and rewards as instructional variables, their influence on language, logice, and fate control: Part One Wait-Time. *Journal of Research in Science Teaching,* 1974, *11,* 81-94.

Rubovits, P., & Maehr, M. Pygmalion analyzed: Toward an explanation of the Rosenthal-Jacobson findings. *Journal of Personality and Social Psychology,* 1971, *19,* 197-203.

Rushall, B.S. Two observation schedules for sport and physical education environments. *Canadian Journal of Applied Sport Sciences,* 1977, *2,* 15-22.

Ryan, E.D. Attribution, intrinsic motivation, and athletics. In L.I. Gedvilas & M.E. Kneer (Eds.), *Proceedings of the NCPEAM/MAPECW National Conference, 1977.* Chicago: Office of Publication Services, University of Illinois at Chicago Circle, 1977.

Ryan, E.D. Attribution, intrinsic motivation, and athletics: A replication and extension. In C.H. Nadeau, W.R. Halliwell, K.M. Newell, & G.C. Roberts (Eds.), *Psychology of Motor Behavior and Sport - 1979.* Champaign, Ill.: Human Kinetics, 1980.

Ryan, D.E. & Lakie, W.L. Competitive and noncompetitive performance in relation to achievement motive and anxiety. *Journal of Personality and Social Psychology,* 1965, *1,* 344-345.

Sales, S.M. Some effects of role overload and role underload. *Organizational Behavior and Human Performance.* 1970, *5,* 595-608.

Sapp, M., & Haubenstricker, J. *Motivation for joining and reasons for not continuing in youth sports programs in Michigan.* Paper presented at the American Association of Health, Physical Education and Recreation National Conference, Kansas City, Missouri, April 1978.

Scanlan, T.K. & Passer, M.W. Factors related to competitive stress among male youth sport participants. *Medicine and Science in Sports,* 1978, *10,* 103-108.

Scanlan, T.K., & Passer, M.W. Factors influencing the competitive performance expectancies of young female athletes. *Journal of Sport Psychology,* 1979, *1,* 212-220. (a)

Scanlan, T.K., & Passer, M.W. Sources of competitive stress in young female athletes. *Journal of Sport Psychology,* 1979, *1,* 151-159. (b)

Scanlan, T.K., & Passer, M.W. Determinants of competitive performance expectancies of young male athletes. *Journal of Personality,* 1981, *49,* 60-74.

Schapp, P. *Instant replay: The Green Bay diary of Jerry Kramer.* New York: World Publishing, 1968.

Schachter, S. *The psychology of affiliation.* Standford, Calif.: Stanford University Press, 1959.

Scheer, J.K. & Ansorge, C.J. Effects of naturally induced judges' expectations on the ratings of physical performances. *Research Quarterly,* 1975, *46,* 463-470.

Scheer, J.K. & Ansorge, C.J. Influence due to expectations of judges: A function of internal-external locus of control. *Journal of Sport Psychology,* 1979, *1,* 53-58.

Schwartz, B. & Barsky, S.F. The home advantage. *Social Forces,* 1977, *55,* 641-662.

Scott, J.P. & Marston, M.V. Non-adaptive behavior resulting from a series of defeats in fighting mice. *Journal of Abnormal and Social Psychology,* 1953, *48,* 417-428.

Shapira, A. and Madsen, M. Cooperative and competitive behavior of Kibbutz and Urban children in Israel. *Child Development,* 1969, *40,* 609-617.

Shaw, G.B. *Pygmalion: A romance in five arts,* New York: Penguin Books, 1941.

Sherif, M., Harvey, O.J., White, B.J., Hood, W.R., & Sherif, C.W. *Intergroup conflict and cooperation: The Robbers Cave Experiment.* Normal, University of Oklahoma Book Exchange, 1961.

Siedentop, The management of practice behavior. In W.F. Straub (Ed.), *Sport psychology: An analysis of athlete behavior,* Ithaca: Mouvement, 1978.

Siedentop, D. & Dawson, J. Eagle effort: Managing practice contingencies in junior high school basketball. Paper presented at meeting of the Midwestern Association of Behavior Analysis, Chicago, Illinois, May, 1978.

Siedentop, D. & Ramey, G. Extrinsic rewards and intrinsic motivation. *Motor Skills: Theory Into Practice,* 1977, *2,* 49-62.

Simon, J.A. & Martens, R. Children's anxiety in sport and nonsport evaluative activities. *Journal of Sport Psychology,* 1979, *1,* 160-169.

Singer, R.N. *Coaching, athletics and psychology,* New York: McGraw-Hill, 1972.

Singer, R.N. *Motor learning and human performance,* 2nd ed. New York: Macmillan & Co., 1975.

Singer, R.N. *Myths and truths in sports psychology.* New York: Harper & Row, 1975.

Skinner, B.F. *The behavior of organisms: An experimental analysis,* New York: Appleton-Century-Crofts, 1938.

Sloggett, B.B. Use of group activities and team rewards to increase classroom productivity. *Teaching Exceptional Children,* 1971, *3,* 54-66.

Smith, M.C. Children's use of the multiple sufficient cause scheme in social perception. *Journal of Personality and Social Psychology,* 1975, *32,* 737-744.

Smith, R.E., Smoll, F.L., & Curtis, B. Coaching behaviors in Little League baseball. In F.L. Smoll & R.E. Smith (Eds.), *Psychological perspectives in youth sports.* Washington, D.C.: Hemsphere Publishing, 1978.

Smith, R.E., Smoll, F.L., & Hunt, E. A system for the behavioral assessment of athletic coaches. *Research Quarterly,* 1977, *48,* 401-407.

Smoll, F.L., & Smith, R.E. *Improving relationship skills in youth sport coaches.* East Lansing, Mich.: Institute for the Study of Youth Sports, 1979.

Spielberger, C.D. Theory and research on anxiety. In C.D. Spielberger (Ed.), *Anxiety and behavior.* New York: Appleton, 1966.

Spielberger, C.D. Anxiety as an emotional state. In C.D. Spielberger (Ed.), *Current trends in theory and research* (Vol. 2). New York: Academic Press, 1972.

Spink, K.S. Win-loss causal attributions of high school basketball players. *Canadian Journal of Applied Sport Sciences,* 1978, *3,* 195-201.

Staats, A.W. Behavior analysis and token reinforcement in educational behavior modification and curriculum research. In C.E. Thoresen (Ed.), *Behavior modification in education.* Chicago, Illinois: The University of Chicago Press, 1973.

Steers, R.M. Task-goal attributes, achievement, and supervisory performance. *Organizational Behavior and Human Performance,* 1975, *13,* 392-403.

Stevenson, H.W. Social reinforcement with children as a function of CA, sex of E, and sex of S. *Journal of Abnormal and Social Psychology,* 1961, *63,* 147-154.

Stevenson, H.W. Social reinforcement of children's behavior. In L.P. Lipsitt & C.C. Spiker (Eds.), *Advances in child development and behavior* (Vol. 2). New York: Academic Press, 1965.

Stevenson, H.W., & Allen, S. Adult performance as a function of sex of E, and sex of S. *Journal of Abnormal Social Psychology,* 1964, *68,* 214-216.

Strang, H.R., Lawrence, E.C., & Fowler, P.C. Effects of assigned goal level and knowledge of results on arithmetic computation: A laboratory study. *Journal of Applied Psychology,* 1978, *63,* 446-450.

Suinn, R.M. Visual motor behavior rehearsal for adaptive behavior. In J. Krumboltz & C. Thoresen (Eds.), *Counselling methods.* New York: Holt, 1976.

Suinn, R. (Ed.), *Psychology in sports: Methods and applications,* Minneapolis: Burgess, 1980.

Swann, W., & Snyder, M. On translating beliefs into action: Theories of ability and their application in an instructional setting. *Journal of Personality and Social Psychology,* 1980, *38,* 879-888.

Swann, W.B., & Pittman, T.S. Imitating play activity of children: The moderating influence of verbal cues on intrinsic motivation. *Child Development,* 1977, *48,* 1128-1132.

Taylor, M. Race, sex, and the expression of self-fulfilling prophecies in a laboratory teaching situation. *Journal of Personality and Social Psychology,* 1979, *37,* 897-912.

Terborg, J.R., & Miller, H.E. Motivation, behavior, and performance: A closer examination of goal setting and monetary incentives. *Journal of Applied Psychology,* 1978, *63,* 29-39.

Terborg, J.R. The motivational components of goal setting. *Journal of Applied Psychology,* 1976, *61,* 613-621.

Tetlock, P.E., & Levi, A. Attribution bias: On the inconclusiveness of cognition-motivation debate. *Journal of Experimental Social Psychology,* 1982, *18,* 68-88.

Thirea, J., & Rampey, M.S. Effects of abrasive spectator's behavior on performance of home and visiting inter-collegiate basketball teams. *Perceptual and Motor Skills,* 1979, *48,* 1047-1053.

Thorndike, E.K. *The original nature of man.* (Educational Psychology I). New York: Teacher's College, 1913. (a)

Thorndike, E.L. *The psychology of learning.* (Educational Psychology II). New York: Teacher's College, 1913. (b)

Tolman, E.C. The determiners of behavior at a choice point. *Psychological Review,* 1938, *45,* 1-41.

Triplett, N. The dynamogenic factors in pace-making and competition. *American Journal of Psychology,* 1897, *9,* 507-533.

Tutko, T.A., & Ogilvie, B.C. The role of the coach in motivation of athletes. In R. Slovenko & J.A. Knight (Eds.), *Motivation in play, games and sports.* Springfield, Ill.: Charles C. Thomas, 1967.

Tutko, T.A., & Richards, J.W. *Psychology of coaching.* Boston: Allyn and Bacon, 1971.

Vallerand, R.J., Reid, G., & Marisi, D.Q. Effects de reinforcements verbaux et materiels sur la motivation intrinseque face a une tache motrice. In C.H. Nadeau, W.R. Halliwell, K.M. Newell, & G.C. Roberts, (Eds.), *Psychology of Motor Behavior and Sport - 1979.* Champaign, Ill.: Human Kinetics, 1980.

Van Schoyck, S.R., & Grasha, A.F. Attentional style variations and athletic ability: The advantages of a sports-specific test. *Journal of Sport Psychology,* 1981, *3,* 149-165.

Varca, P.E. An analysis of home and away game performances of male college basketball teams. *Journal of Sport Psychology,* 1980, *2,* 245-257.

Wankel, L.M. Competition in motor performance: An experimental analysis of motivational components. *Journal of Experimental Social Psychology,* 1972, *8,* 427-437.

Wankel, L.M. The effects of social reinforcement and audience presence upon the motor performance of boys with different levels of initial ability. *Journal of Motor Behavior,* 1975, *7,* 207-216.

Wankel, L.M., & Pabich, P. *The minor sport experience: Factors contributing to or detracting from enjoyment.* Paper presented at the Fifth World Congress of Sport Psychology, Ottawa, Canada, August 1981.

Watt, T. What I want from sport psychology. In P. Klavora & J.V. Daniel (Eds.), *Coach, athlete, and the sport psychologist.* Champaign, Ill., Human Kinetics, 1979.

Weinberg, R.S. Motivating athletes through goal setting. *Journal of Physical Education Recreation and Dance,* 1982, *53,* 46-48.

Weinberg, R.S., Gould, D., & Jackson, A. Expectations and performance: An empirical test of Bandura's self-efficacy theory. *Journal of Sport Psychology,* 1979, *4,* 320-331.

Weiner, B. A theory of motivation for some classroom experiences. *Journal of Educational Psychology,* 1979, *71,* 3-25.

Weiner, B., & Kukla, A. An attributional analysis of achievement motivation. *Journal of Personality and Social Psychology,* 1970, *15,* 1-20.

White, R.W. Competence and psychosexual stages of development. In M.R. Jones (Ed.), *Nebraska symposium on motivation, Vol. 8.* Lincoln: Univ. of Nebraska Press, 1960.

White, S.E., Michell, T.R., & Bell, C.H. Goal setting, evaluation apprehension, and social cues as determinants of job performance and job satisfaction in a simulated organization. *Journal of Applied Psychology,* 1977, *62,* 665-673.

Winterbottom, M.R. *The relation of childhood training in independence to achievement motivation.* Unpublished doctoral dissertation, University of Michigan, 1953.

Wood, N.L. *Incentive motivation in sport: A theoretical analysis and the development of a measuring instrument.* Unpublished doctoral dissertation, University of Alberta, Edmonton, Alberta, 1980.

Wood, N.L. Improving the motivation of your athletes. In N.L. Wood (Ed.), *Coaching Science Update: 1980/81 Edition.* Ottawa: Coaching Association of Canada, 1981.

Zander, A. *Motives and goals in groups.* New York: Academic Press, 1971.

Zander, A., Forward, J., & Albert R. Adaptation of board members to repeated failure or success by their organization. *Organizational Behavior and Human Performance*, 1969, *4*, 56-76.

Zajonc, R.B. Social facilitation. *Science*, 1965, *149*, 269-274.

AUTHOR INDEX

SUBJECT INDEX

Feedback (also see Social reinforcement),
- coaching behavior and, *37, 41*
- goal setting and, *15, 26*
- Hawthorne effect and, *26*

Fitness,
- incentive motivation and, *76, 83*